Wolfgang Pauli (1900 – 1958)

his photo was taken in 1953 in Zurich on the occasion of his nomination as
Foreign Member of the Royal Society

Wolfgang Pauli
Writings on Physics and Philosophy

T

Wolfgang Pauli

Writings on Physics and Philosophy

Edited by
Charles P. Enz and Karl von Meyenn

Translated by
Robert Schlapp

Springer-Verlag
Berlin Heidelberg New York
London Paris Tokyo
Hong Kong Barcelona
Budapest

Professor Dr. *Charles P. Enz*

University of Geneva, 24, quai Ernest Ansermet
CH-1211 Geneva 4, Switzerland

Dr. *Karl von Meyenn*

Max-Planck-Institut für Physik, Werner-Heisenberg-Institut
Föhringer Ring 6, D-80805 München, Germany

Translator

Dr. *Robert Schlapp* †

ISBN 3-540-56859-X Springer-Verlag Berlin Heidelberg New York
ISBN 0-387-56859-X Springer-Verlag New York Berlin Heidelberg

Library of Congress Cataloging-in-Publication Data.
Pauli, Wolfgang, 1900–1958. Writings on physics and philosophy / Wolfgang Pauli; edited by C. P. Enz und K. von Meyenn. p. cm. Includes bibliographical references and index. ISBN 3-540-56859-X (Berlin: alk. paper). – ISBN 0-387-56859-X (New York: alk. paper) 1. Physics–Philosophy. 2. Philosophy. I. Enz, Charles P. (Charles Paul), 1925 – . II. Meyenn, K. v. III. Title. QC6.2.P38 1994 530' .01–dc20 94-15098

© Springer-Verlag Berlin Heidelberg 1994
Printed in Germany

Cover Design: Struve & Partner, Atelier für Grafik-Design, Heidelberg
Typesetting: Data conversion by K. Mattes, Heidelberg
SPIN: 10081498   55/3140 - 5 4 3 2 1 0 - Printed on acid-free paper

Contents

Preface

The History of this Translation:
Paul Rosbaud, Friend and Publisher of Wolfgang Pauli

Wolfgang Pauli wrote a highly sophisticated and beautiful German. This very fact is at the origin of the delay of almost 37 years since Pauli signed a contract on 15 July 1957 to publish the translation by Robert Schlapp contained in the present volume [Ref. 1, p. 5]. Anybody who has tried to translate Pauli's German into English must have experienced the dilemma of the choice between accurately reproducing Pauli's ideas and rendering the flavour of his particular style. Thus L. Rosenfeld comments on Schlapp's translations "I have found them competently done; the meaning is clearly and accurately rendered and the English, though lacking distinction, is reasonably smooth. . . . I did try to modify the translation at one or two critical places, but did not succeed – at least not without departing rather much from the literal rendering, which again is dangerous!" [2].

In the *Memorandum* quoted above Rosbaud writes [Ref. 1, p. 1] "Pauli was insistent, from the outset, that to preserve the precise meaning and the individuality of presentation, the translation *must* be literal and not freely smoothed into 'good' English." Pauli himself seems to have adhered to this rule when he wrote in English, as may be concluded from the following remark of Rosbaud [Ref. 1, p. 2]: "When in 1955 I was instrumental in publishing a volume dedicated to Niels Bohr's 70th birthday [see Ref. 3], one of the Editors objected strongly to the English of Wolfgang Pauli's contribution. However, the co-editor quite rightly insisted that it should remain unchanged. Pauli's contribution to the Niels Bohr volume has since become a very famous scientific document."

The last quotation shows Paul Rosbaud's activity in science publishing which, in fact, went back to the late twenties in Berlin where he was offered the job of editor with the newly founded weekly magazine *Metallwirtschaft* [see Ref. 4 for biographical information on P. Rosbaud]. Born in Graz on 18 November 1896 he was the brother of the well-known conductor and expert in modern music Hans Rosbaud. In 1926 he graduated in chemistry at the

Paul Rosbaud (1896–1963)

Darmstadt Polytechnic and subsequently made a doctorate in Berlin in the
new field of X-ray physics. His editing activity there allowed Paul Rosbaud
to travel widely all over Europe. And his Austrian charm and his enthusiasm
made it easy for him to make friends with the elite in science and particularly
in physics.

In the early thirties Dr. Ferdinand Springer offered Paul Rosbaud the
position of scientific adviser with the prestigious publishing house run by
him and his brother Julius in Berlin. His most important deed in this function was to assure that Otto Hahn's report on nuclear fission got immediately
published in *Naturwissenschaften* in January 1939. Forseeing very clearly the
catastrophic political development in Germany, Rosbaud became increasingly hostile to the Nazi regime. And when he met Edward Foley who then
became associated with the Secret Intelligence Service at the British Lega-
tion in Berlin, this was the beginning of a liaison which made Paul Rosbaud
the most valuable scientific informer of the British government throughout
World War II. Rosbaud's material covering all scientific developments in
Germany but particularly nuclear research was channeled through the Nor-

wegian, French and other Resistances. Towards the end of the war Rosbaud got trapped in Berlin and, after a mysterious incident of an alleged kidnapping by the Russians, he was moved out in late 1945 by British intelligence [4].

In London, Rosbaud resumed his editing activity, first with the publishing house of Butterworth and then with its new branch Butterworth Scientific, which in 1949 became Butterworth-Springer. In this year he was brought together with Robert Maxwell who then was buying and selling scientific journals and later also books and who for that purpose founded the firm Lange, Maxwell and Springer [see Ref. 5 for a biography of R. Maxwell]. For financial reasons the association of the two men became inevitable and at the end of 1951 Rosbaud accepted Maxwell's invitation to become Scientific Director of a new venture called Pergamon Press. This name as well as the colophon had its origin in the head of Athena on a coin minted in the Asian city of Pergamon. Clearly, Rosbaud, who was an expert on ancient Greek coins, was involved in this choice [6]. While at the beginning of Pergamon Press decision making concerning new journals and books was largely in Rosbaud's competence, Maxwell started to interfere more directly after having suffered his first bankrupcy in 1954; in September 1956 Rosbaud left Pergamon Press in profound bitterness. But his enormous reputation quickly brought him consulting functions with the leading scientific publishing houses, an activity he carried on until his death from leukaemia in 1963 and which was honoured a year before by the Tate Medal for scientific editing awarded by the American Institute of Physics.

This brings the story back to the start: Paul Rosbaud's friendship with Pauli and the history of the present volume. "Pauli was very much in favour of such a book, but at this stage [1955–56] we had no particular publisher in mind: Subsequently, he decided on Interscience Publishers, Inc., New York" [Ref. 1, p. 1]. Concerning the choice of the translator "Professor Pauli proposed Professor Kemmer, who, in turn, suggested Dr. Schlapp, Lecturer at his Department as an 'extremely suitable person to take this job, having just the right qualifications, both scientific and linguistic.' (2nd April, 1957). Dr. Schlapp consented, and met Professor Pauli in Edinburgh to discuss style and other matters of detail." [Ref. 1, p. 2].

Although Pauli's interest in the English translation of his essays was genuine, he was reluctant to read them himself. "To chat with you would be nice (to read myself in English, however, definitely not charming. Then I even prefer to write new articles)" he writes to Rosbaud on 2 November 1957 (my translation) [7]. In the *Memorandum* Rosbaud writes "October 1957: I persuaded Professor Pauli to spend an afternoon with me in Zurich, in his own home, going through a batch of four or five of the translations. He offered several minor suggestions, raised one or two queries, ... he sent me a 'One-way Street' diagram as a constant reminder to me that the postal traffic between Zurich-London must be in one way only: No more translations to be sent to him for his approval. ... Professor Pauli agreed to see the translation of *Die Wissenschaft und das abendländische Denken* and added to it a few pencilled notes. He asked that translation of the more philosophical papers should be checked by Professor Pryce, Kemmer or Rosenfeld. This was done. Very nearly all the translations were completed during Pauli's lifetime." [Ref. 1, pp. 3–4].

So why this delay of nearly 37 years? The tragedy was that Pauli unexpectedly died of cancer of the pancreas on 15 December 1958. His wife Franca very courageously took command of all editorial projects concerning her late husband. These projects now also included an agreement with Vieweg, Braunschweig, that Pauli himself had signed on 29 October 1958 to publish a German edition of the essays with the title "Aufsätze über Physik und Erkenntnistheorie" [8] and a plan suggested by Rosbaud to publish the Collected Papers with Interscience [9]. The "Aufsätze" were published in 1961 with the addition of "und Vorträge" in the title and of an obituary speech (Trauerrede) by V. F. Weisskopf. A second edition including an historical introduction and an index by K. von Meyenn appeared in 1984 [10]. On the other hand, the Collected Papers appeared in 1964 [11]. While none of these publications acknowledges the important rôle played by Paul Rosbaud, a memorial volume which originally had been planned to celebrate Pauli's 60th birthday on 25 April 1960 does mention Rosbaud in the Preface [12].

It is a sad fact that the relations between Franca Pauli and Paul Rosbaud – who with the Pauli's carried the nickname 'Steinklopfer Hansl' – came apart because, confused by the contradicting advice she received concerning the Schlapp translations, Mrs. Pauli lost confidence in Rosbaud. A letter Franca Pauli wrote on 27 January 1960 to E. Proskauer, the editor-in-chief with Interscience, contained plainly wrong statements concerning Rosbaud's handling of these translations and was personally offensive towards him [9]. Deeply hurt Paul Rosbaud whom I had met when I was Pauli's assistant and with whom I stayed in contact by letters, wrote in his defense the documents quoted in Refs. 1, 2 and 7. In a letter dated 12 February 1960 Proskauer then proposed to Franca Pauli not to publish Schlapp's translations but to honour the conditions of the contract concluded on 15 July 1957 concerning pay – and to wait for a satisfactory translation [9].

Thus the Schlapp translations went into total oblivion, and I was convinced that they were lost. So my surprise was immense when Professor Kemmer, having secured the single carbon copy of the whole translation in Schlapp's home in Edinburgh, contacted Springer Publishers in December 1988 and, after examining the legal situation with them, sent the whole package to the Pauli Estate at CERN for reconsideration. Having accepted to act, together with K. von Meyenn, as editor I considered it my duty to tell this story as a tribute to Paul Rosbaud. As to the translations, I have read them only in recent times but thoroughly and in every detail. And although I have interfered at many places, but with the sole aim of achieving greater precision (particular German expressions which have no precise translation are given in parantheses), I agree with Paul Rosbaud when he writes on 27 April 1959 in one of his many letters to Robert Schlapp: "It is only when comparing the translations with the original German manuscripts that I saw how terribly difficult your task must have been and how superbly you have mastered this" [13]. The translations, in fact stand as a worthy memory to Robert Schlapp who, unfortunately has not lived to see at last the fruit of his efforts of half a lifetime ago [for biographical notes on R. Schlapp see the following account by N. Kemmer as well as Ref. 14].

In the contract signed by Pauli on 15 July 1957 the selection of essays arranged by Paul Rosbaud did not include what might well be considered Pauli's most important work outside physics: the study on Johannes Kepler. This omission may seem surprising and even regrettable, particularly since the Kepler paper is hard to get because of its publication in a separate book, together with an essay on synchronicity by C. G. Jung [15]. However, we learn from Fierz's commentary to this book that in response to suggestions by some friends to publish his article separately from Jung's, Pauli told Fierz: "I have thought about it and I believe I should not do this. For, indeed, there comes the time when I must give documentary evidence of what I owe this man" (my translation) [Ref. 16, p. 191].

Today the motivation for keeping Pauli's and Jung's essays together has vanished, particularly because both have long since been included in the respective collected works [for Pauli it is contained in Ref. 11, vol. 1, p. 1023]. The most beautiful manifestation of the high mutual esteem of the two men, however, is the recent publication of the Pauli-Jung correspondence [17]. I am pleased therefore to point out that the Kepler paper is included here in the original translation as the highlight to close this collection (again, particular German expressions which have no precise translation are given in parantheses). The translator, Mrs. Priscilla Silz of Princeton, had been proposed by Pauli's friend, Erwin Panofsky, who personally and actively oversaw the English edition of the Kepler paper [18].

Finally, I wish to address the thanks of the editors to Professor Nicholas Kemmer and to the Pauli committee at CERN for their cooperation.

Charles P. Enz

References

[1] *Memorandum. 4th April 1960.* Signed P. Rosbaud, enclosure in letter of P. Rosbaud to C. P. Enz of 16 May 1960.

[2] *Professor L. Rosenfeld to Dr. P. Rosbaud. August 31st, 1959.* Excerpt of letter, enclosure in letter of P. Rosbaud to C. P. Enz of 16 May 1960.

[3] *Niels Bohr and the Development of Physics*, ed. W. Pauli, with the assistance of L. Rosenfeld and V. Weisskopf (Pergamon, London, 1955).

[4] A. Kramish, *The Griffin* (Houghton Mifflin, Boston, 1986). I am particularly indebted for valuable biographical information to the nephew of Paul Rosbaud, Dr. Vincent C. Frank-Steiner, Basel, who also is the owner of the Pauli-Rosbaud correspondence of the period 1952–59.

[5] T. Bower, *Maxwell the Outsider* (Mandarin, London, 1991).

[6] R. W. Cahn, *The Origins of Pergamon Press: Rosbaud and Maxwell*, European Review **2**, No. 1, 37–42 (1994).

[7] *Excerpts from letters from Professor Pauli to Dr. Rosbaud*, enclosure in letter of P. Rosbaud to C. P. Enz of 16 May 1960.

[8] *Vereinbarung* signed on 16 October 1958 by Friedr. Vieweg & Sohn. Copy dated by Pauli, in the Pauli Estate, CERN Archive, Geneva.

[9] Correspondence between Franca Pauli and Eric S. Proskauer, Editor-in-Chief, Interscience Publishers, Inc., in Pauli Estate, CERN Archive, Geneva.

[10] Wolfgang Pauli, *Aufsätze und Vorträge über Physik und Erkenntnistheorie*, ed. W. Westphal (Vieweg, Braunschweig, 1961; second edition 1984).

[11] Wolfgang Pauli, *Collected Scientific Papers*, eds. R. Kronig and V. F. Weisskopf (Interscience, New York, 1964).

[12] *Theoretical Physics in the Twentieth Century*, eds. M. Fierz and V. F. Weisskopf (Interscience, New York, 1960).

[13] Letters of Paul Rosbaud to Robert Schlapp, in Pauli Estate, CERN Archive, Geneva.

[14] N. Kemmer, *Robert Schlapp*, in *Yearbook of the Royal Society of Edinburgh* (Edinburgh, to be published).

[15] C. G. Jung, W. Pauli, *Naturerklärung und Psyche* (Rascher, Zürich, 1952).

[16] M. Fierz, *Naturwissenschaft und Geschichte. Vorträge und Aufsätze* (Birkhäuser, Basel, 1988).

[17] C. A. Meier (ed.), *Wolfgang Pauli und C. G. Jung. Ein Briefwechsel 1932–1958* (Springer, Berlin Heidelberg, 1992).

[18] Correspondence between W. Pauli, the Bollingen Foundation (New York) and E. Panofsky (The Institute for Advanced Study, Princeton), in Pauli Estate, CERN Archive, Geneva.

Robert Schlapp
(1899 – 1991)

Robert Schlapp – or 'Robin', as all his many friends called him, was born in Edinburgh on July 18th 1899 of German parents who had arrived and settled in Edinburgh in 1887. Robin's father Otto Schlapp almost immediately gained a reputation teaching German and as soon as 1894 the University of Edinburgh established a lectureship for him and later a Department which he headed as the Professor of German until his retirement.

Robin finished College in 1917 with the highest honours and, after serving in the army with the war still continuing, he embarked on the Honours MA course of Mathematics and Natural Philosophy at Edinburgh University. This course was shared by the two Departments of Mathematics and Natural Philosophy, the former having (Sir) Edmund Whittaker, the latter the aging Charles Barkla, as Professors. Robin's total record over the three years of studies was so unblemished that his acceptance in Cambridge was unassailable.

Robin was accepted by St. John's College and by the University as a Research Student, and he enrolled for the Ph.D. He was possibly the first student assigned to Sir Joseph Larmor for supervision. Robin describes his stay in Cambridge as not particularly rewarding and Larmor as shy and not very inspiring. The subject that Larmor had suggested to him was "The Reflexion of X-Rays from Crystals" – it was precisely the subject for which Barkla gained his Nobel Prize. The examiners deemed Robin's work worthy, and the assessment of its quality was proven by its appearance in the Philosophical Magazine.

A happy fact about Robin's last year in Cambridge was that the great Paul Dirac was admitted to the same College as Robin, St. John's. On a mention of the name Schlapp many years later Dirac's eyes lit up, indicating warm memories. As Dirac was a very withdrawn, shy man of very few words no other explanation seems possible than that Robin must have been acceptable to him to share the regular Sunday morning walks that Dirac was famous for. This friendship was sufficient for us in Edinburgh to win Dirac to give a Robin Schlapp Lecture, an event that was instituted at the time of Robin's retirement. It was the only other time the two old gentlemen met again.

Members of the Theory Department of Edinburgh University,
in the eighties. Centre, left to right:
Prof. Nicholas Kemmer, his secretary and Robert Schlapp

However, in Robin's life there is quite a different further linking thread. In the summer of 1924 at the end of Robin's Cambridge period he was entitled to do some travelling. He chose to spend a period in Göttingen where a galaxy of authorities in Theoretical Physics were offering a series of lectures. Among them was a local Ordinarius, Max Born, who was later to play an important part in Robin's life. Just one year later was the *annus mirabilis* of the birth of Quantum Mechanics, begun by Werner Heisenberg who, as an assistant of Max Born in Göttingen, took the first step in the comprehension of the structure of the atom. Though Paul Dirac was at the time a mere novice research student, his Research Supervisor received a private communication from Max Born on Heisenberg's new ideas long before publication. The Supervisor sought help from his phenomenal young student, Dirac – and before long the Quantum Mechanics idea was enlarged and reinforced.

A new scheme of Commonwealth Fellowships had been created and Robin already had an offer of one to spend several years at Yale University, but in his own home of Edinburgh there had been changes of great interest to Robin. The University decided to found a Chair in mathematical physics which, keeping to local tradition they decided to name the *Tait Chair of Natural Philosophy* thus keeping up the memory of P. G. Tait who had occupied the single chair before. An excellent choice for that Chair was Charles Galton Darwin who understood the new ideas of Quantum Mechanics and all the many related developments. Nobody in Scotland could have been better suited to fill the lectureship that would be needed to support Darwin than Robin. In his own words "the family ties and the old environment" led him to accept Darwin's offer rather than the Commonwealth Fellowship to Yale, even though that option would involve considerable teaching duties.

At the very start Darwin suggested that Robin should study the Stark Effect of the Fine Structure of Hydrogen. Robin tackled this without delay and reported the results at a meeting of the British Association where a visiting American noted that a pupil of his had obtained the same results, but heard from Robin that the two workers had used very different methods. The outcome of this was that van Vleck invited Robin to spend the academic year 1931–32 in his department in Madison, Wisconsin. There he produced ample proof that he was an up-and-coming theoretical physicist. He also found two firm friends for life. One was van Vleck himself, the second was a British scientist whose name was to become very familiar to every Briton: William, later Lord Penney, hard not to associate with Los Alamos and Aldermaston.

Van Vleck's central interest was paramagnetism and he assigned to the two Britons a study of two groups of ionic crystals – rear earths and the iron group. In his speech accepting his (shared) Nobel Prize for 1977 van Vleck tells: "In ... 1931 ... I had two postdoctorate students.... [Penney and Schlapp's] calculations ... are particularly striking and form the basis of modern magnetochemistry. Each time I read the paper [by Schlapp] I am impressed how it contains all the ingredients of modern crystalline field theory...." Schlapp published one more paper in the Physical Review where the paper from Madison had appeared – and that was the last of Robin's papers on Theoretical Physics.

Darwin resigned the Tait Chair when he was appointed to the Mastership of Christ's College Cambridge in 1936. His successor was Max Born, whom Robin had met in Göttingen in 1924. Under Hitler, Born had lost his post of Ordinarius there at the age of 50 when with a wife and still young family he had to seek a new home abroad. After a few years in Cambridge the vacant Chair at Edinburgh seemed the solution that he sought. The new Born School at Edinburgh became widely known to the relief of the scientific world. But Born was unaware of what a Scottish professor was also expected to do: take a share in a four-year course for undergraduates, including lectures at a very much more elementary level that he had long ceased to deliver, with an elaborate structure of examinations and tutorials – quite unknown on the Continent. In his post it was expected for the Professor to have a personal assistant. It is hardly surprising that Robin did not come up to Born's expectations as an assistant, nor did he realise what the extent of his organisational and teaching commitments was. The University offices soon accepted that this one Department gets its business done not by the Professor but by Dr. Robert Schlapp.

Theoretical Physics research was for Robin at an end but he was far from becoming just an administrator, nor was he merely turning into a superb teacher – he became an important scholar in another, entirely different field. The lives of eminent mathematicians and scientists had for a long time been an interest for him, and as he was well known as a brilliant lecturer, he was invited to speak at many functions. Our Edinburgh Royal Society recognised his early achievements and elected him to Fellowship at the early age of 27, later he served on the Society's Council and held many of its offices. On the occasion of the Society's Bicentenary the Society's Medal was bestowed on him by Her Majesty the Queen. However, the most serious recognition of his scholarship came to him when Professor H.W. Turnbull F.R.S. of St. Andrews University arranged for Robin to join him in the Isaac Newton Committee that was publishing Newton's full correspondence. He remained on the committee, with frequent trips to London, until Turnbull's death.

Halfway towards Born's retirement, in 1953, the very heavy duties expected of Robin were lightened by the recruitment of a student of Robin's, Andrew (Drew) Nisbet to a second lectureship (in Applied Mathematics). As I had the honour of succeeding Born, the duties in my new post were measurably eased for me – there was much in a Scottish Department that was unfamiliar to me as it was for Born, and my gratitude to Robin and Drew is difficult to express. But things started off very smoothly and I must admit that I was not even aware of what additional loads Robin was constantly ready to bear. In 1958 it was Britain's turn to welcome the huge International Congress of Mathematicians. Edinburgh was chosen and the mathematical world knew that the man to turn to was Robin Schlapp.

But Robin had not let me know that the Congress was giving him the enormous added load of work just when Paul Rosbaud, whom I knew very well, was looking for a translator from the German of a collection of essays by Wolfgang Pauli, my own old teacher. I was sure that Robin was ideal for the job. As I can confirm, he got on very well with Pauli, who could sometimes be difficult to satisfy, but just before he was completing the translation Pauli died. Robin's work, soon completed was sent to several eminent referees, who hardly differed in returning favourable reports that Robin had tackled an extremely difficult task. "I can't think of how it could have been done better" was a typical phrase, except that one of the referees added the words "I felt that Pauli's unique personality does not quite come through". This one phrase was enough for Pauli's widow to exercise her right to veto the publishing of the translation.

A number of friends tried very earnestly to convince Mrs Pauli to change her mind; we did not succeed. Despite much effort, we were unable to induce Robin to accept more than a trifling sum from the publisher. The affair was left to rest for 29 years, until Pauli's widow's death. Then, when Robin's home in Edinburgh was just being emptied and Robin had settled in a home in the south near his daughters, I had the good fortune to discover one of the typist's flimsy copies of the entire translation from which the work done so long ago can be reconstructed. I cannot describe the many obstacles that had to be overcome. I had hoped that all could be completed while Robin still lived. But that was not to be; he died on 31 May 1991.

Nicholas Kemmer

Wolfgang Pauli

(1900–1958)

A Biographical Introduction by Charles P. Enz

1. The Family

Wolfgang Pauli's grandfather Jacob W. Pascheles had inherited from his father Wolf a bookshop in Prague which he operated with considerable success so that he was able to acquire a house on the Old Town Square. Interestingly, in the past this house had been a convent of the congregation of the Paulans. Jacob Pascheles was a respected member of the Jewish community of Prague. As elder of the congregation of the well-known 'Gipsy's Synagogue' he had presided over the "confirmation" (bar mitzwah) of Franz Kafka whose family also lived on the Old Town Square. Jacob's son Wolfgang Joseph, the father of Wolfgang Pauli, was born in Prague on 11th September 1869 and studied Medicine at Charles University together with Ernst Mach's son Ludwig. There he obtained his doctor's degree in 1893 [1].

Ernst Mach was professor of experimental physics at Charles University until 1895 when he moved to the University of Vienna. Wolfgang Joseph Pascheles had come to Vienna already in 1892 where he was offered an assistantship at the Medical Faculty. There he later became a professor and a well-known expert in the physical chemistry of proteins [2]. Vienna became his home; there he joined the catholic faith and chose the new name Pauli (see the speculation in Ref. 1 concerning this choice). There also he married Bertha Camilla Schütz on 2nd May 1899. On 25th April 1900 his only son Wolfgang was born and on 31st May the newborn was baptized with the names Wolfgang Ernst Friedrich. The second of these names was chosen in honour of Ernst Mach who had agreed to be the godfather.

Much later Pauli describes this relationship in a letter to C. G. Jung (Ref. 3, letter [60] of 31 March 1953), an excerpt of which is exhibited in the Pauli room at CERN, Geneva, together with the christening cup and the card of Ernst Mach. There one reads: "It so happened that my father was very friendly with his family, and at that time was intellectually entirely under his influence. He (Mach) had thus graciously agreed to assume the role of my godfather. ... He evidently was a stronger personality than the catholic priest, and the result seems to be that in this way I am baptized 'antimetaphysical' instead of catholic. In any case, the card remains in the cup and in spite of my larger spiritual transformations in later years it still remains a label which I myself carry, namely: 'of antimetaphysical descent'." (see Ref. 4, pp. 766 and 787).

Pauli's third given name was chosen in honour of his grandfather Friedrich Schütz, a well-to-do Viennese whose wife Bertha born Dillner von Dillnersdorf was of noble descent. Young "Wolfi" loved this grandmother who was a singer at the Imperial Opera in Vienna and spent hours with him playing the piano and singing. Between her and his mother Bertha who was a correspondent of the *Neue Freie Presse* he lived a well-protected childhood which was only disturbed when in 1909 Pauli's sister Hertha was born who, much like her mother, became a writer and, in fact, made herself a name with some of her novels.

2. The Infant Prodigy

During the first World War Pauli was a pupil in the humanistic section, including ancient Greek and Latin in its curriculum, of the Gymnasium (high school) of Döbling, a district of the city of Vienna. He soon became an infant prodigy in mathematics and physics but he also took a vivid interest in the history of classical antiquity. His father regularly consulted with godfather Mach concerning the mathematics and physics literature to be recommended to young Wolfgang. Thus when Pauli passed his Abitur (final exams) at the end of the war as a member of the "class of geniuses" of the Döbling Gymnasium (see Ref. 4, p. 767) he was already in possession of the mathematical and physical knowledge to write three papers on general relativity, all published in 1919 [5a,b,c] (also Ref. 6, vol. 2) which immediately attracted the attention of the illustrious mathematician Hermann Weyl.

It was clear that Pauli was going to study theoretical physics, and his choice was Sommerfeld in Munich where Pauli went in autumn 1918. Arnold Sommerfeld, together with Niels Bohr in Copenhagen, was one of the authorities in the quantum theory of the atom and an accomplished teacher. And although Pauli could afford not to follow Sommerfeld's lectures regularly he later considered the stimulation received from Sommerfeld and his circle of pupils as essential for his scientific development (see Pauli's *Autobiographie* reproduced in Ref. 7, English translation in Ref. 6, vol. 1, p. X ; see also essay 5 in this volume). He even retained a life-long almost submissive devotion to his teacher.

Sommerfeld had suggested that the 19-year old Pauli write in his place the encyclopedia article on relativity theory. Published in 1921 this article established Pauli's fame and evoked the admiration of Einstein himself. Apart from supplements in English written by Pauli in his last year of life to complement the English translation of the encyclopedia article, this work has survived to this day as a still valid account on the subject [8].

Surprisingly, Pauli's later contributions to the theory of relativity are rather modest as compared to his other achievements. Nevertheless, he clearly kept a vivid interest in the subject which is evidenced not only by the mentioned supplements but also by his critical survey of the current problems in his *Schlußwort durch den Präsidenten der Konferenz* at the congress *Fünfzig Jahre Relativitätstheorie*, Bern 1955 [9] (see also the essay 11 in this volume).

The same year 1921 of his encyclopedia article Pauli received his doctor diploma "summa cum laude" from the University of Munich. In his PhD thesis he had investigated the hydrogen molecule ion $(H_2)^+$ in the framework of the Bohr-Sommerfeld quantum theory [10]. A short account of this work, written in the sophisticated and precise German typical for Pauli is reproduced in Ref. 7. From this time in Munich also dates Pauli's life-long friendship with Werner Heisenberg who, one year younger, was also a student of Sommerfeld.

3. Exclusion Principle and Spin

Pauli's work on problems of the old quantum theory begun with his thesis led him to the principal research centers in this field in Europe. As may be seen from his *Autobiographie* mentioned above, he spent the winter term 1921–1922 in Göttingen as assistant of Max Born with whom he formulated the systematic application of the astronomical perturbation theory to atomic physics [11]. Also in Göttingen but later in 1922 he met Bohr personally for the first time. Bohr, to Pauli's great surprise, invited him to his institute for one year (see Ref. 12 which is a more personal version of the first part of Pauli's Nobel Lecture reproduced as essay 18 in this volume).

Thus, after a summer spent in Hamburg as assistant of Wilhelm Lenz, whom he had met in Munich among Sommerfeld's pupils, Pauli went to Copenhagen. This was the beginning of his occupation with the irregularities induced by a magnetic field in the atomic spectra, the so-called anomalous Zeeman effect. Pauli comments on this activity as follows [12]: "A colleague who met me strolling rather aimlessly in the beautiful streets of Copenhagen said to me in a friendly manner, 'you look very unhappy'; whereupon I answered fiercly, 'How can one look happy when he is thinking about the anomalous Zeeman effect?' ".

This research culminated at the end of the year 1924 in the formulation of the *exclusion principle* [13] for which Pauli received the Nobel Prize of 1945. While this exclusion principle left none of Pauli's colleagues indiffer-

Physics Department from Debye. It is at this moment also that Pauli drops the "jun." attached to his name on his publications, an attribute that he had kept because his father published under the same name and was also well known.

The first years in Zurich turned out to be very difficult for Pauli; not that anything transpired in his scientific life, as will be seen shortly. The year before, on 15 November his evangelical mother died from poisoning at the age of 48 years. His father who had separated from her, later married the much younger sculptor Maria Rottler [2]. On 6 May 1929 Pauli left the catholic church, and on 23 December of that year he married in Berlin Käthe Deppner, a young performer from the dance school Trudi Tschopp in Zurich. However, this marriage seems to have been rather unstable from the start since Pauli writes to his friend Oskar Klein on 10 February 1930 (my translation): "In case my wife should run away one day you (as well as all my other friends) will receive a printed notice." (Ref. 14, Vol. II, p. 4). True, Pauli was not Käthe's choice, she spent most of her time in Berlin and before the marriage had already met the chemist Paul Goldfinger whom she married later. The divorce took place in Vienna on 26 November 1930. Pauli commented later: "Had she taken a bullfighter I would have understood but an ordinary chemist . . .".

In his despair Pauli started to drink and to smoke. His father recommended him to see the psychiatrist Carl Gustav Jung in Zurich. Jung, realizing that he had to do with an extraordinary personality, assigned the young analyst Erna Rosenbaum to Pauli and stayed in the background (see the footnote on p. 9 of Ref. 3). However, he kept supervising the treatment, being particularly interested in Pauli's abundant dreams. This was the beginning of the life-long association between the two men which led to a deeply fascinating correspondence [3]. In 1934 the analysis was successfully terminated, and already on 4 April 1934 Pauli married Franca Bertram, born in Munich on 16 December 1901, who was a devoted and caring spouse for the rest of his life.

During this time of crisis came Pauli's proposal of the *neutrino*. A few days after his divorce Pauli writes the famous letter "to the radioactive ladies and gentlemen" at a physics meeting in Tübingen, in which he excuses himself for being unavailable because of a dance taking place in Zurich that night. This letter is reproduced in essay 20 in this volume which contains all the essential points of the early history of the neutrino. The content of this letter, however, was so revolutionary that Pauli waited to give a written report on it until the situation had cleared. This was at the 7th Solvay Congress in October 1933 [23].

To appreciate the boldness of the neutrino idea one has to realize that before 1932 the only known elementary particles (apart from the photon) were the proton and the electron. The problem had been an energy deficit in the beta-decay of Radon (Radium Emanation). While Bohr, taking up an earlier speculation, was prepared to sacrifice energy conservation in the sub-atomic domain, this conservation law was for Pauli one of the pillars of modern physics. However, as is particularly lucidly described in Pauli's conference paper on *The conservation laws in the theory of relativity and in nuclear physics* given in Moscow on 27 October 1937 (reprinted in Ref. 7), this conviction was not just a credo but was based on the following argument: In the realm of Einstein's general relativity, energy conservation plays formally the same role as charge conservation in Maxwell's electrodynamics. Since violation of charge conservation has never been observed, violation of energy conservation is unacceptable.

Proof of the existence of the neutrino was slow to come. The first news of its detection reached Zurich late in 1953. To celebrate the event Pauli and a group of faithfuls climbed Uetliberg above Zurich. On the way down late that evening, recounts William Barker, "Pauli was a little wobbly from the red wine we had at dinner. (He had graciously responded to many individual toasts.) [Konrad] Bleuler said to me: 'Take his left arm – I'll take his right arm, we can't afford to lose him now.' Later when we were about midway, Pauli turned to me with a comment I shall always treasure, 'Remember, Barker,' he said, 'all good things come to the man who is patient.' " [24].

The news of the definitive detection, however, reached Pauli only on 15 June 1956. The telegram from Los Alamos where, during the war, the atomic bomb had been developed, announced: "We are happy to inform you that we have definitely detected neutrinos from fission fragments by observing inverse beta decay of protons. Observed cross section agrees well with expected six times ten to minus forty-four square centimeters. Frederick Reines, Clyde Cowan", to which Pauli answered by night letter: "Thanks for message. Everything comes to him who knows how to wait. Pauli".

Although Reines and Cowan's result was a personal triumph for Pauli "this crazy child of the crisis of my life" (letter to Max Delbrück of 6 October 1958, Ref. 14, Vol. II, p. 38) had other surprises in store. Less than six months later several experiments discovered a birth defect: the neutrino was left-handed (see essay 20 in this volume). This news of *parity violation* even made *The New York Times* of 16 January 1957 (see Ref. 3, p. 218). Again later in 1957 it was the neutrino that motivated Pauli to collaborate with Heisenberg on his nonlinear spinor equation (for details see C. P. Enz, *Paulis Schaffen der letzten Lebensjahre*, Ref. 7, p. 105). Towards the end of the year this collaboration developed into a real euphoria, which ended when Pauli met severe criticism at a special meeting convened at the end of January 1958 at Columbia University, New York (for details see Ref. 25). The result of this collaboration was a manuscript entitled *On the Isospin Group in the Theory of the Elementary Particles* which, however, was not published until recently [26].

6. Field Quantization. Princeton

When Pauli settled at ETH in 1928 his main interest was in quantum field theory. In Hamburg he had already written a paper together with Jordan on the relativistically covariant quantization of the electromagnetic field [27]. However, in this form, quantization did not seem at that time to be generalizable to other fields and interactions. Thus the two fundamental papers by Heisenberg and Pauli were based on the canonical formalism [28]. Although the lack of explicit covariance in this work turned out to be a handicap some 20 years later, the general quantization prescriptions formulated in the first of these papers were of great use.

An important application of this work was the (second) quantization of massive charged particles of spin 0 obeying Bose-Einstein statistics and the relativistic wave equation or Klein-Gordon equation. Pauli analysed this system in collaboration with his assistant Victor Weisskopf in 1934 [29]. The surprising result was the existence of antiparticles with the same mass but opposite charge. Thus the theory achieved exactly the same thing as the second-quantized Dirac equation but "without introducing a vacuum full of particles", a feature which had strongly displeased Pauli who therefore called their work the "anti-Dirac paper" [30].

At the time this work seemed to be an academic exercise without physical meaning. Weisskopf comments: "We had no idea that the world of particles would abound with spin-zero entities a quarter of a century later. This was the reason why we published it in the venerable but not widely read *Helvetica Physica Acta*." [30].

But the most important consequence of the Pauli-Weisskopf paper certainly was that it "led Pauli to formulate the famous relation between spin and statistics." [30]. In its most general form this relation was proven by Pauli in his first paper submitted from Princeton in August 1940, shortly after his arrival at the Institute for Advanced Study [31]. The relation says that particles with integer or half-integer spin must be quantized according to Bose-Einstein or Fermi-Dirac statistics, respectively. In a footnote to this paper Pauli writes: "This paper is part of a report which was prepared by the author for the Solvay Congress 1939 and in which slight improvements have since been made. In view of the unfavorable times, the Congress did not take place, and the publication of the reports has been postponed for an indefinite length of time."

A second paper that Pauli submitted from Princeton and which also was planned as a report to the Solvay Congress of 1939 reviewed the relativistic field theories of particles with spin 0, 1 and 1/2 [32]. This paper is noteworthy because it calls attention to the fact that the cases of spin 1 and 1/2 admit arbitrary anomalous magnetic moments. These "Pauli terms" were later found to exist for all elementary particles with non-zero spin.

In July 1940 Pauli and his wife had left Zurich under difficult circumstances, travelling by train through southern France to Lisbon and by boat to New York and finally to Princeton where Pauli had accepted an invited professorship offered by the Institute for Advanced Study. Switzerland had become increasingly isolated and insecure due to the German occupation of Austria and France. To his regret Pauli had not been able to obtain Swiss citizenship. He left behind the new house in Zollikon on the lake of Zurich and his dog Dixi (for more details see the introduction to Vol. III of Ref. 14). His friend Gregor Wentzel who was professor at the University of Zurich replaced Pauli at ETH during the whole war and vigorously defended Pauli's chair for him.

But otherwise Pauli did not have any particular attachment to a home. As may be seen from the correspondence of this period (Ref. 14, Vol. III) physics continued for Pauli without respite. However, a definite change of focus is easily noticeable: Instead of general field-theoretic questions, it is the more concrete problem of meson physics that commands his attention. As Pauli says himself, this change was mainly due to the influence of Robert Oppenheimer (see the introduction to Vol. III of Ref. 14). These efforts published in several papers with his collaborators in Princeton were discussed by Pauli in a series of lectures given at MIT in Boston in autumn 1944 [33].

At the beginning, Pauli encountered a very active scientific atmosphere in the US. However, when the atomic bomb project got organized in Los Alamos at the beginning of 1943, Pauli started to feel somewhat lonesome. Of course, he had good contacts with his colleagues at the Institute, above all with the art historian Erwin Panofsky (see the Prefatory Note in essay 21 in this volume) and with Albert Einstein (in essay 13 in this volume, Pauli mentions his discussions with Einstein speaking of Einstein's work with Rosen and Podolsky). Although very suspicious of any political interference with science, Pauli had asked Oppenheimer's opinion concerning the propriety of Pauli's association with the war-related research. But Oppenheimer thought it more important that Pauli assured the continuity of basic research in the US (see Oppenheimer's letter [671] of 20 May 1943 and Pauli's answer [672] in Ref. 14, Vol. III).

It was in Princeton that the news of the Nobel Prize reached Pauli in November 1945. His lack of a valid passport rendered the preparations to travel to Stockholm quite complicated, and finally Pauli decided not to go. Instead, a splendid dinner party was organized at the Institute for Advanced Study on 10 December 1945; Ref. 12 is Pauli's address to this party. To everybody's surprise, Einstein rose and offered a toast in which he designated Pauli as his successor at the Institute and as his spiritual son (see the footnote on page 213 of Ref. 12). Pauli has described this scene in a letter to Max Born on

24 April 1955, shortly after Einstein's death: "Never will I forget the speech that he has pronounced about me and for me in Princeton in 1945, after I had received the Nobel Prize. It was like a king who abdicates and installs me, as sort of 'son of choice', as successor. Unfortunately, no records of this speech of Einstein exist (it was improvised, and a manuscript does not exist either)." [34].

Pauli was about to become a permanent member of the Institute for Advanced Study and received American citizenship in 1946; he also had an offer from Columbia University. However, in spring 1946 he decided to return to his chair at ETH in Zurich and to his house in Zollikon where on 25 July 1949 he also became a Swiss citizen. In December 1946 he attended the Nobel festivities in Stockholm and gave his Nobel Lecture.

7. Zurich. Physis and Psyche

Back in Zurich Pauli's enormous reputation soon attracted the most brillant young theorists so that his institute became a world center of field theory and the problems of renormalization. In a course given at ETH in the academic year 1950–51 Pauli critically reviewed the new covariant methods developed by Tomonaga, Schwinger, Feynman, Dyson and others [35].

However, the "larger spiritual transformations" mentioned in Pauli's letter exhibited at CERN and quoted at the beginning of this introduction are visible in the increasingly philosophical aspect of Pauli's work during this last period of his life. This aspect is manifest in the content of the present volume.

Back from Princeton he resumed his discussions and exchange of letters with Carl Gustav Jung [3]. A similarly fascinating exchange also developed with Pauli's former assistant Markus Fierz who had become a professor at the University of Basel and regularly participated in the Monday-afternoon theory seminars in Zurich (the first part of this correspondence is published in Ref. 14, Vol. III). A deep and very personal correspondence linked Pauli and Marie-Louise von Franz, one of the principal collaborators of Jung who had translated most of the texts in Latin of Pauli's Kepler article (see the Prefatory Note in essay 21 in this volume). Pauli also renewed his regular meetings with his friend C. A. Meier who had been assistant of Jung and later became president of the Curatorium of the C. G. Jung Institute in Zurich and professor at ETH.

Repetedly Pauli discussed in his essays the meaning of the measuring process in quantum mechanics and, in particular, the role of the observer in this theory. In *The Philosophical Significance of the Idea of Complementarity* (essay 2) and again in his Kepler article (essay 21) he stresses the fact that in microphysics the observer is different in an essential way from the "detached observer" of classical physics and compares the effect of an observation of a quantum system (the "reduction of the wave packet") with a transformation (Wandlung) in the alchemist sense. This alchemist transformation is described in *Science and Western Thought* (essay 16) as follows: "According to the alchemist conception, the deliverance of substance by the man who transforms it, which culminates in the production of the stone, is, in consequence of a mystic correspondence between macroscosm and microcosm, identical with the redeeming transformation (Wandlung) of the man through the *opus*, which comes about only 'Deo concedente'."

The notion of the "detached observer" occurs surprisingly often in Pauli's essays and always designates a world view, namely the classical one, that has been left behind once and for all. More astonishing is Pauli's conjecture in *Phenomenon and Physical Reality* (essay 15) "that the observer in present-day physics is still too completely detached, and that physics will depart still further from the classical example." Within the strictly physical domain Pauli here has in mind a future quantum field theory capable of describing the field and its source (the test charge) as dual or complementary (see also Ref. 25). This opinion is vibrantly expressed in the concluding remarks of *Albert Einstein and the Development of Physics* (essay 13, see also the essays 1, 15, 17 and 18).

An important detail in this thinking about duality is the meaning of the numerical value of the electric charge which in the form of Sommerfeld's fine-structure constant is approximately 1/137. Pauli repeatedly stressed that progress in quantum field theory was linked to an understanding of this number (see the essays 9, 10, 15, 18, also Ref. 29 and Ref. 8, Supplementary Note 23). But the number 137 also had an irrational, magic meaning for Pauli; it was the room number 137 in the Red Cross Hospital in Zurich where he died on 15 December 1958 (see Ref. 4, p. 792, Ref. 7, pp. 11 and 110 and Ref. 34).

The enigmatic conjecture "that the observer in present-day physics is still too completely detached" also has a meaning beyond physics. Indeed, in his article for Jung's 80th birthday (essay 17), Pauli compares the observational situation in physics with that in psychology: "Since the unconscious is not quantitatively measurable, and therefore not capable of mathematical description and since every extension of consciousness ('bringing into consciousness') must by reaction alter the unconscious, we may expect a 'problem of observation' in relation to the unconscious, which, while it presents analogies with that in atomic physics, nevertheless involves considerably greater difficulties."

For Pauli this analogy had implications in both directions: On the one hand, in the concluding remarks of the birthday article for Jung (essay 17) he expresses the expectation that in the future the idea of the unconscious should emerge from the purely therapeutical realm and become more a problem of *objective* research. On the other hand, he thought that in physics the remedy for the too complete detachement of the observer may lie in the integration of the *subjective*, psychic. Indeed, in *Science and Western Thought* (essay 16) Pauli asks the question: "Shall we be able to realise, on a higher plane, alchemy's old dream of psycho-physical unity, by the creation of a unified conceptual foundation for the scientific comprehension of the physical as well as the psychical?"

This quest for a unity of physis and psyche is a recurrent theme in the exchange between Pauli and Jung and is the main concern in Pauli's *Background Physics* in which he was guided by his dream motives (*Hintergrundsphysik*, Ref. 3, Appendix 3). It was also a motivation for his Kepler article (essay 21) in which he describes the polemic between the rational Kepler representing the new scientific attitude and the irrational Fludd who defends the old alchemist world view. Kepler, like Newton after him, firmly believed in the Trinity of the Christian God while Fludd got his inspiration from the Pythagorean quaternity which for him was a symbol for the unity of the world.

Pauli admits that his sympathy is not only on Kepler's side, remembering that the discovery of the exclusion principle had been possible only after realizing that the electron's state depends on a *fourth* quantum number. Towards the end of Section 6 of his Kepler article Pauli characterizes Fludd's vision of unity as follows: "Even though at the cost of consciousness of the quantitative side of nature and its laws, Fludd's 'hieroglyphic' figures do try to preserve a *unity* of the inner experience of the 'observer' (as we should say today) and the external processes of nature, and thus a *wholeness* in its contemplation – a wholeness formerly contained in the idea of the analogy between microscosm and macrocosm but apparently already lacking in Kepler and lost in the world view of classical natural sciences."

Charles P. Enz

References

[1] F. Smutný, *Ernst Mach and Wolfgang Pauli's Ancestors in Prague*, Gesnerus **46**, 183 (1989).
[2] E. I. Valko, *Professor Wolfgang Pauli zum achzigsten Geburtstag*, Österreichische Chemiker-Zeitung, 50. Jahrgang, Heft 9, 1949, p. 183.
[3] C. A. Meier (ed.), *Wolfgang Pauli und C. G. Jung. Ein Briefwechsel 1932–1958*, (Springer, Berlin, 1992).
[4] C. P. Enz, *W. Pauli's Scientific Work*, in *The Physicist's Conception of Nature*, ed. J. Mehra (Reidel, Dordrecht-Holland, 1973).

[5] W. Pauli, *Physikalische Zeitschrift* **20**, 25 (a), 457 (b) (1919); *Verhandlungen der Deutschen Physikalischen Gesellschaft* **21**, 742 (c) (1919).

[6] W. Pauli, *Collected Scientific Papers*, Vol. 1 and 2, eds. R. Kronig and V. F. Weisskopf (Wiley, New York, 1964).

[7] C. P. Enz und K. von Meyenn (eds.), *Wolfgang Pauli. Das Gewissen der Physik* (Vieweg, Braunschweig, 1988).

[8] W. Pauli, *Relativitätstheorie*, in *Encyklopädie der mathematischen Wissenschaften*, Vol. 5, Part 2, pp. 539–775 (Teubner, Leipzig, 1921); *Theory of Relativity*, transl. G. Field (Pergamon, London, 1958).

[9] W. Pauli, *Helv. Phys. Acta*, Supplement **IV**, 261 (1956); reprinted in Ref. 7.

[10] W. Pauli, *Annalen der Physik* **68**, 177 (1922).

[11] M. Born und W. Pauli, *Zeitschrift für Physik* **10**, 137 (1922).

[12] W. Pauli, *Science* **103**, 213 (1946); reprinted in Ref. 7.

[13] W. Pauli, *Zeitschrift für Physik* **31**, 765 (1925); reprinted in Ref. 7.

[14] W. Pauli, *Scientific Correspondence with Bohr, Einstein, Heisenberg and others*, Vol. I: 1919–1929, eds. A. Hermann, K. von Meyenn and V. F. Weisskopf (Springer, New York, 1979); Vol. II: 1930–1939, ed. K. von Meyenn (Springer, Berlin, 1985); Vol. III: 1940–1949, ed. K. von Meyenn (Springer, Berlin, 1993).

[15] W. Pauli, *Naturwissenschaften* **12**, 741 (1924).

[16] S. Goudsmit, *Pauli and Nuclear Spin, Physics Today*, June 1961, p. 18.

[17] W. Pauli, *Zeitschrift für Physik* **36**, 336 (1926); reprinted in Ref. 7.

[18] W. Pauli, *Zeitschrift für Physik* **43**, 601 (1927); reprinted in Ref. 7.

[19] W. Pauli, *Zeitschrift für Physik* **41**, 81 (1927); reprinted in Ref. 7.

[20] W. Pauli, *Die allgemeinen Prinzipien der Wellenmechanik*, in *Handbuch der Physik*, eds. H. Geiger and K. Scheel, 2nd ed., Vol. 24, Part 1, pp. 83–272 (Springer, Berlin, 1933); revised second edition without the section on quantum electrodynamics (B, Ziff. 6–8), in *Handbuch der Physik*, ed. S. Flügge, Vol. 5, Part 1, pp. 1–168 (Springer, Berlin, 1958); reprinted in Ref. 6; *General Principles of Quantum Mechanics*, original version translated and edited by P. Achuthan and K. Venkatesan (Springer, Berlin, 1980); reprinted second edition (with B, Ziff. 6–8 from first edition as appendices I–III), edited and commented by N. Straumann (Springer, Berlin, 1990).

[21] W. Pauli, *Zeitschrift für Physik* **80**, 573 (1933); reprinted in Ref. 7.

[22] M. Fierz, *Naturwissenschaft und Geschichte. Vorträge und Aufsätze* (Birkhäuser, Basel, 1988).

[23] W. Pauli, in *Septième Conseil de Physique Solvay, Noyaux Atomiques. Discussions, Bruxelles 1933*, p. 324 (Gauthier-Villars, Paris, 1934); reprinted in Ref. 7 but missing in Ref. 6.

[24] W. Barker, letter to *Physics Today*, February 1979, p. 11.

[25] C.P. Enz, *Wolfgang Pauli between Quantum Reality and the Royal Path of Dreams*, in *Symposia on the Foundation of Modern Physics 1992. The Copenhagen Interpretation and Wolfgang Pauli*, p. 195, eds. K. V. Laurikainen and C. Montonen (World Scientific, Singapore, 1993).

[26] W. Heisenberg, *Collected Works*, eds. W. Blum, H.-P. Dürr and H. Rechenberg, Series A/Part III (Springer, Berlin, 1993), p. 337, final version, March 1958, including the circular letter (postscript) by Pauli of 8 April 1958.

[27] P. Jordan and W. Pauli, *Zeitschrift für Physik* **47**, 151 (1928).

[28] W. Heisenberg and W. Pauli, *Zeitschrift für Physik* **56**, 1 (1929); **59**, 168 (1930); reprinted in Ref. 7.

[29] W. Pauli and V. F. Weisskopf, *Helvetica Physica Acta* **7**, 709 (1934); reprinted in Ref. 7.

[30] V. F. Weisskopf, *The development of field theory in the last 50 years*, *Physics Today*, November 1981, p. 69.

[31] W. Pauli, *Physical Review* **58**, 716 (1940).

[32] W. Pauli, *Reviews of Modern Physics* **13**, 203 (1941).

[33] W. Pauli, *Meson Theory of Nuclear Forces* (Interscience, New York, 1946); second edition 1948.

[34] C. P. Enz, *Wolfgang Pauli, Physicist and Philosopher*, in *Symposium on the Foundations of Modern Physics*, eds. P. Lahti and P. Mittelstaedt (World Scientific, Singapore, 1985), p. 241.

[35] W. Pauli, *Ausgewählte Kapitel aus der Feldquantisierung*, ausgearbeitet von U. Hochstrasser und M. R. Schafroth (Verlag VMP ETH, Zürich, 1957); reprinted by Boringhieri, Torino, 1962; *Selected Topics in Field Quantization* transl. S. Margulis and H. R. Lewis, in *Pauli Lectures on Physics*, ed. C. P. Enz, Vol. 6 (MIT Press, Cambridge, Mass., 1973).

1. Matter*

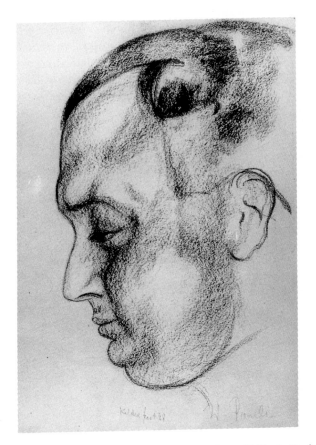

I would like to see Tom Kelder's sketch of me. (The sculptor Haller in Zurich has made a bust which makes me look rather introspective – i.e. Buddha-like.)

Letter from Pauli to Ralph Kronig, December 22, 1949

* First published in English in *Man's Right to Knowledge*, 2nd Series, p. 10 (Columbia University, New York 1954).

Matter has always been and will always be one of the main objects of physics. By speaking on "matter as an aspect of the nature of things," I intend therefore to give you an impression of how laws of nature concerning matter and belonging to physics can be found and how they gradually develop. It is true that these laws and our ideas of reality which they presuppose are getting more and more abstract. But also, for a professional, it is useful to be reminded that behind the technical and mathematical form of the thoughts underlying the laws of nature, there remains always the layer of everyday life with its ordinary language. Science is a systematic refinement of the concepts of everyday life revealing a deeper and, as we shall see, not directly visible reality behind the everyday reality of colored, noisy things. But it should not be forgotten either that this deeper reality would cease to be an object of physics, different from the objects of pure mathematics and pure speculation, if its links with the realities of everyday life were entirely disconnected.

Let us take as an example the fundamental laws of mechanics that we now call classical, but which were entirely unknown about three hundred years ago. The law of inertia says that bodies move with a velocity constant both in direction and magnitude, if external causes are absent. What was most revolutionary in this statement, when it was new, was the recognition that a uniform movement is an ultimate fact without any cause. This was alien to the views of earlier times which assumed that in absence of any moving cause there is rest and that any velocity is due to a cause. On the other hand, most problematical to later times was the question of how the uniformity of the motion of a body could be judged without reference to other moving bodies. After many critical works in the last century, the latter question led to a new formulation of the laws of gravitation at the hands of *Einstein*.

Let us return, however, in the spirit of classical mechanics, to the further problem of how external causes influence the motion of a body. *Newton* called the external causes "force" and defined them as mass times acceleration. Let us assume, for the sake of simplicity, that we know what acceleration is; then this explanation still seems to contain a logical circle: force is defined by mass, and mass by force. But this is not so bad as it sounds at first, due to the other law of *Newton* that action and reaction are equal and opposite. This implies that the sum of all forces in a closed system is always zero. That has the consequence that something is conserved, is constant in time, namely, the sum of the velocities multiplied by their masses taken over all bodies of a closed system for every possible direction.

In this way we see that we have already made certain steps in the direction of abstracting concepts which have their origin in everyday life. Mass, originally weight measured with balances, is now an abstract coefficient of velocities determined in such a way that the sum is constant. Later one had even to take a dependence of the mass on velocity into account. I wish to say here that the product of mass and velocity is called momentum. Just as velocity, it is a directed quantity, a vector, as the professionals say. Force, originally related to the efforts made by human muscles, has become now something that is measured by mass times acceleration. The forces have to be known somehow in their dependence on the distances of the bodies, so that the assumed laws of mechanics can be checked by experience. This was actually the case for the movement of the celestial bodies under the influence of gravity, due to the famous inverse square law of *Newton*.

Whatever the forces may be, it is an immediate consequence of these mechanical laws that the initial conditions determine uniquely the motion of all bodies, if both the position and velocity or momentum of the bodies at a given time are included in the initial conditions. In order to check the laws of classical mechanics, the terrestrial experimenter chooses the initial conditions in an arbitrary way at his free will, while the astronomer takes advantage of the different conditions realized by different celestial bodies in nature.

As a consequence of these mechanical laws, there is another quantity conserved which we call energy, and which consists of two parts. One of them, the so-called potential energy, is a function of the position of the bodies from which the forces can be computed. The sum of the two is constant in time. Energy, in contrast to momentum, has no direction.

The chemists found another conservation law, namely, the law of the conservation of mass in chemical reactions. But *Einstein* showed by a careful analysis of the laws of electricity and magnetism – which since *Maxwell* includes optics, the physics of light – that these two conservation laws are actually only one. Whenever energy is changed, then mass is changed too. However, the amount is very small, as the factor involved is the square of the velocity of light. It needs very large changes of energy to obtain a measurable change of mass.

This means now an important step of abstraction for the very concept of matter itself. What is matter? The paper on which I am writing is matter, the air is still matter, but even light has become matter now, due to *Einstein*'s discoveries. It has mass and weight; it is not different from ordinary matter, it too having both energy and momentum. The only difference is that light is never at rest, but always moving with the same characteristic velocity.

I alluded already to the laws of electromagnetism. Are they consequences of the mechanical laws of *Newton*? No, they are of a different type, in spite of fundamental similarities regarding the supposed complete determination of the course of events by initial conditions. Since the days of *Faraday* and *Maxwell* in the last century, we speak here of a field. What is a field? Another refinement of a concept of everyday life – something which is continuous in space and time, physical qualities of the points of space and time, continuously varying with them. What is the nature of these physical qualities? The modern answer is: it does not matter; I only need a means to measure them, and whenever they vary continuously, then it is a field. In the last century one had a very different answer: the nature of the qualities involved should be mechanical, deformations, strain and stress, perhaps of a hypothetical medium, but in any case mechanical. Gradually the physicists abandoned the mechanical premise. An objective scientific description was not any longer a mechanical description in absolute space and time. It became a more abstract description of phenomena, in which continuous functions depending on a frame of reference occurred. The laws of nature, however, are the same, whatever this system of reference may be. Not only does a common uniform movement of observer and apparatus have no influence on the phenomena, but even an accelerated movement, according to *Einstein*, is at least locally equivalent to a gravitational field. I shall not try here to explain to you the mathematical ideas of group theory that serve to formulate exactly such an equivalence, and which are one of the most fundamental tools of modern physics, the fruitfulness of which, as I believe, is not yet exhausted at all. I only say briefly that also this part of mathematics is a generalization of everyday experiences, as we meet the underlying ideas already in the problem of distinguishing left from right. In carrying through the equivalence of acceleration and gravitation, *Einstein* succeeded in establishing a field theory of gravitation, analogous to the older field theory of electromagnetism, enriched by the idea of the invariance of the laws of nature with respect to transformations of space-time co-ordinates – continuously varying numbers co-ordinated to the points.

At this stage of the development of the general concepts of physics we meet the old question of whether or not there is a limit to the divisibility of matter, in other words, is matter continuous or discontinuous? Experience decided in favour of the existence of last units of matter in agreement with the ideas of the atomists of ancient Greece. The chemists already had found that the idea of stable molecules and atoms as constituents of matter are the simplest way to describe chemical transformations, but only the physicists of the last century invented methods to count these atoms and molecules. They measured the key number that tells us how many real atoms are in the chemical units. The radioactive phenomena showed that the atoms characterizing the chemical nature of a substance are composed of a relatively small nucleus of positive electricity surrounded by electrically negative particles called electrons, just as the sun is surrounded by planets. Later experiments showed that the nuclei, much heavier than the electrons, are also capable of transformations and consist of other particles, the so-called nucleons. These are the protons of positive charge and the electrically uncharged neutrons of nearly the same mass as the protons. I shall not speak here of the so-called mesons revealed by the cosmic rays and later also artificially produced in the laboratory, with masses intermediate between electrons and protons. I only mention the existence of positrons, which are of equal mass but of opposite electric charge to the electrons. When a positron and an electron meet, they annihilate each other, becoming electromagnetic radiation; and, conversely, this radiation can create electrons and positrons in pairs.

Taking the existence of all these transmutations into account, what remains of the old ideas of matter and of substance? The answer is *energy*. This is the true substance, that which is conserved; only the form in which it appears is changing. There is another quantity, too, which is conserved, but in contrast to energy it is capable of both positive and negative values, namely, *electric charge*. This is not only conserved; it has an atomistic, discrete character: every electric charge occurring in nature has an amount which is an integral multiple of a certain number, the elementary quantum of electricity. We do not know yet why this is so. Theory registers the fact, but does not interpret it yet.

This problem is closely connected with other features of nature, which are comprehended under the name "quantum of action," invented by *Planck*. He found that the laws of electromagnetic radiation, including light, in thermal equilibrium with ordinary matter, could only be explained by making an entirely new assumption regarding the possible values of radiation energy of given frequency. These values can only be integral multiples of a certain amount proportional to the frequency. The universal constant of proportionality involved here is *Planck*'s quantum of action. It has to be recalled here that action is another abstraction of Newtonian mechanics, namely, a quantity with the dimension of energy times time, replacing the merely qualitative concept of action in everyday life. The new assumption soon gave rise to the idea of a "photon," a light particle keeping its energy and momentum together in space so that only its whole amount could be absorbed or emitted at the same time. There are, however, other optical phenomena, the so-called interference and diffraction phenomena, which can only be explained by using the wave-picture. A still deeper analysis was necessary to get rid of these contradictions. Paradoxically this became possible only by the fact that the electrons, just as all other material particles, have also wave properties besides their particle properties, just as light has particle properties besides its wave properties.

These paradoxes of the quantum of action made our atoms into something very different from the objects of Newtonian mechanics. Indeed, although effects of a single atom can be made visible in the form of collective or avalanche effects by suitably constructed apparatus, it should not be forgotten that we are dealing here with an invisible reality, in which features are becoming fundamental which are at least negligible and without practical importance for macroscopic objects. It was *Bohr* who not only developed *Planck*'s ideas concerning a theory of atomic structure and spectral lines, but who also worked out the epistemological consequences of the new quantum mechanics or wave mechanics, which since 1927 removed the logical contradictions from the theoretical explanation of the quantum phenomena. These consequences are not quite easy to understand; and the point of view called "complementarity", which was developed by *Bohr* and others for this purpose, though shared by the majority of physicists, did not remain without opposition.

In order to understand the meaning of complementarity, you have to imagine objects, which always start to move as soon as you look at them with help of an apparatus suitable to locate their position. That would not matter if you could compute this motion and so theoretically determine the disturbance caused by the measurement. What if this disturbance could not be kept under control in principle? If the empirical measurement of this disturbance would introduce new measuring instruments, the interaction of which with the old ones would introduce new disturbances indeterminable and uncontrollable in principle?

This is indeed the actual situation created by the finiteness of the quantum of action. One is here, as *Heisenberg* first pointed out, always in the position of the dilemma between the sacrifice and the choice, a situation which implies a certain freedom on the side of the observer to choose his experimental arrangement as one of at least two possibilities, excluding each other. The old initial conditions of the classical law of inertia consisting of position and velocity or momentum appear now as a real pair of opposites, consisting of independent quantities. According to the theory, to one of these can be ascribed a sharply defined value, only if the other is undetermined in principle in such a way that the product of the uncertainties of the two quantities is given by the quantum of action. As this indeterminacy is an unavoidable element of every initial state of a system that is at all possible according to the new laws of nature, the development of the system can never be determined as was the case in classical mechanics. The theory predicts only the *statistics* of the results of an experiment, when it is repeated under a given condition. Like an ultimate fact without any cause, the *individual* outcome of a measurement is, however, in general not comprehended by laws. This must necessarily be the case, if quantum or wave mechanics is interpreted as a rational generalization of classical physics, which takes into account the finiteness of the quantum of action. The probabilities occurring in the new laws have then to be considered to be primary, which means not deducible from deterministic laws. As an example of these primary probabilities I mention here the fact that the time at which an individual atom will undergo a certain reaction stays undetermined even under conditions where the rate of occurrence of this reaction for a large collection of atoms is practically certain.

It was on these lines that the contradiction between the wave and the particle idea was overcome, since the above-mentioned relation of indeterminacy, which is inherent in the laws of nature, just makes mutually exclusive the experiments which serve to check the wave properties of an atomic object, and the other experiments which serve to check its particle properties.

The significance of this development is to give us insight into the logical possibility of a new and wider pattern of thought. This takes into account the observer, including the apparatus used by him, differently from the way it was done in classical physics, both in Newtonian mechanics and in Maxwell-Einsteinian field theories. In the new pattern of thought we do not assume any longer the *detached observer*, occurring in the idealizations of this classical type of theory, but an observer who by his indeterminable effects creates a new situation, theoretically described as a new state of the observed system. In this way every observation is a singling out of a particular factual result, here and now, from the theoretical possibilities, thereby making obvious the discontinuous aspect of the physical phenomena.

Nevertheless, there remains still in the new kind of theory an *objective reality*, inasmuch as these theories deny any possibility for the observer to influence the results of a measurement, once the experimental arrangement is chosen. Therefore particular qualities of an individual observer do not enter the conceptual framework of the theory. On the contrary, it describes the phenomena on the microscopic scale of atomic objects in a way that is valid for all kinds of observers and by mathematical laws with group theoretical properties, which can be taught to all with a sufficient general knowledge of mathematics and physics. In this wider sense the quantum-mechanical description of atomic phenomena is still an objective description, although the state of an object is not assumed any longer to remain independent of the way in which the possible sources of information about the object are irrevocably altered by observations. The existence of such alterations reveals a new kind of wholeness in nature, unknown in classical physics, inasmuch as an attempt to subdivide a phenomenon defined by the whole experimental arrangement used for its observation creates an entirely new phenomenon.

There is a general agreement that present-day quantum mechanics leaves many fundamental facts unexplained, as for instance the atomistic character of electricity that I mentioned already. Besides that, no satisfactory interpretation is given of the characteristic variety of mass values and of the very different degrees of stability of the many particles, which in a very provisional way are called "elementary". The limitations of the applicability of our present theory admitted, there is, naturally, a wide divergence of opinions about the direction of further development in future. Some physicists hope for the possibility of a return to the classical idea of the detached observer, whose effect on the observed system could always be eliminated by theoretically determinable corrections. Others, with whom I belong myself, have, on the contrary, hopes just in the opposite direction. What has impressed me most in the development which in 1927 eventually led to the establishment of present wave mechanics is the fact that real pairs of opposites, like particle versus wave, or position versus momentum, or energy versus time, exists in physics, the contrast of which can only be overcome in a symmetrical way. This means that one member of the pair is never eliminated in favour of the other, but both are taken over into a new kind of physical law which expresses properly the complementary character of the contrast.

It seems to me likely that the situation is similar in the case of the concepts of field versus test bodies. A field can only be measured by its effects on test bodies, and the test bodies can also be considered as sources of the field. This does not give rise to difficulties for the ordinary large-scale, or macroscopic, phenomena, since the disturbance of the field by the test bodies can here always be supposed to be small and kept under control. This is, however, no longer the case for test bodies, the atomic constitution of which is essential, and particularly not for the elementary particles like electrons or nucleons themselves, the location and motion of which is no longer under control as with macroscopic test bodies.

While in the present theory there exists still a duality between the concepts of fields and of test bodies, I think that a new mathematical form of the physical laws is required, which makes fields without test bodies not only physically but also logically impossible. It must also express properly the complementarity between the measurement of a field with an atomic object on the one hand, and the description of the same object as source of the field on the other hand. Indeed, these two possibilities should become automatically mutually exclusive as a result of a suitable form of the laws of nature.

Similar ideas have been uttered already by *Bohr* and others. I do not need to stress, however, that we are here in a very hypothetical domain where nothing is proved yet and every possibility is still a question of success. I mentioned these hypothetical possibilities only to recommend generally that one should not think simply in traditional forms of the explanation of nature, even if these forms are well formulated in historical philosophical systems, but should be open-minded for new logical and empirical possibilities, not foreseen by these systems.

We have confidence that the human spirit will always be able to create ideas fitting somehow to the external objects that are conveyed to us by our sense data as witnesses of matter or energy in the sense of physics, because both the human spirit inside and the perceived object outside are subjugated to the same cosmic order.

2. The Philosophical Significance of the Idea of Complementarity*

The situation called "complementarity" by *N. Bohr* is explained with the aid of the example furnished by the spheres of application of the contrasting concepts of "wave" and "particle" in modern atomic physics. It consists in the fact that the experimental arrangements to which the one or the other of these intuitive pictures is applied necessarily are mutually exclusive as a consequence of the fundamentally never completely determinable interaction between instruments of observation and the observed system. The analogy is pointed out between this complementary situation and the paradoxes in the relation "subject-object" in general, as well as the pair of opposites employed in more recent psychology, "conscious-unconscious" in particular.**

1. This lecture is published in the hope of furthering by this small contribution those major efforts which have the general aim of once more bringing into closer contact the various partial disciplines into which our intellectual life (Geistigkeit) has fallen apart. The splitting off of the exact sciences and of mathematics as independent partial disciplines from an originally unified but pre-scientific natural philosophy, which began in the 17th century, was of course a necessary condition for the subsequent intellectual development of the western world (Abendland). At the present time, however, the conditions for a renewed understanding between physicists and philosophers on the epistemological foundations of the scientific description of nature seem to be satisfied. As a result of the development of atomistics and quantum theory

---

* Published under the title "Die philosophische Bedeutung der Idee der Komplementarität" in *Experientia* **6** (Heft 2), p. 72–75 (1950). Lecture delivered to the Philosophical Society in Zürich in February 1949. – It has not been possible to give more than a brief qualitative sketch of the physical situation in §2 of the lecture. For details the reader is referred to relevant papers by N. Bohr on *Atomic Theory and the Description of Nature* (Cambridge 1934) as well as his article in the Einstein volume of the *Library of Living Philosophers* (Evanston 1949); also to W. Heisenberg, *The Physical principles of Quantum Theory* (Chicago, 1930). The author's earlier lecture to the Philosophical Society in Zürich, "Raum, Zeit und Kausalität in der modernen Physik", has been published in the periodical *Scientia* **59**, 65–76 (1936), (English translation in this volume, essay 10).

**This *Summary* in English appended to the original version is not reproduced in the German Edition of Pauli's *Aufsätze über Physik und Erkenntnistheorie*.

since 1910 physics has gradually been compelled to abandon its proud claim that it can, in principle, understand the whole universe. All physicists who accept the development that reached a provisional conclusion in 1927 in the systematic construction of the mathematical formalism of wave mechanics, must admit that while at present we have exact sciences, we no longer have a scientific picture of the universe (Weltbild). It is just this circumstance that may contain in itself, as a corrective to the earlier one-sided view, the germ of progress towards a unified total world-picture, of which the exact sciences are only a part. In this I would like to see the more general significance of the idea of complementarity, an idea that has grown out of the soil of physics, as a result of the work of the Danish physicist *Niels Bohr*.

Only a small number of philosophical specialists have hitherto taken cognizance of this new tendency in modern physics, as compared with the theory of relativity. On the other hand some physicists have interpreted modern quantum physics as confirming particular philosophical trends, e. g., positivism. In opposition to this view I shall here adopt the standpoint that the epistemological situation confronting modern physics had been foreseen by no philosophical system.

In what follows I wish to explain by simple examples how the idea of complementarity has made possible, within the field of physics, a synthesis of contrasted and at first sight mutually contradictory hypotheses. To achieve this aim, far-reaching generalizations of the old ideal of causality, and even of the idea of physical reality, were of course necessary.

2. The example of two mutually contradictory ideas that has become celebrated in physics, and which will engage our attention here, is that of the "particle picture" and the "wave picture". That particles are not waves and waves are not particles can readily be recognized by interposing a semi-transparent plate in the path of an energy stream. If the stream consists of a wave process or of *many* particles, a definite fraction of the energy will be reflected at the plate, and the remainder will pass through it. What happens if, in the case of the stream of particles, the intensity of the stream is diminished to such an extent that during the experiment practically only a single particle strikes the plate? In contrast to the case of the wave process, the particle, being an indivisible entity, will either pass through the plate or be reflected by it, but can certainly not appear on both sides of the plate at once. The difference in the consequences of the two pictures is thus just as irreconcilable as the analogous difference between the two logical relations "either-or" and "both-and".

Now it has turned out empirically that light possesses properties describable only by means of the wave picture, as well as others describable only by the particle picture. Among the former are the phenomena of interference and diffraction, which have now become classical. Their common

feature is that light from the same source is divided into at least two different paths, which meet again later. In the latter process it is however not the
intensities of the constituent rays that add, but their amplitudes (principle
of superposition), to whose squares the intensities are proportional. The resultant intensity thus depends in a periodic manner on the phase difference
of the constituent waves, which is determined by the lengths of the paths
traversed, as well as by the optical constants of the media through which the
light has passed. The exact geometric determinacy of this phase difference
is accordingly a necessary condition for the occurrence of interference phenomena. These phenomena prove to be independent of the intensity of the
light, provided only that the apparatus used to detect the light is in action
for a sufficiently long time.

On the other hand the photoelectric effect provides a particularly con-
spicuous example of a phenomenon for the interpretation of which the particle picture is the natural one. This effect consists in the release of electrons
from a metal plate by the action of light. While the intensity of the incident
light determines only the *number* of electrons released in unit time, the energy of the electrons is found to be independent of the intensity of the light,
and to depend only on the wave length (or frequency) of the incident light.
As *Einstein* showed in 1905, the phenomenon of the photoelectric effect can
be described quantitatively by means of the idea that the energy E, and the
momentum P, of light of given wave length and direction of propagation
remains concentrated in space and time into "light quanta" or "photons" of
magnitude

$$E = h\nu , \quad P = \frac{h}{\lambda} . \tag{1}$$

Here ν denotes the frequency, λ the wave length, related to it by

$$\nu = \frac{c}{\lambda} ; \tag{2}$$

c is the velocity of light and h the universal constant introduced by *Planck*
into the theory of thermal radiation, and known as the *quantum of action*.
To understand the photoelectric effect it is sufficient to assume that the elementary amounts of energy and momentum given by (1) can be emitted
and absorbed only in their entirety. This assumption has also held good for
the interpretation of other phenomena involving the transformation of light
energy.

One is forced to the conclusion that the experiment with the semi-transparent plate described above will, for light of low intensity, come out in
favour of either-or: a single photon will produce an effect in a photocell
or photographically either behind or in front of the plate, but not on both
sides at once. However the application of this particle picture to interference
phenomena turns out to be impracticable. For if we assume that a single

photon traverses only *one* of the optical paths, on whose joint action the interference phenomenon depends, the number of times it produces an effect at a point, which is always proportional to the light intensity at this point deduced from the wave theory (i. e., to the square of the resultant amplitude) would have to depend on the existence of paths, perhaps some distance away, which it had not traversed. Indeed this probability of registering a hit would have to undergo an essential change if the observer were for instance to close an aperture through which the photon had not passed. For in the wave picture such an operation essentially alters the possible paths of the partial waves that determine the resultant distribution of hits of the photon. Moreover the result is particularly striking at those points where wave theory predicts zero intensity, since then the mere *possibility* of the appearance of a photon at this point (instead of the number of photons in the general case) depends on the totality of possible paths of the photon. The interference experiment thus decides in favour of "both-and".

For a long time this dilemma appeared to be insoluble. However the situation took an unexpected turn when the dualism between the wave and particle pictures was found to be *universal*. It holds not merely for light but also for all material particles. They too exhibit interference effects, which can be described only by means of a wave picture. Moreover, according to *De Broglie*, frequency and wave length of these waves must be related to the energy and momentum of the particles by the identical formula (1) which also holds for light. (For matter waves, however, (2) must be replaced by a more general formula.)

The first consequence of this is that there is also a characteristic limitation on the particle picture, not only for light but also for matter. In wave kinematics it is readily shown, in general, that superpositions of waves, so-called *wavepackets*, must contain a range $\Delta(1/\lambda)$ of wave-numbers (reciprocal wave lengths), in their spectrum, which is greater the smaller the spatial extension of the packet, and vice-versa. In general the product

$$\Delta x \cdot \Delta\left(\frac{1}{\lambda}\right) \sim 1 \tag{3}$$

is at least* of order of magnitude 1. In accordance with the fundamental connection (1) between wave length and momentum, it follows that

$$\Delta P \Delta x > h \tag{4}$$

(where P and x relate to components in the same direction of the corresponding vectors). This is the content of the celebrated uncertainty principle of *Heisenberg*. It is not possible to ascribe to a material body, whether it

---

* This corrects a mistake in the original.

be macroscopic or atomic, electrically charged like an electron or neutral like a photon, an exact position and at the same time an exact value of its momentum. For in the wave picture no "packets" exist which contradict the relation (3). (Analogous results hold for energy and time, but we do not need to discuss these.)

This universal principle of indefinition or uncertainty enables us to understand that the application of the wave and particle pictures can no longer conflict with each other, since the experimental arrangements whose result supports "both-and" (wave picture) and the other experimental arrangements whose result supports "either-or" (particle picture) are *mutually exclusive*. For in order to decide whether a photon has followed one or other of two (or of several) paths, it is necessary to detect a recoil exerted by the photon on certain parts of the apparatus (screens, diaphragms, mirrors etc.). The direction of propagation of the photon can then be deduced by means of the *theorems of conservation of energy and momentum*. For measurement of such a recoil to be possible it is necessary, not only that certain parts of the apparatus should be freely moveable relative to others, but also that their momentum should be known with sufficient accuracy before they interact with the photon. In accordance with the uncertainty relation (4), however, this means that the positions of those portions of the apparatus before the experiment are then known only with an unavoidable uncertainty. A quantitative discussion, which I cannot reproduce here, shows that the amount of this uncertainty is always exactly such that the definition of the phase difference requisite for carrying out an interference experiment is lost. So if one has shown that a photon has certainly not followed a particular path, this path need not be taken into account in calculating the probabilities of hits. On the other hand an interference setup requires portions of the apparatus to be fixed in space, the momentum imparted to which must always remain indeterminate. An interference setup for a photon is accordingly a single whole; it cannot be decomposed into causal sequences which can be followed in space and time, of further events in which the photon is concerned. Every attempt in this way to follow the photon in space and time would destroy the interference phenomenon by indeterminable changes in the position of parts of the apparatus.

3. The finiteness of the quantum of action, which precludes a subdivision of individual quantum processes, thus confronts the physicist with the following situation: it is impossible to take account, by determinable corrections, of the whole influence of the measuring apparatus on the object measured. Every gain in knowledge of atomic objects by observation has to be paid for by an irrevocable loss of some other knowledge. For example, the laws of nature prevent the observer from attaining a knowledge of the energy and momentum of an object, and at the same time of its localization in space and

time. What knowledge is gained and what other knowledge is irrevocably lost is left to the experimenter's free choice between mutually exclusive experimental arrangements. This situation was designated "complementarity" by *Bohr*. The impossibility of controlling the interference of the act of observation with the system observed is taken into account by the impossibility of describing atomic objects in a unique way by the usual physical properties. Thus the precondition for a description of phenomena independently of the mode of their observation is no longer fulfilled, and physical objects acquire a two-valued, or many-valued, and therefore symbolic character.

The observers or instruments of observation which modern microphysics has to consider thus differs essentially from the detached observer of classical physics. By the latter I mean not necessarily one without influence on the system observed, but one whose influence on it can in any case be eliminated by determinable corrections. In microphysics, on the other hand, every observation is an interference of indeterminable extent, both with the instruments of observation and with the observed system, and interrupts the causal connection between phenomena preceding and subsequent to it. The indeterminable interaction between observer and observed system in every measurement thus makes it impossible to carry through the deterministic conception of phenomena postulated in classical physics. Even under well-defined physical conditions it is in general possible to make only statistical predictions of the results of future observations, while the result of the single observation is not determined by any laws. In this sense we may say that irrationality presents itself to the modern physicist in the shape of selecting (auswählende) observation. The course of events, taking place according to predetermined rules, is interrupted by this observation, and a transformation (Wandlung)* is evoked with an unpredictable result, a modification which is therefore conceived of as happening in an essentially non-automatic manner.[1]

---

* Pauli here has in mind the alchemist meaning; see *Science and Western Thought*, essay 16, this volume.

[1] The formal mathematical operation which is correlated with an actual observation, and whose result the theoretical laws do not determine, is the so called "reduction of wave packets". The abstract wavefunction involved (in general a complex quantity in a multidimensional space) has a significance of a symbol uniting the contradictory features of the visualisable pictures (anschauliche Vorstellungen). The statistical connection of this wavefunction with series of observations on systems of the same nature, which have been subjected to the same previous treatment, is analogous to the connection, mentioned above, between the probability of a hit for a photon and the classical wavefield. This new type of natural law forms a link between the ideas of a discontinuum (particle) and the continuum (wave), and can therefore be regarded as "correspondence" in *Bohr*'s sense, which forms a rational generalisation of the classical deterministic type of a law of nature.

4. This situation in regard to complementarity within physics leads naturally beyond the narrow field of physics to analogous situations in connection with the general conditions of human knowledge. Of course the concept of consciousness does not need to be used directly within physics, since the instruments of observation can be supposed to be an automatic registering device. The only assumption that has to be made about the latter is that it should be describable in ordinary language, supplemented if necessary by the terminology of classical physics. The instruments of observation thus take the place of an apprehending subject with enlarged technical resources. In this way modern physics generalizes the old placing in opposition of apprehending subject on one hand and object apprehended on the other to the idea of the cut between the observer or instrument of observation and the system observed. While the *existence* of such a cut is a necessary condition of human cognition, modern physics regards the *position* of the cut as to a certain extent arbitrary, and as the result of a choice partly determined by considerations of expediency, and therefore partly free.

The relation between subject and object does in fact possess paradoxical features having a far-reaching analogy with the relation between the instruments of observation and the system observed, as we meet it in quantum physics. *Bohr* characterizes this paradox of cognition as follows:[2]

"For describing our mental activity, we require, on the one hand, an objectively given content to be placed in opposition to a perceiving subject, while, on the other hand, ... no sharp separation between object and subject can be maintained, since the perceiving subject also belongs to our mental content".

In this connection *Bohr* also points out that "the conscious analysis of any concept stands in a relation of exclusion to its immediate application."

The concept of consciousness in fact demands a cut between subject and object, the *existence* of which is a logical necessity, while the *position* of the cut is to a certain extent arbitrary. Failure to recognize this state of affairs gives rise to two different kinds of metaphysical extrapolation, which may themselves be described as mutually complementary. One of these is that of the material, or more generally, physical object whose nature is supposed to be independent of the manner in which it is observed. We have seen that modern physics, compelled by facts, has had to abandon this abstraction as too restrictive. The complementary abstraction is that of Hindu metaphysics, with its pure apprehending subject, without any object standing opposed to it. Personally I have no doubt that this idea must also be recognized as an untenable extrapolation. The western mind (abendländischer Geist) cannot accept such a conception of a supra-personal cosmic consciousness without a corresponding object, and must hold the middle course prescribed by the idea

---

[2] N. Bohr, *Atomic Theory and the Description of Nature* (Cambridge 1934), p. 96.

of complementarity. Regarded from this point of view a duality of subject and object is already postulated by the concept of consciousness.

In the place of the oriental universal consciousness lacking an object, western psychology has set up the idea of the unconscious, whose relation to consciousness exhibits paradoxical features similar to those we meet in physics. On one hand modern psychology demonstrates a largely objective reality of the unconscious psyche; on the other hand every bringing into consciousness, i. e., observation, constitutes an interference with the unconscious contents that is in principle uncontrollable; this limits the objective character of the reality of the unconscious and invests reality with a certain subjectivity.

It would lead me too far afield to discuss other analogies with physical complementarity that fall within the biological sphere and have to do with psychophysical parallelism.

I hope I have succeeded in giving you an impression of the synthetic power of the idea of complementarity, which, by setting a limit in principle to the field of application of contrasted conceptions, ensures that a system of concepts operating with them will be free from contradictions.

3. Probability and Physics*

As you will see in the reprint of my lecture on "probability and physics", which I have sent to you, it seems to me quite appropriate to call the conceptual description of nature in classical physics, which Einstein so emphatically wishes to retain, "the ideal of the detached observer". To put it drastically the observer has according to this ideal to disappear entirely in a discrete manner as hidden spectator, never as actor, nature being left alone in a predetermined course of events, independent of the way in which the phenomena are observed. "Like the moon has a definite position" Einstein said to me last winter, "whether or not we look at the moon, the same must also hold for the atomic objects, as there is no sharp distinction possible between these and macroscopic objects. Observation cannot *create* an element of reality like a position, there must be something contained in the complete description of physical reality which corresponds to the *possibility* of observing a position, already before the observation has been actually made." I hope, that I quoted Einstein correctly; it is always difficult to quote somebody out of memory with whom one does not agree. It is precisely this kind of postulate which I call the ideal of the detached observer.

Letter from Pauli to Niels Bohr, February 15, 1955

The mathematical concept of probability arose from the endeavour to render objective, as far as possible, the subjective expectation of a single event. To do this the expectation must be replaced by the objective average frequency of an event when it is repeated under like conditions. It is assumed that when the number of repetitions is large, the probability of an event A differs only little from the quotient m/n, where n is the number of repetitions, and m the number of occurrences of A. Thus we here encounter the theme of the *one* expectation to be rendered objective and the *many* events.

A closer analysis of this state of affairs is not easy; in particular, the transition from the logico-mathematical formulation to experience raises profound epistemological problems. I believe that every physicist is glad to have available an unexceptionable set of mathematical axioms, since it allows him to make a clean separation between problems of mathematics and logic

---

* Amplified version of a review given on the occasion of the meeting of the *Swiss Society of Natural Sciences* in Bern in 1952. First published in *Dialectica* **8**, 112–124 (1954).

on the one hand, and physical problems of natural philosophy on the other. As *van der Waerden* in particular has emphasised,[1] the axioms of the calculus of probabilities do not include a reduction of the concept of probability to other concepts; on the contrary, the concept of "probability" cannot be eliminated from the system of axioms which are the basic rules for its proper treatment; that is, it is defined only implicitly and not explicitly.

I do not need to give a system of axioms *in extenso* here, as this has been done from the mathematical side. The British school (*Keynes, Jeffreys, Broad*) have a preference for *contingent* probability (probability of *p* when *k* is given).[2] The mathematician *Kolmogorov*[3] formulates the axioms from the point of view of the theory of sets, which is perhaps less familiar to the physicist.

The most important axioms are the conjunctive and disjunctive axioms of the addition and multiplication of probabilities. Frequencies of the elements of finite classes certainly satisfy the axioms automatically.[4]

In passing I may mention the curious fact, that it was not a mathematician, but a physicist, *P. A. M. Dirac*, who had the idea of dropping the axiom according to which probabilities must be numbers lying between 0 and 1, while retaining the remaining axioms, and of admitting "negative probabilities" as well (the sum of all probabilities being constant and normalised). Naturally these generalised "probabilities" can no longer be interpreted as frequencies. Consequently the extensive application in physics, which *Dirac* originally expected them to have, has turned out not to be practicable. None the less they are occasionally useful as mathematical auxiliary quantities, which have no direct physical significance.

But let us return once more, after this digression, to ordinary probabilities lying between 0 and 1: The most important logical consequence of the axioms is *Bernoulli*'s theorem, also known as the law of large numbers. The theorem presupposes that on each of a number of occasions (repetitions) the chance of occurrence of a particular event is always the same, say *p*. The assertion of the theorem, in mathematical language, is this: corresponding to "all" pairs of positive numbers (ε, δ) "there always exists" a large integer *N* having the following property: "the probability that the fraction of the number of occasions on which the event happens, from *N* occasions upwards, should ever differ from *p* by more than ε, is less than δ.

---
[1] B. L. van der Waerden: "Der Begriff der Wahrscheinlichkeit." *Studium Generale* **4** (Heft 2), 65–68 (1951).

[2] Cf. Harold Jeffreys, *Theory of Probability*, 2nd Edition, Oxford 1948.

[3] A. Kolmogorov, "Grundbegriffe der Wahrscheinlichkeitsrechnung", *Ergebnisse der Mathematik und ihrer Grenzgebiete* **2** (Heft 3), 195–262 (1933).

[4] Let *B* be a given finite class and *A* another class; form the quotient of the number of those *B*'s which are *A*'s, divided by the total number of *B*'s.

It should be observed that this assertion is not an assertion about a limit. It would be so only if δ were replaced by 0, which is however not permissible. The calculus of probabilities expressly demands the existence of a very small but non-vanishing probability for a subsequent occurrence of a discrepancy greater than ε between the empirical frequency and the mathematical probability p.

In this purely mathematical form, *Bernoulli*'s theorem is thus not as yet susceptible to empirical test. For this purpose it is necessary somewhere or other to include a rule for the attitude in practice of the human observer, or in particular the scientist, which takes account of the subjective factor as well, namely that the realisation, even on a single occasion, of a very unlikely event is regarded from a certain point on as impossible in practice. Theoretically it must be conceded that there is still a chance, different from zero, of error; but in practice actual decisions are arrived at in this way, in particular also decisions about the empirical correctness of the statistical assertions of the theories of physics or natural science. At this point one finally reaches the limits which are set in principle to the possibility of carrying out the original programme of the rational objectivation of the unique subjective expectation.[5]

The first application of the calculus of probabilities in physics, which is fundamental for our understanding of the laws of nature, is the general statistical theory of heat, established by *Boltzmann* and *Gibbs*. This theory, as is well known, led necessarily to the interpretation of the entropy of a system as a function of its state, which, unlike the energy, depends on our *knowledge* about the system. If this knowledge is the maximal knowledge which is consistent with the laws of nature in general (micro-state), the entropy is always null. On the other hand thermodynamic concepts are applicable to a system only when the knowledge of the initial state of the system is inexact; the entropy is then appropriately measured by the logarithm of a volume in phase space. The most beautiful and important result of this theory was the conception of thermodynamic "irreversibility" of processes as a transition in the direction of more probable states. Furthermore, this conception led to the expectation that there would be real departures from the behaviour of systems as postulated by phenomenological thermodynamics, namely the so-called fluctuation phenomena, subsequently brilliantly confirmed by experience.

This application of the probability concept in physics, fundamental though it is, was logically consistent with a deterministic form of the laws of nature. The view has however been widespread that the more satisfactory possibility would be that the concept of probability, dissociated from any deterministic and causal form of the laws of nature, should turn out to be

---

[5] Cf. also van der Waerden, loc. cit.

incapable of further reduction, that is, to be a primary fundamental notion of physics. The fact also that the inductive conclusions of the sciences are always probability conclusions has been held to support this view.

It must, however, be emphasised that such general considerations are not by themselves sufficient to decide the question of the presence or absence of a deterministic frame work for the laws of nature. It was wave or quantum mechanics that was first able to assert the existence of *primary probabilities* in the laws of nature, which accordingly do not admit of reduction to deterministic natural laws by auxiliary hypotheses, as do for example the thermodynamic probabilities of classical physics. This revolutionary consequence is regarded as irrevocable by the great majority of modern theoretical physicists – primarily by *M. Born*, *W. Heisenberg* and *N. Bohr*, with whom I also associate myself.

Opposition to this has not been lacking, but having got stuck in the stage of regressive hopes, it has remained fruitless. It is moreover in the nature of the case that this opposition should have fallen into two classes from the outset. Those in one class (to which *Schrödinger* belongs) consider waves to be more beautiful than particles, and would accordingly like to eliminate the latter concept. The others, following *De Broglie*'s earlier theory of the "pilot wave" in one of its possible variants, would like to introduce particles and waves as two separate co-existing halves of a physical reality thus falling into two parts.

I do not wish to embark here upon a detailed discussion of recent attempts which have been made to revive these old ideas, but rather to characterize the epistemological consequences of the statistical interpretation of wave mechanics, which in my view is the only satisfactory one. According to this conception every experimental arrangement is accompanied by an undeterminable interaction between the measuring instrument and the system observed; as a result, any knowledge gained by an observation must be paid for by an irrevocable loss of some other knowledge. What knowledge is gained and what other knowledge is irrevocably lost, is left to the experimenter's free choice between mutually exclusive experimental arrangements. It is on this possibility of a free choice of mutually complementary experimental arrangements that the indeterministic character of natural laws postulated by quantum mechanics rests.

Observation thereby takes on the character of *irrational, unique actuality* with unpredictable outcome. Moreover, the impossibility of subdividing the experimental arrangement without essentially altering the phenomenon, brings a new feature of *wholeness* into physical happenings. Contrasted with this *irrational aspect* of concrete phenomena which are determined in their *actuality*, there stands the *rational aspect* of an abstract ordering of the *possibilities* of statements by means of the mathematical concept of probability and the ψ-function.

Mathematically the new form of the quantum-mechanical laws of nature solves, in a very elegant way, the question of the measure of the probability: this is given by the square of the absolute value of a complex number, the probability amplitude, which obeys simpler laws than the probability itself. These simpler laws give the amplitudes the significance of linearly superposable vectors in an Hilbert space, which by definition carries a positive definite form as intrinsic metric.[6]

If in spite of the logical closure and mathematical elegance of quantum mechanics there is on the part of some physicists a certain regressive hope that the epistemological situation we have sketched may turn out not to be final, this is in my opinion due to the strength of traditional thought-forms embraced in the designation "ontology" or "realism". Even those physicists who do not reckon themselves entirely "sensualists" or "empiricists" must ask themselves the question, which it is possible to ask on account of the postulational character of these traditional thought-forms, and is unavoidable on account of the existence of quantum mechanics – namely the question whether these thought-forms are a necessary condition that physics should be possible at all, or whether other, more general thought-forms can be set up in opposition to them. The analysis of the theoretical foundations of wave or quantum mechanics has shown that the second alternative is the correct one.

The postulates of the thought-forms in question, in their application to physics, have been formulated most clearly by *Einstein*, for instance, recently, in the following form[7] "There is such a thing as the real state of a physical system, which exists objectively, independently of any observation or measurement, and can in principle be described by the modes of expression used in physics." However, these formulations of *Einstein*'s are only a paraphrase of the ideal of a special form of physics, namely the "classical" form. This ideal, so pertinently characterised by *Einstein*, I would call that of the *detached observer*. In point of fact "existent" and "non-existent", or "real" and "unreal", are not unique characterisations of complementary qualities, which can be checked only by statistical sequences of experiments using different arrangements, freely chosen, which may in some cases be mutually exclusive. The new theory on the contrary generalises these classical ideals and postulates. Under the pressure of the physical facts summed up under the heading "finiteness of the quantum of action", this logical generalisation has emerged into a higher synthesis as a finally satisfactory solution of earlier contradictions: The mathematical inclusion, in quantum mechanics, of the *possibilities* of natural events has turned out to be a sufficiently wide framework to embrace the irrational *actuality* of the single event as well. It may

---

[6] For the "negative probabilities" mentioned above the corresponding metric is an indefinite quadratic form.

[7] Louis de Broglie, *Physicien et penseur*, Paris 1952, p. 6.

also, as comprehending the rational and irrational aspects of an essentially paradoxical reality, be designated as a theory of becoming.[8]

The fact that the mathematical concept of probability has also justified itself in this new situation denoted by the term "complementarity" seems to me highly significant. It appears that there corresponds to it, at a very deep level, a reality in nature; for it has provided a solid logical basis for the type of natural law which generalises the classical and deterministic explanation of nature and provides the link between continuum (wave) and discontinuum (particle), and for which I have suggested the name "statistical correspondence".[9] *

---

[8] One may, following F. Gonseth, denote the interplay of the two aspects as "dialectical".
[9] Experientia 6 (Heft 2), 72–75 (1950).
* Compare footnote 1, this volume, essay 2.

4. Niels Bohr on His 60th Birthday*

Niels Bohr (1885–1962)

Photo published in the *Reviews of Modern Physics* **17**, 97 (1945) on the occasion of his 60th birthday celebration (Courtesy: The Niels Bohr Archive, Copenhagen)

* First published in English in *Reviews of Modern Physics* **17**, 97 (1945).

Bohr's sixtieth anniversary was celebrated with grand festivities, but in the true Copenhagen spirit. In the morning there was a meeting at the institute with Rozental as conferencier. Speeches were made and gifts presented by Møller, Jacobsen and other members of the institute, Klein, Rosenfeld, Hylleraas and Gustafson. The Danish and Norwegian dedication publications were handed over, and, of course, a new issue of the 'Journal of Jocular Physics'. Among the presents there was a beautiful and well-shaped van de Graaff-baby (Broström and his people had worked all night to make it 'go'. It did.) Some jocose films and pictures were also shown. Obviously Bohr enjoyed this form of birthday celebration as much as we all did.

In the afternoon there was an official reception at Carlsberg, attended by representatives of the Danish government and 'Videnskabernes Selskab', foreign ministers etc. A gift of about 400.000 danish crowns, intended for a Niels Bohr Foundation and collected in Danish financial circles, was presented to Bohr.

The dinner at Carlsberg was very festive and pleasant. You know what a charming hostess is Mrs. Bohr. During the dinner we first heard the special Bohr program broadcast by the Danish Radio. Bohr then made a long speech (not very easy to understand) which was later answered by his old friend Bjerrum, the chemist. Bohr was also waited upon by a torchlight procession of 3.000 students and addressed them in a most wonderful speech. He seemed to be deeply moved. Truly it was an unforgettable day and evening to us all.

Letter from Lamek Hulthén to Pauli, November 13, 1945

The present volume to which scientists of many nations from three continents have contributed, notwithstanding the adverse times, gives proof indeed that Professor *Niels Bohr*'s 60th birthday, on October 7, 1945, is not only his private, personal day of celebration, but a day of observance throughout the scientific community of physicists.[1]

While many outstanding scholars of all times have obtained their fundamental insights in solitary labor secluded from the world, *Niels Bohr*, thanks to his inspiring personality, has gained contact, in proportion as his scientific work grew and shaped itself, with an ever-increasing number of people among

---

[1] Each of the authors contributing to this issue would like to express his individual debt and gratitude to Professor Bohr, but editorial arrangements leave it to this author to convey that message from the entire group. – The author is greatly indebted to Dr. M. Delbrück, Physics Department, Vanderbilt University, for the translation of the original manuscript into English, and for suggestions concerning its content.

whom he found many collaborators and pupils. After two decisive years in *Rutherford*'s laboratory in Manchester, he returned in 1916 as a professor to his birthplace, Copenhagen, where in 1920 the "Institut for Teoretisk Fysik" was founded. Soon this institute made Copenhagen attract scientists from all parts of the planet as the "Capital of Atomic Physics". As director of the laboratory which was attached to the institute, *Bohr* found an opportunity, along with his main theoretical work, to supervise experimental research in which he had been taking a keen interest since his early youth. The discovery in this laboratory of the element hafnium by *Coster* and *Hevesy* was the result of a close collaboration between theoretical and experimental research as well as between physics and chemistry, which, in *Bohr*'s theory of atomic structure, were for the first time founded upon common principles. As *Bohr*'s theory united distinct branches of science, thus *Bohr* himself integrated, in lectures at international congresses and at those carefully planned conferences in Copenhagen, the diverse scientific standpoints and epistemological attitudes of the physicists, and thereby imparted to all participants in those conferences the feeling of belonging, in spite of all their dissensions, to one large family.

Without going into the details of *Bohr*'s work we shall briefly characterize some aspects of the general development of the fundamental concepts of the quantum theory of the structure of atoms. This theory took its proper inception when *Bohr* succeeded in the happy synthesis of *Rutherford*'s nuclear atom with the ideas based on the existence of a quantum of action which were implied in *Planck*'s theory of heat radiation and the further development of these ideas in *Einstein*'s interpretation of the photoelectric effect. *Bohr* formulated his postulates originally in the following form:[2]

"(1) That the dynamical equilibrium of the systems in the stationary states can be discussed by help of the ordinary mechanics, while the passing of the systems between different stationary states can not be treated on that basis.
(2) That the latter process is followed by the emission of a *homogeneous* radiation, for which the relation between the frequency and the amount of energy emitted is the one given by *Planck*'s theory."

With these postulates *Bohr* achieved a theoretical interpretation of the previously baffling regularities of the spectra. The ambiguity of the conceptual basis – clearly expressed in *Bohr*'s formulation of the first postulate – by means of which this interpretation was accomplished, became particularly apparent in the assumption of two kinds of frequencies which were supposed to differ from each other in the general case, according to the two postulates,

---

[2] N. Bohr, *Philosophical Magazine* **26**, 1 (1913), contained as Paper I in *Abhandlungen über Atombau.* (Friedrich Vieweg und Sohn, Braunschweig, 1921); translated from the *Philosophical Magazine* of the years 1913–1916, including a paper which was withdrawn from publication in 1916.

although they coincide in the classical picture – an objectionable feature to many physicists. On the one hand there were the frequencies of the emitted radiation associated with a pair of stationary states, the initial and the final state of a "transition process"; and on the other hand, the kinematical frequencies of the particles in the mechanical orbits corresponding with their stationary states.

However, the later development which led to the elimination of the concept of the mechanical orbit from the theoretical description was foreshadowed in *Bohr*'s famous "correspondence principle," or "correspondence argument." He could show, first for systems with simple periodic motions, that in the limiting case of large quantum numbers where the energy values of different stationary states come to lie relatively close together, the emission frequencies, calculated by means of the second postulate coincide asymptotically with the harmonics $\tau\omega$ of the fundamental frequency ω of the periodic mechanical orbit, if one identifies the integer τ with the difference $n' - n''$ of the values of the quantum numbers in the initial and final states, respectively.[3] However, according to the classical conception, these frequencies should all be emitted simultaneously; according to the quantum theory, the occurrence of the various transitions is described by statistical laws, first given by *Einstein* in their general form (spontaneous emission, induced emission, absorption). In the limiting case of large quantum numbers, mentioned above, the frequency of occurrence of a transition is proportional to the square of the amplitude of the "corresponding" harmonic, the amplitudes of the mechanical motion thus becoming "amplitudes of probability". *Bohr*'s pupil *Kramers* has shown how this correspondence may be utilized for the estimation of intensities of spectral lines also in the case of small quantum numbers.

Already in 1913, *Bohr*[4] proved that the postulate of the asymptotic identity of the mechanical frequencies with the frequencies given by the quotient of the energy differences of the stationary states and *Planck*'s constant suffices to calculate the constant of *Balmer*'s formula of the hydrogen spectrum, also called *Rydberg*'s constant, from charge and mass of the electron and the quantum of action (including the correction due to the finite mass of the nucleus). It was clear from the arguments given in this paper that, for the calculation of this constant, the assumption of the exact validity of classical

---

[3] N. Bohr, *Philosophical Magazine* **27**, 506 (1914) and **28**, 394 (1915), contained in N. Bohr: *Abhandlungen über Atombau.* (Friedrich Vieweg und Sohn, Braunschweig, 1921) as Papers VI and IX. See also especially Paper X, which was earlier withheld from publication.

[4] Compare Essay I in N. Bohr: *The Theory of Spectra and Atomic Constitution.* (Cambridge University Press, Teddington, England, 1922), which is a translation of an address delivered before the Physical Society of Copenhagen in December, 1913 and printed in *Fysisk Tidsskrift* **12**, 97 (1914).

mechanics for the stationary states is unnecessary, if one accepts *Balmer's* formula as an empirical law. On the basis of the extension of the rules of quantization, particularly by *Sommerfeld* and his students, *Bohr*[5] generalized the correspondence principle so that it could also be applied to the so-called multiple periodic systems. Simultaneously he advanced the theory of these systems by giving the method of secular perturbations of which *Kramers* made interesting applications.

In a qualitative way this theory was successful in interpreting the properties even of complicated atoms. One could classify their energy levels by quantum numbers, establish selection rules, interpret X-ray spectra, describe the formation of inner shells in the periodic system, including the rare earths. Notwithstanding these successes, it became more and more apparent that a quantitative formulation of the endeavor expressed in the correspondence principle, particularly the calculation of transition probabilities and of the energy levels of atoms with more than one electron, would be possible only if one abandoned the idea of visualizing stationary states by means of classical kinematics. During my stay at *Bohr's* institute in Copenhagen in 1922 and 1923, I was impressed by the cautiousness with which these classical models were used by *Bohr* in contrast to other physicists. He always emphasized their provisional character, and in his deductions preferred to fall back on the limiting case of large quantum numbers, for which alone there existed a dependable correspondence between classical and quantum theory. This attitude is reflected in a formulation of the first postulate which *Bohr* gave at this time,[6] and which may here be given for comparison with the original formulation:

"The first postulate of the quantum theory for an isolated atomic system states that, among the kinematically conceivable relative motions of the particles of the atom, there exist certain states, the so-called stationary states, which are distinguished by a peculiar stability, shown by the fact, that every permanent change in the motion of the isolated system must consist in a complete transition from the original to another of these stationary states."

The assumption of the validity of classical mechanics for the stationary states was formulated separately from the fundamental postulates. There is here an example of the subtlety of *Bohr's* style. For those readers who are not familiar with the developmental history of *Bohr's* papers, these shades of meaning are difficult to appreciate. He knew well what he wished *not* to say when he strove in long sentences to express himself in his scientific papers.

---

[5] N. Bohr: "On the quantum theory of line spectra", Parts **I** and **II**. *Det Kongelige Danske Videnskabernes Selskabs, matematisk-fysiske Meddelelser* [8] **IV**, No. 1 (1918).

[6] N. Bohr: "On the application of quantum theory to the structure of atoms. Part I: The fundamental postulates." Supplement of the *Proceedings of the Cambridge Philosophical Society*, 1924. Translated from *Zeitschrift für Physik* **13**, 117 (1923).

The critical attitude towards the use of kinematic-mechanical pictures led to another development. Although momentary doubts as to the exact validity of the law of conservation of energy and momentum as applied to individual elementary processes were soon abandoned, the picture of virtual oscillators introduced in this connection as a generalization of the oscillators in the classical electron theory of light refraction proved useful. Using this concept, and boldly extrapolating the result of classical mechanics, *Kramers* established the first law which held exactly even for the case of small quantum numbers, a formula which correlated dispersion phenomena with transition probabilities for the spontaneous emission of light. It was later extended to the incoherent scattering of light; also in other cases one was able to guess correctly quantitative rules which the energies of stationary states and the probability amplitudes had to fulfill.

The ground was thus prepared for the decisive advance which came with *Heisenberg*'s matrix theory (1925). In this theory the probability amplitudes of the virtual oscillators and the energy values of the stationary states were for the first time derived by means of a coherent mathematical formalism. Soon thereafter (1926) *Schrödinger*, using *de Broglie*'s idea of matter waves, discovered his famous wave equation, the periodic solutions of which proved to be equivalent with the matrix theory. The formal methods were now at hand for a consistent description of the quantum phenomena, but many problems of physical interpretation had yet to be solved in order to elucidate the foundations of the theory. The discussions of the Solvay congress of 1927, in which *Bohr* participated, give a vivid picture of these difficulties. After *Born*'s statistical interpretation of *Schrödinger*'s function and the establishment of the general quantum-mechanical transformation theory which was carefully worked out by *Dirac*, the clarification of the issues made further progress. Finally *Heisenberg* discovered his principle of indeterminacy, and intuitively realized its great importance. It was *Bohr*, however, who gave the simple and correct derivation of this principle from the properties of wave packets, a derivation which today can be found in all textbooks.[7] He also emphasized the importance of the general, time-dependent, solution of *Schrödinger*'s equation for the discussion of the transition to classical mechanics in those cases in which the scattering of the wave packets is insignificant.

By means of a thorough discussion of numerous imaginary experiments *Bohr* showed that the concept of complementarity characterizes the essential physical content of the new theories. In harmony with the principle of indeterminacy he defines this concept in the following words:

---

[7] See Essay I in N. Bohr: *Atomic Theory and the Description of Nature.* (Cambridge University Press, Teddington, England, 1934.)

"Any given application of classical concepts precludes the simultaneous use of other classical concepts which in a different connection are equally necessary for the elucidation of the phenomena."[8]

Well-known examples of this mutual exclusion of concepts are: momentum and position of a particle, recoil at the emission of a photon and the coherence of light emitted in different directions, wave and corpuscle. According to Bohr[9] the notion of complementarity serves

"to symbolize the fundamental limitation, met with in atomic physics, of our ingrained idea of phenomena as existing independently of the means by which they are observed."

It is indeed this limitation which makes the theory logically consistent. The "transition processes" of the theory in its earlier form are now replaced by the discontinuous selection from the theoretical possibilities of one case by the act of observation "here and now." The theoretical possibilities themselves are subject to statistical laws with probability amplitudes that vary continuously as functions of time.

Bohr has always looked upon quantum mechanics as the precise fulfillment of the program which he had in mind in his original formulation of the fundamental postulates. In harmony with quantum mechanics, he[10] characterizes the "correspondence argument" as expressing

"our endeavor, by means of a suitably limited use of mechanical and electromagnetic concepts, to obtain a statistical description of the atomic phenomena that appears as a rational generalization of the classical physical theories, in spite of the fact that the quantum of action from their point of view must be considered as an irrationality."

Indeed, wave mechanics or quantum mechanics in their present form may be considered as the key for translating the results of classical theory into a quantum language compatible with the existence of the quantum of action. For such a translation the canonical formalism, which derives the form of the equations of motion from the so-called Hamilton function or Hamiltonian, was shown to be an excellent tool. However, quantum mechanics, in borrowing the form of the Hamiltonian from classical theory, takes over also a duality in its foundation, namely the concepts of particle mechanics and the concepts of the theory of the electromagnetic field of *Maxwell* and *Lorentz*. As a consequence, the present form of quantum theory does not explain the

---

[8] Introductory survey in *Atomic Theory and the Description of Nature*, p. 10.
[9] See N. Bohr: "Light and Life", address delivered at the International Congress on light-therapy in Copenhagen, August 1932; *Nature* **131**, 421 and 457 (1933), p. 423. [Compare also *Die Naturwissenschaften* **21**, 245 (1933).]
[10] See N. Bohr: "Light and Life", *Nature* **131**, p. 422.

atomicity of electric charge and forms no logical connection between the elementary quantum of charge and the quantum of action.

Whatever one may think about the foundation of quantum mechanics from an epistemological point of view, it is quite apparent from the situation which arose by the creation of this theory that the road for future developments will not lead back but forward. Clues as to the specific direction of this way forward will come, we think, not so much from philosophic discussions and postulations as from new experimental results concerning the reactions of elementary particles, particularly in the high energy region, and possibly from the enrichment, by the introduction of new formal concepts, of the theoretical study of those consequences of the theory which reveal a limitation in the applicability of its mathematical formalism. We meet with one such limitation in the application of quantum mechanics to the interaction between electromagnetic radiation and electrons. On the one hand, this interaction when developed into a power series of the fine structure constant, due to the smallness of this constant, yields a usable approximation for processes of emission, absorption, and scattering of photons, when only that term of the development is used in which the particular process first occurs. On the other hand, in the logically complete form of the theory in which the electromagnetic field itself is quantized (quantum electrodynamics), the higher approximations are divergent. As a result certain small (but experimentally measurable) effects cannot, on the basis of the present theory, be calculated accurately. As an example we may cite the influence of the emission of a small amount of energy, in the form of many photons of small frequency, on the scattering cross section of electrons under a specified angle by a Coulomb field of force, an effect which must give rise to correction terms in *Rutherford*'s well-known formula. Ingenious attempts of very recent date to extend the theory to those electrodynamic effects expected as being small do not seem to be sufficiently successful. It is therefore probable that the divergence difficulties of the theory cannot be overcome without directly attacking the more basic problems which are left untouched by the present theory. Of these the most important ones are the interpretation of the elementary quantum of electric charge and the theoretical prediction of the types of elementary particles occurring in nature, and of their masses.

It would seem that this view is also in harmony with an interesting paper by *Bohr* and *Rosenfeld*[11] concerning the physical interpretation of the uncertainty relations as implied in quantum electrodynamics for the electromagnetic field of free radiation. In this paper *Bohr* proves himself, as so often, the master in the use of imaginary experiments. It is shown that the uncertainty relations required by quantum electrodynamics for the values of

---

[11] N. Bohr and L. Rosenfeld: "Zur Frage der Messbarkeit der elektromagnetischen Feldgrössen." *Det Kongelige Danske Videnskabernes Selskabs, matematisk-fysiske Meddelelser* **XII**, No. 8, (1933).

the various components of the field strengths, averaged over finite space-time areas, are actually verifiable, on principle. This paper is a good illustration of a remark which, much earlier, *Bohr* once made to the present author. He said that his interest in physics was not so much that of a mathematician as that of a craftsman and of a philosopher. In the paper referred to, this fruitful combination is reflected in the circumstance that the complicated mechanisms of springs and frames are based on the simple principle that it is permissible to use as test-bodies extended bodies with practically homogeneous distribution of charge and mass, as long as no restricting assumptions are introduced regarding the elementary particles occurring in nature. As *Bohr* and *Rosenfeld* point out, a new epistemological situation may be expected only if the atomic constitution of the test bodies is made an essential feature of the argument.

Space does not permit the discussion here of *Bohr*'s interesting applications of his epistemological point of view of complementarity to the domains of biology and psychology.[12] Physics however will, in all likelihood, transcending the correspondence argument, turn to the problems of the elementary particles and to the closely related problem of the nature of the nuclear forces. It is clear that this physics of the future will be in need, just as the earlier development of atomic physics was, of intellectual coherence and of a unifying order. Professor *Niels Bohr*, whose interest in the problems of nuclear structure and of radioactivity reaches back to those early days which he spent with his teacher Lord *Rutherford* and his collaborators, will be called upon, more than anybody else, to play a leading role in the accomplishment of this difficult task. His friends and students may therefore be permitted to express, on his 60th birthday, the hope that circumstances may permit him soon to resume the physics conferences in Copenhagen, so fruitful and stimulating for all who participated.

---

[12] See N. Bohr: *Atomic Theory and the Description of Nature.* (Cambridge University Press, Teddington, England, 1934), Introductory Survey, and Essays III and IV.

5. Sommerfeld's Contributions to Quantum Theory*

Arnold Sommerfeld (1868–1951)

Photo from the early twenties, when Pauli and Heisenberg were studying physics in Munich. On the blackboard the Balmer formula with Paschen's line in the infrared and the drawing of the corresponding orbits according to the Bohr-Sommerfeld atomic theory (From: Albert Einstein / Arnold Sommerfeld, Briefwechsel, hg. von Armin Hermann, Schwabe & Co. AG, Basel 1968)

---

* Dedicated to A. Sommerfeld on his 80th birthday on 5th December, 1948. – First published in *Die Naturwissenschaften* **35**, 129 (1948).

Ich bin gerne bereit, für das Festheft der Zeitschrift für Naturforschung zu Sommerfelds 80. Geburtstag eine Arbeit beizusteuern, unter der Voraussetzung, daß ich bis zum 31. Juli 1948 etwas Geeignetes zu publizieren habe.

Es ist dies wohl möglich, da ich in letzter Zeit wieder in die Quantenelektrodynamik hineingeraten bin in Verbindung mit den in Amerika ausgeführten Experimenten über die Verschiebung der S-Terme des H-Atoms (neuerdings bestätigt durch einen analogen Effekt an den He^+-Linien) und den weitern Experimenten, die dafür sprechen, daß das magnetische Moment des freien Elektrons um 0.12% größer ist als ein Magneton. Vielleicht komme ich später auf diese Frage zurück.

Letter from Pauli to Werner Heisenberg, January 22, 1948

The early work of *A. Sommerfeld* had been concerned partly with applications of the mathematics of wave theory, such as the integration of *Maxwell*'s equations in problems of diffraction and wireless telegraphy, and partly with problems of classical electron theory. The X-rays emitted when electrons are decelerated had already brought him up against quantum theory;[1] and *Voigt*'s formal theory of the anomalous Zeeman effect of doublet spectra, which he was able to simplify substantially by considering emission instead of absorption,[2] had brought him into contact with the great complex of problems connected with the explanation of spectra. Shortly afterwards, through *Bohr*'s fundamental work (from 1913 onwards) *Rutherford*'s nuclear model of the atom was linked up with *Planck*'s quantum theory of thermal radiation, and *Rydberg*'s constant of spectra was reduced to the quantum of action and the charge and mass of the electron (with a supplementary correction for the motion of the nucleus). It was at the end of 1915 that *Sommerfeld*, greatly impressed by this new development, turned his attention to the theoretical interpretation of spectra and the associated problems of atomic structure. It can be said that this period marked the beginning of a new chapter in *Sommerfeld*'s scientific activity, which entailed not only a change in the object of study, but also a fundamental change in the methods employed in his work. It was a fortunate circumstance that *Sommerfeld* recognised the formal significance of the phase integrals over the so-called separation coordinates of a mechanical system and immediately applied them in his first papers "On the quantum theory of spectral lines"[3] to the motion of a single electron in

---

[1] A. Sommerfeld, Report to the Solvay Congress, Brussels, 1911.

[2] A. Sommerfeld, *Göttinger Nachrichten*, math.-phys. Klasse (1914).

[3] A. Sommerfeld, *Sitzungsberichte der Münchener Akademie der Wissenschaften*, pp. 425, 459 (1915); p. 131 (1916). *Annalen der Physik* **51**, 1, 125 (1916) (Quantum theory of spectral lines).

simply periodic Keplerian ellipses under the influence of the Coulomb attraction of the nucleus, without misgivings on account of the degeneracy of this system. By equating the phase integrals of each of the two polar coordinates r and φ over their full periods to integral multiples of the quantum of action, he had introduced into the theory an azimuthal quantum number n_φ in addition to the radial quantum number n_r. As long as Newtonian mechanics were assumed, however, this led to no new results as compared with *Bohr*'s theory, since in this case the total energy depends only on the sum $n = n_r + n_\varphi$, also called the principal quantum number. None the less *Sommerfeld*'s calculation enabled him to generalise his result to the case in which the dependence of the mass of the electron on its velocity, required by the special theory of relativity, is taken into account; this leads to a superposed rotation of the perihelion of the ellipse, and consequently to a removal of the degeneracy. The energy of the system then depends on the two quantum numbers n_r, n_φ separately, a result which broke through the framework of the then current theory of simply periodic systems. *Sommerfeld* immediately recognised the possibility of applying the theory to the fine-structure of hydrogenic spectra, (a result soon fully confirmed by *Paschen*'s measurements of the spectrum of ionised helium) and to the analogous relativistic doublets of X-ray spectra, as well as to the series spectra of higher atoms, in which the influence of the atomic core on an outer electron (Leuchtelektron) can be approximately represented by a non-Coulombic central field. In this case the degeneracy is absent even when the relativistic variability of mass is neglected, and the terms which lie close together in the hydrogen atom are here widely separated (s, p, d terms). The general quantum theory of so-called multiply periodic mechanical systems rapidly developed out of *Sommerfeld*'s work. It was formulated independently in 1916 by *Epstein*[4] and *Schwarzschild*,[5] and successfully applied to the *Stark* effect of the hydrogen spectrum. In spite of complete agreement in the results, a certain difference is recognisable in the points of view of these authors. While in the work of *Epstein*, a pupil of *Sommerfeld*, the separation of the variables of the mechanical problem in suitable point-coordinates stands in the forefront, *Schwarzschild* lays the main emphasis on the periodicity properties of the mechanical orbit. The phase integrals over the separation variables are very closely related to the problem of the division of phase space into finite cells, which arises naturally from a thermodynamic standpoint, and was dealt with in a paper by *Planck*[6] published at the same time. On the other hand the method of "an-

---

[4] P. S. Epstein, *Physikalische Zeitschrift* **17**, 148 (1916); *Annalen der Physik* **50**, 489; **51**, 168 (1916).

[5] K. Schwarzschild, *Sitzungsberichte der Berliner Akademie der Wissenschaften*, phys.-math. Klasse, p. 548 (1916); cf. also J. M. Burger's Dissertation, Haarlem (1918).

[6] M. Planck, *Verhandlungen der Deutschen Physikalischen Gesellschaft* **17**, 407, 438 (1915); *Annalen der Physik* **50**, 385 (1916).

gle variables" with which *Schwarzschild* was conversant as an astronomer
has proved most useful in regard to *Bohr's* correspondence principle and the
method of secular perturbations derived from celestial mechanics. The angle
variables are coordinates of the system such that the ordinary momenta and
positional coordinates are periodic functions of them (for convenience the
period can be normalised to either 1 or 2π) but which are themselves linear
functions of time. All frequencies in the Fourier components of the motion of
a system of this kind are then linear combinations, with integer coefficients,
of a certain number of basic frequencies, whose number s is certainly not
greater than the number f of degrees of freedom of the system, but which in
some circumstances may be less (degeneracy). The basic frequencies must be
chosen so that there are no homogeneous linear relations with integer coefficients between them. Only those "action variables" possess a direct physical
significance and a unique definition which are canonically conjugate to the
angle variables corresponding to these independent basic frequencies, whose
number therefore coincides with s. Since the energy of a multiply periodic
system depends only on these s action variables, *Schwarzschild* proposed
that such a system should be characterised by precisely s quantum conditions which determine these action variables as integral multiples of *Planck's*
constant.

It was this formulation of the quantum conditions which *Bohr* followed
closely when he succeeded in adapting his correspondence principle, already
mentioned, which he had previously formulated only for simple periodic systems, to the general theory of multiply periodic systems.[7] The correspondence
principle asserts that the general combination oscillation in the mechanical
motion having frequency $\tau_1 \nu_1 + \tau_2 \nu_2 + \cdots + \tau_s \nu_s$ (where $\tau_1 \ldots \tau_s$ are positive
or negative integers or zero, and $\nu_1 \ldots \nu_s$ the chosen basis of fundamental
frequencies) is associated with a transition in which the values $n'_1 \ldots n'_s$ and
$n''_1 \ldots n''_s$ of the quantum numbers in the initial and final states respectively
differ by precisely $\tau_1 \ldots \tau_s$. It is in fact easy to show that *in the limit of large
quantum numbers* the frequency of the emitted light calculated from the frequency condition $h\nu = E(n'_1 \ldots n'_s) - E(n''_1 \ldots n''_s)$ coincides asymptotically
with the expression $(n'_1 - n''_1)\nu_1 + \cdots + (n'_s - n''_s)\nu_s$, as a consequence of
the assumed form of the quantum conditions of multiply periodic systems.
Which mechanical orbit is it whose fundamental frequencies are here to be
substituted for $\nu_1 \ldots \nu_s$? As long as each n is large compared with the corresponding τ, the differences between the values of the $\nu_1 \ldots \nu_s$ in the initial
and final states may be neglected, and it is unnecessary to answer this embarrassing question. *Bohr* had the happy idea that at any rate in the limit of
large quantum numbers the squares of the amplitudes of each component

---

[7] N. Bohr, *Kongelige Danske Videnskababernes Selskab Skrifter, naturvidensk. og mat.
Afd.* **8** Raekke IV, 1, Parts **I** and **II** (1918); German translation by P. Hertz under the
title *Über die Quantentheorie der Linienspektren* (Braunschweig 1923).

oscillation must determine the intensity of the "corresponding" transition. In extrapolating to small quantum numbers, one was however reduced to guesswork. Nevertheless *Bohr* was able in a few cases to obtain from his principle *selection and polarisation rules* valid even for small values of the quantum numbers, namely in those cases in which for *all* mechanical orbits of a system the oscillations with certain values of $\tau_1 \ldots \tau_s$ are absent (have zero amplitude) or belong to a particular form of the oscillation. By this means it proved possible for *Sommerfeld*[8] and *Debye*[9] to complete the theory of the normal Zeeman effect.

Bohr had already clearly indicated that his correspondence principle could not in any way serve to obliterate the distinction between classical mechanics and quantum theory; but rather that it was a pointer towards the goal of a general translation of the treatment of a given system by classical mechanics into a logically coherent quantum-theoretical treatment. Yet *Sommerfeld* himself evinced a certain disinclination towards the use of the correspondence principle, probably mainly because it was not possible, in the state of the theory at the time, to use this principle to obtain general quantitative results for small quantum numbers. He was also somewhat reluctant to characterise a degenerate system by fewer quantum numbers than the number of its mechanical degrees of freedom, although he was perfectly well aware that the orbital constants, which differ from the s action integrals determined by *Schwarzschild*'s rule, are very sensitive to perturbation by weak external fields of force, in that their values undergo cumulative changes in course of time (secular perturbation, as contrasted with periodic perturbation of the s action integrals). It must be remarked at this point that this situation has an analogue in present-day wave mechanics. If an energy value has g-fold degeneracy, there exists an associated g-dimensional linear subspace of the general Hilbert space of the eigenfunctions; just *which* particular vector in this subspace describes the state of the system (*every* such vector can be represented as a linear combination of g linearly independent base vectors) depends, before the removal of the degeneracy, on chance circumstances, and is sensitive to external perturbations of the system.

It was however always my own impression that the differences between the methods of *Sommerfeld* and his school on the one hand and those of *Bohr* on the other exercised a purely favourable and fertilising influence on the subsequent development of the theory. In the succeeding period the problem was to delimit more clearly the range of validity of classical mechanics. While it soon became manifest that classical mechanics must already break down in the case of the helium spectrum, since the problem of two electrons does not lead to multiply periodic orbits, erroneous ideas had at first been entertained

---

[8] A. Sommerfeld, *Physikalische Zeitschrift* **17**, 491 (1916) (Theory of the Zeeman effect of the hydrogen lines, with an appendix on the Stark effect).

[9] P. Debye, *Physikalische Zeitschrift* **17**, 507 (1916).

as to the scope of the theory of multiply periodic systems. Later it transpired that in the case of these multiply periodic systems too the treatment of the stationary states by means of classical mechanics did not necessarily lead to correct results; and indeed that the usefulness of this theory even for small quantum numbers is restricted to very special systems and is more or less fortuitous. In this connection the correspondence principle was very useful in separating those applications of the theory in which classical mechanics were used merely to interpret the selection and polarisation rules on the basis of the general orbital type or only in the limit of large quantum numbers (as for example in the derivation of the formula for *Rydberg*'s constant) from those other applications in which details of mechanical models were appealed to in an essential way (as for instance in excluding certain orbits in the hydrogen atom).

Sommerfeld found himself at this time logically driven to abandon classical models more and more, and to turn to the classification of spectral terms by quantum numbers and the search for simple empirical laws governed by whole numbers. We cannot any more think of this time without his fundamental treatise "Atombau und Spektrallinien",[10] which combines in such masterly fashion a unified treatment of the wealth of material with the ability to give something essential to readers of the most diverse kinds. In the preface to the first edition he conjured up, along with *Kepler*'s ellipses, the spirit of *Kepler* as well, when he wrote:*

What we are nowadays hearing of the language of spectra is a true music of the spheres within the atom, chords of integral relationships, an order and harmony that becomes ever more perfect in spite of the manifold variety. The theory of spectral lines will bear the name of *Bohr* for all time. But yet another name will be permanently associated with it, that of *Planck*. All integral laws of spectral lines and of atomic theory spring originally from the quantum theory. It is the mysterious *organon* on which Nature plays her music of the spectra, and according to the rhythm of which she regulates the structure of the atoms and nuclei.

It is as though there was here an echo of *Kepler*'s search for the harmonies in the cosmos, guided by the musical feeling for the beauty of just proportion in the sense of Pythagorean philosophy, – an echo of his "geometria est archetypus pulchritudinis mundi" (geometry is the archetype of the beauty of the universe). And how admirably did *Sommerfeld* understand the art of communicating to his large circle of pupils his infallible feeling for the just proportion and for the harmonious! It was in the years before the new

---

[10] A. Sommerfeld, *Atombau und Spektrallinien*. Vieweg, Braunschweig: 1st ed. (1919); 2nd ed. (1920); 3rd ed. (1922); 4th ed. (1924); *Wellenmechanischer Ergänzungsband* (1929); 5th ed. Vol. **I** (1931), Vol. **II** (1939).

* English translation by Henry L. Brose in A. Sommerfeld: *Atomic Structure and Spectral Lines*, London and New York, Dutton 1923.

quantum mechanics was set up that the saying was current among young physicists (modifying the advertising slogan of a well-known optical firm of those days) "if it's integers, go to Sommerfeld".

By comparing successive editions of his book, from the first edition in 1919 to the final form of the "Wellenmechanischer Ergänzungsband" of 1939 it is possible to follow in all its detail the development of the theory of atomic structure and of spectral lines during these twenty years. Here we can mention briefly only the most significant landmarks in this development. The similarity between the spark spectra of the alkaline earths and the arc spectra of the alkali elements led *Sommerfeld*, in conjunction with *Kossel*,[11] to the setting up of the "spectroscopic displacement law". Later on the exceptions to this rule acquired importance for those elements in which an inner shell of electrons is in process of filling up. Work on term representation (energy levels in a magnetic field) in the anomalous *Zeeman* effect led *Sommerfeld* to the formulation of the "magneto-optic decomposition rule" for *Runge*'s denominators,[12] which was followed shortly afterwards by the introduction of the "inner" quantum number j and its selection rules for doublet and triplet spectra.[13] Both researches were carried further by substantial contributions of *A. Landé* who was the first to give a completely successful representation of the terms in the anomalous Zeeman effect, and who also derived for singlet terms the values of the inner quantum number, which was soon interpreted as the quantum number of the resultant angular momentum. In continuation of his earlier work on *Voigt*'s theory of the anomalous *Zeeman* effect *Sommerfeld* succeeded in reinterpreting this theory in a quantum-theoretical manner, and thereby also in representing by a formula the positions of the energy levels in an external magnetic field for all terms of doublet spectra, over the whole range of the magneto-optical transition from weak to strong fields discovered by *Paschen* and *Back*.[14] He also discussed the relation of the spectroscopic data of the Zeeman effect to paramagnetism.[15] After the experimental discovery of the multiplets he could readily assign his third quantum number j to these terms as well.[16] It

---

[11] A. Sommerfeld and W. Kossel, *Verhandlungen der Deutschen Physikalischen Gesellschaft* **21**, 240 (1919) (Selection principle and displacement law in series spectra).

[12] A. Sommerfeld, *Die Naturwissenschaften* **8**, 61 (1920) (A numerical puzzle in the theory of the Zeeman effect).

[13] A. Sommerfeld, *Annalen der Physik* **63**, 221 (1920) (General spectroscopic regularities, especially a magneto-optic decomposition rule).

[14] A. Sommerfeld, *Zeitschrift für Physik* **8**, 257 (1922) (Reinterpretation in terms of quantum theory of Voigt's theory of the anomalous Zeeman effect in lines of the D type).

[15] A. Sommerfeld, *Physikalische Zeitschrift* **24**, 360 (1923) (Spectroscopic magneton numbers); *Zeitschrift für Physik* **19**, 221 (1923) (Theory of the magneton).

[16] A. Sommerfeld, *Annalen der Physik* **70**, 32 (1923) (Interpretation of complex spectra such as Mn, Cr etc. by the method of inner quantum numbers); *Annalen der Physik* **73**, 209 (1924) (Theory of multiplets and their Zeeman effect).

was of the greatest importance for the development of the theory that *Sommerfeld* turned his attention to the question of the *intensity of spectral lines*, after measurements at Utrecht had brought to light regularities determined by whole numbers in this quantity as well. On the basis of these measurements *Sommerfeld*'s pupil *Hönl*[17] and independently of him *Goudsmit* and *Kronig*[18] succeeded in guessing the quantitatively correct mode of rendering precise the formulae which *Sommerfeld* and *Heisenberg*[19] had derived earlier as estimates following from the correspondence principle. In a similar way *Sommerfeld* and *Hönl*, simultaneously with *Russell* and *Kronig*, were able to guess the correct formulae for the intensities of multiplet lines.[20]

In this way the ground was prepared for the quantum mechanics of *Sommerfeld*'s pupil *Heisenberg*, who recognised the calculus of matrix multiplication as the appropriate key to a quantitative translation of classical mechanics into a rational quantum mechanics – a translation which *Bohr*'s correspondence principle had indeed aimed at but had not been able to carry through. In this quantum mechanics a harmonic component oscillation is actually assigned to a pair of stationary states. By this abandonment of the mechanical picture – there is no such thing as a development in time of a single stationary state – the embarrassing question mentioned above as to the values of the mechanical frequencies of revolution which are to be substituted becomes superfluous, since the conception of such frequencies is now completely eliminated from the theory.

To this period of clarification of fundamental principles of the new quantum mechanics belong contributions by *Sommerfeld* which are concerned not with spectra but with the electron theory of metals. When I applied *Fermi*'s statistics, based on the exclusion principle, to the paramagnetism of metals, *Sommerfeld*, more enterprising than myself, immediately extended the range of application of the theory to other properties of metals such as electrical conductivity, thermal conductivity (the constant of the *Wiedemann-Franz* law) and thermoelectric phenomena.[21] A new and wide field for quantum me-

---

[17] H. Hönl, *Zeitschrift für Physik* **31**, 340 (1925).

[18] S. Goudsmit and R. Kronig, *Die Naturwissenschaften* **13**, 90 (1925).

[19] A. Sommerfeld and W. Heisenberg, *Zeitschrift für Physik* **11**, 131 (1922) (Intensity of multiplet lines and their Zeeman components).

[20] A. Sommerfeld and H. Hönl, *Sitzungsberichte der Berliner Akademie der Wissenschaften*, phys.-math. Klasse, p. 141 (1925) (Intensity of multiplet lines); H. W. Russell, *Nature* **115**, 835 (1925); *Proceedings of the American Academy of Arts and Sciences* **11**, 314, 322 (1925); R. Kronig, *Zeitschrift für Physik* **31**, 885 (1925).

[21] A. Sommerfeld, *Die Naturwissenschaften* **15**, 825 (1927); *Zeitschrift für Physik* **47**, 1 (1928) (Electron theory of metals).

chanics thereby opened up, a comprehensive account of which may be found in the article by *Sommerfeld* and *Bethe*[22] in the "Handbuch der Physik".

Sommerfeld himself did not intervene in the discussions of matters of principle connected with *Heisenberg*'s uncertainty relation as well as with causality and probability which followed *Schrödinger*'s setting up of his celebrated wave equation. None the less he found in the wave-mechanical form of the new quantum theory a rich field of application for the mathematical methods, so familiar to him, of the integration of partial differential equations and of eigenvalue problems. These can be found collected in *Sommerfeld*'s supplementary volume on wave mechanics. In the same place there will also be found a detailed account of the theory of the relativistic fine structure of the spectra of atoms with one electron, which follows from *Dirac*'s spinor equations for the electron. It is surprising how *Sommerfeld*'s original formula of 1916 for the energy levels can also be deduced from this new theory which takes electron spin into account. There is however an important difference in the selection rules as compared with the old theory, connected with the fact that the spin of the electron leads, even in atoms with a single electron, to a duplication of the number of energy levels. This duplication had previously escaped the notice of physicists, since in these atoms each pair of levels which differ only in the sign of *Dirac*'s quantum number coincide.

According to *Dirac*'s theory this coincidence should be exact. About a year ago a significant new development began in this connection in which several experimental and theoretical physicists are already taking part. The refinement of techniques of measurement with short waves in the U.S.A. has made it possible to establish by means of measurements of the lines of the H-atom corresponding to transitions between terms of the same principal quantum number the result that this degeneracy required by *Dirac*'s theory is removed by a small upward displacement of the *S*-terms. Later an analogous effect was detected by ordinary spectroscopic measurements for the terms of ionised helium. It can probably be said that quantum electrodynamics, rightly interpreted, permits an interpretation of this effect. It must however not be forgotten that here, on account of the well-known divergencies in the results following from the quantum theory of *wave fields*, we already find ourselves outside the range of a logically closed theory, and are once more reduced to guessing the correct final formulae. The smallness of these new effects is a consequence of the smallness of the so-called fine structure constant, which is often linked with *Sommerfeld*'s name, since its fundamental significance first came clearly to light through his theory of 1916 of the fine structure of hydrogenic spectra. The theoretical interpretation of its numerical value is one of the most important unsolved problems of atomic physics.

---

[22] A. Sommerfeld and H. Bethe, *Handbuch der Physik* (Springer, Berlin) volume **XXIV/2**, 2nd ed., pp. 333-620 (1933) (Electron theory of metals). The first chapter of this report is by Sommerfeld himself.

On 26th April 1951 the death occurred in Munich in the 82nd year of his age, as the result of a street accident sustained some four weeks previously, of *A. Sommerfeld*, one of the most outstanding German physicists of his generation. It was vouchsafed to him to pass on to posterity in their final form five of the six projected volumes of his lectures on theoretical physics. One volume only remained uncompleted, that on thermodynamics, the preparation of which he had purposely deferred to the last.

Sommerfeld was versatile to an astonishing degree. He was a master of the technical applications of mathematics, of the partial differential equations of physics (cf. in this connection his articles in the Mathematical Encyclopaedia and in the new edition by *Ph. Frank* and *R. von Mises* of the classical "Riemann-Weber"); of the formal classification of spectra; and again of wave mechanics, and in all alike he made decisive advances.

Of his applications of theory to technical problems it is *Sommerfeld*'s theory of friction of lubricants and his contributions to wireless telegraphy that have become best known. The standard treatise on the "theory of the top", which he wrote in conjunction with his teacher *F. Klein* in his early days, while he was still a "Privatdozent" in Göttingen, and in which many technical problems are discussed, possesses a significance going far beyond applied mathematics. It contains, on the basis of work by *Euler* and *Cayley*, and of *Hamilton*'s quaternions, the essential foundations of what considerably later was called the theory of representations of the rotation group in three-dimensional space. In particular, *Klein* had, following *Cayley*, clearly worked out the relation of this group to the "covering group" of linear unitary unimodular transformations of two complex variables. Thus in this treatise, now a classic, the mathematical basis is developed for the two-component "spinors" which turned up much later in wave mechanics.

F. Klein's plans for enrolling his favourite pupil *Sommerfeld* in the ranks of applied mathematicians were modified in consequence of the far-sighted initiative of *W. C. Röntgen*, who in 1906 called *Sommerfeld* to the Chair of Theoretical Physics in Munich, which was henceforth to be his permanent home. At first it was the special theory of relativity, particularly the geometrical form given to this theory by *H. Minkowski*, which engaged his interest. *Sommerfeld* made original contributions elucidating four-dimensional vector and tensor calculus, and also wrote explanatory comments on *Minkowski*'s work after the latter's untimely death. *Sommerfeld* always remained an adherent of the special and later also of the general theory of relativity, of whose creator, *A. Einstein*, he would speak only in terms of the greatest veneration and admiration.

Following the decisive and revolutionary introduction of *Bohr*'s model of the atom (1913), suggestions received earlier in Göttingen from *C. Runge* and *W. Voigt* for a theory of spectral lines bore abundant fruit. After *Sommerfeld*'s fundamental extension of *Bohr*'s theory of purely periodic systems to multiply periodic systems (1915–1916), which he was immediately able to apply to the theory of the relativistic fine-structure of hydrogenic spectra and to X-ray spectra, his contributions to the classification of spectra found visible expression in the successive editions of his fundamental treatise "Atombau und Spektrallinien". His pupils will always remember how with his fine sense of harmonies based on whole numbers he conjured up anew the spirit of *Kepler*, and how in this way his assured touch guided him in the discovery and formulation of general spectroscopic laws, even when the failure of models of the atom based on classical mechanics was becoming more and more evident. After the discovery of the new quantum mechanics (1927) *Sommerfeld* was able to employ now also in the service of the theory of atomic structure his old mastery in handling the mathematics of wave theory on paths in the complex plane, which he knew so well. The "Wellenmechanischer Ergänzungsband" which followed his book "Atombau und Spektrallinien" gives greater completeness to *Sommerfeld*'s scientific work.

Although the epistemological side of physics in general and of quantum mechanics in particular is not discussed in any special detail in *Sommerfeld*'s work, he always maintained an open mind in regard to fundamental problems, such as the duality of wave and corpuscle, which kept him from one-sided solutions when it was a question of recognising the opposition in the sense of complementarity.

To an extent granted to only few men, *Sommerfeld* united in himself in happy fashion the types of the researcher and the teacher. Handing on his own inspiration to the younger generations, he created a numerous band of disciples, whose members already occupy many chairs of theoretical physics in different countries. Thus will his spiritual children and grandchildren, mourning his loss, now continue his work.

7. Rydberg and the Periodic System of the Elements*

Johannes Robert Rydberg (1854–1919)

Photo published in the *Proceedings of the Rydberg Centennial Conference on Atomic Spectroscopy* held in the Physics Laboratory of the University of Lund, July 1–5, 1954

* First published in English in the *Proceedings of the Rydberg Centennial Conference on Atomic Spectroscopy*, Lund 1954. Vol. **50**, No 21. *Universitetes Årsskrift*, Lund, Schweden, 1955.

It is not so well known as it should be that *Rydberg*'s occupation with spectral lines had its origin in his interest in the periodic system of the elements, an interest which accompanied him through his whole life.

After an early attempt (1885) to discover new laws by a Fourier analysis of the famous *Lothar Meyer* curve for the atomic volumes of the elements, already in 1889 in his first larger paper[1] on the emission spectra of the chemical elements he clearly formulated the idea, that these spectra should give the clue to the understanding of the periodic system. The connexion between spectra and chemical properties had been empirically well established by *Kirchhoff* and *Bunsen*, but the attempts at a theoretical explanation of this connexion were very vague. *Rydberg* said rather generally that the periodic system of elements shows us "that the effective force between the atoms must be a periodic function of the atomic weight". This he considered to be a hint that periodic motions of the atoms have something to do with it, which lead to the analysis of the spectra. Therefore he concluded that the spectral analysis will lead nearer to the goal of a mechanics of the atoms and of an understanding of the periodic system than "investigations of any other physical property".

I quote here *Rydberg*'s own words:[2]

"Durch Mendelejeffs Entdeckung des periodischen Systems der Elemente ist ein neuer Ausgangspunkt aller einschlägigen Arbeiten gewonnen worden und doch hat man sich dessen selten bedient. Um solche Untersuchungen wenigstens in Schub zu bringen, habe ich in einer früheren Abhandlung (Bihang till K. Svenska Vet.-Akad. Handlingar, 10, No 2) mit etwas größerer Genauigkeit die periodische Beziehung zwischen dem spezifischen Gewichte und dem Atomgewichte der Elemente zu bestimmen versucht. Ich habe dort gefunden, daß man annähernd diese Beziehung durch eine Sinusreihe mit veränderlichen Koeffizienten darstellen kann. Daraus habe ich ferner geschlossen, daß die Periodizität sehr vieler physikalischer Konstanten davon abhängen muß, daß die wirksame Kraft zwischen zwei Atomen eines und desselben oder verschiedener Elemente eine periodische Funktion des Atomgewichtes sei. Steigt man noch weiter vor, so gelangt man zu der sehr wahrscheinlichen Annahme, daß Kohäsion, Adhäsion und chemische Affinität im Grunde auf periodische Bewegungen der Atome zurückzuführen seien. Es läge somit am nächsten, die periodischen Bewegungen überhaupt zu untersuchen, und da die Spektren der chemischen Elemente auf Bewegungen dieser Art beruhen, werden wir in den Bereich der Spektralanalyse hingewiesen. Zwar können wir nicht wissen, ob diese periodischen Bewegungen dieselben sind, die wir anfänglich aufsuchten, aber eine Untersuchung dieser Schwingungen wird uns jedenfalls wertvolle Erkenntnisse vermitteln über die Beschaffenheit der Atome und wird uns unserem Ziele mehr nähern als eine Untersuchung irgendeiner anderen physikalischen Eigenschaft."

---

[1] J. R. Rydberg: "Recherches sur la constitution des spectres d'émission des éléments chimiques", *Kongl. Svenska Vetenskapsakademiens Handlingar*, Vol. **23**, Nr. 11, Stockholm 1890. (In German: "Untersuchungen über die Beschaffenheit der Emissionsspektren der chemischen Elemente", *Ostwalds Klassiker der exakten Wissenschaften* Nr. **196**, Leipzig 1922.)

[2] From *Ostwalds Klassiker*, Nr. **196**, p. 9 f.

I think, one has to admit that *Rydberg*'s speculations were sometimes rather wild, but on the other hand they were always controlled again by his study of the empirical material. In a paper of 1897[3] he expressively stated (Chap. XI): "In investigations on the periodic system the ordinals (Ordnungszahlen) of the elements instead of the atomic weight should be used as independent variables". His argument for it was that the atomic numbers simply run through all integers.

At that time no sufficient attention had been paid to *Rydberg*'s claim and only later the work of *Julius Thomsen* and others on the periodic system of the elements followed.

In this same paper *Rydberg* finds an interesting simple rule for the relation between mass-number M and atomic number Z. Today we must add, that the rule concerns the mass of the most frequent isotope of this Z value. The rule is:

if Z is odd (odd chemical valence) $\quad M = 2Z + 1$;

if Z is even $\quad M = 2Z$.

Rydberg was aware that nitrogen ($Z = 7$, $M = 14$) is an exception, but it is true that otherwise this rule holds until about Ca. *Rydberg* trusted this rule so much that he always assumes holes and shifts the atomic numbers upwards, till the rule fits. In this way he has the general tendency to assume too many holes in the periodic system and too high values for the atomic numbers.

After the lecture of Professor *Bohr* I only briefly mention *Rydberg*'s idea of a relation between the parity of multiplicity of the spectral lines and the parity of the chemical valence. If the one is even the other is odd and vice versa. However, *Rydberg* was not sure of this idea being unable to give a general proof of it. The reason for it was first that the order and the resolution of more complicated spectra (as for instance copper) was not sufficiently advanced at that time to determine correctly this multiplicity. Secondly the difference between spark spectra and arc spectra made complications, as it was not known at that time that the first are emitted by ions. Only much later it became clear that the rule holds without exception if the chemical valence is replaced by the number of electrons in the emitting atom. This exact rule of alternation ("Wechselsatz") was called after *Rydberg* by *Sommerfeld*.

A further progress in the order of the periodic system was made by *Rydberg* in his paper "Elektron, der erste Grundstoff" of 1906.[4] Here (p. 11) he said for the first time that the 3 numbers 2, 8, 18 for the periods in the system of the elements are represented by $2 \cdot 1^2$, $2 \cdot 2^2$, $2 \cdot 3^2$. There was

[3] J. R. Rydberg: "Studien über Atomgewichtszahlen", *Zeitschrift für anorganische Chemie* **14**, 66 (1897).

[4] J. R. Rydberg: *Elektron, der erste Grundstoff* (Lund 1906).

8. Paul Ehrenfest †*

Paul Ehrenfest (1880–1933)

Photo taken in Leyden in the twenties (Courtesy: Martin J. Klein)

---

* First published in *Die Naturwissenschaften* **21**, 841 (1933).

> Einmal hat *Ehrenfest* einen Brief voller Bosheiten an *Ein-*
> *stein* geschrieben – es war über die Einstein-Bosestatistik,
> besonders über die 'kondensierte Phase' – und Einstein
> schrieb dann zurück: "Deine Witze sind großartig, Deine
> Argumente schwach!"
>
> Letter from Pauli to Gunnar Källén, January 21, 1955

On 25th September 1933, under tragic circumstances and to the dismay of his family and numerous friends and acquaintances, *Paul Ehrenfest* carried out his calamitous resolve to cast off the burden of a life grown too heavy for him to bear. It is now our task to hold in remembrance his scientific work and the picture of his personality unencumbered by those cares and feelings of inferiority which increasingly clouded his spirit in his later years. The picture is of a man of scintillating intellect and wit, intervening in discussions with mordant criticism, and at the same time with profound insight into the foundations of the scientific attitude, drawing attention to some essential point hitherto unnoticed or insufficiently regarded.

Ehrenfest was born on 18th January 1880 in Vienna, and studied at the University there. It was there that he received from his teacher, *Boltzmann*, the decisive stimulus destined permanently to make the kinetic theory of matter and statistical mechanics the favourite object of his creative work. He always followed attentively the later developments in this field, which took place under the rising star of the quantum theory, and he was able to intervene decisively at some fundamental points in furthering this development.

Ehrenfest first became known to a wider circle through his great article in the Encyclopaedia "The conceptual foundations of the statistical point of view in mechanics", which he wrote in conjunction with his wife, *T. Ehrenfest-Afanasjewa*, in Russia, where he worked for some years. In the encyclopaedia article in question, which is even now a most valuable work of reference, *Ehrenfest* was not so much concerned to give an account of the statistical theory of heat as a self-contained compact doctrine; he was rather concerned to vindicate against all possible objections, and to establish as final, the consistency of *Boltzmann*'s point of view, especially his celebrated H-theorem on the increase of the entropy in the statistical average. In this connection he achieved greater conceptual precision in many points, even as compared with the excellent earlier accounts of the H-theorem by *H. A. Lorentz*. In particular, he emphasised the necessity of distinguishing between "fine-grained" and "coarse-grained" (i. e., already averaged over finite cells) density in phase-space, which is essential for establishing the H-theorem in a rigorous and general manner.

It is said that it was just this circumstance that was not without influence on *H. A. Lorentz*'s decision to recommend *Ehrenfest* as his successor in Leiden (Holland). There he worked from 1912 until the end of his life, developing a lively teaching activity and passing on to many a young man his own high enthusiasm for physical science.

At a time when developments in quantum theory were taking place in rapid succession through the fundamental work of *Planck, Einstein, Debye* and others, it was one particular question, the consistent following up of which led *Ehrenfest* to his greatest discovery. As formulated by him (as so often drastically and most impressively from the didactic point of view) the question was: "how is it that *Wien*'s displacement law, which is after all deduced from classical foundations, stands unshaken amidst the breakers of quantum theory?" In order to obtain a general statement embracing the statistical statements of classical and quantum theory, *Ehrenfest* first introduces the idea of the *a priori statistical weight* by which the various regions of phase-space are to be multiplied in forming the continuous or discrete partition functions used in calculating the thermodynamic functions. In the special case of the harmonic oscillator, first treated by *Planck*, all regions of phase-space corresponding to the same range of total energy have equal weight in classical theory (which as is well known leads for black-body radiation to the "violet-catastrophe", to use once again *Ehrenfest*'s expression). In quantum theory on the other hand only those regions which correspond to the discrete energy values $E_n = nv + E_0$ (E_0 = zero-point energy, v = frequency of the oscillator) are to be counted, and these with equal weight. *Ehrenfest* investigated the most general weight-function $g(E, v)$ which is consistent with *Wien*'s displacement law, and found the result

$$g(E, v) = f(E/v) \, ;$$

the weight-function can depend only on the quotient of the energy of the oscillator and the frequency. Since *Planck* had put his elementary regions of energy proportional to the frequency, *Wien*'s displacement law was satisfied.

What did this result mean physically? Further work by *Ehrenfest* gave the answer to this question; in this he directed attention to so-called *adiabatic processes*, which are characterised in thermodynamic-statistical terms by the property that only work and not heat is communicated to the system from outside. In mechanical terms they are characterised by the condition that the system passes through a succession of equilibrium states in consequence of "infinitely slow" alterations in the external parameters; "infinitely slow" is here to be understood in the sense that the fractional change in the values of the parameters is negligibly small in times of the order of the orbital periods of the system, regarded as periodic or quasi-periodic. *Ehrenfest* now showed, first, that the above statistical weight-function must remain generally invariant in such adiabatic processes, if the statistically defined entropy is not to change its value in this process, which is required for thermodynamic reasons (*principle of the adiabatic invariance of the a priori weights*). In the second place he showed, following earlier ideas of *Rayleigh*, that it is precisely this expression E/v that remains invariant when the eigen-frequency of the oscillator undergoes adiabatic change or when applied to a normal mode of the radiation cavity which is adiabatically compressed, if this process is followed out on the basis of classical mechanics. For arbitrary periodic mechanical systems the time-integral

$$\int_0^T 2E_{\text{kin}}\, dt$$

of twice the kinetic energy extended over the period T of the system had to be substituted for E/v. This led *Ehrenfest* to set up the *adiabatic hypothesis*, according to which the quantum conditions must always be such that *adiabatic invariants* of classical mechanics are equated to integral multiples of the quantum of action.

Ehrenfest himself has given an account,[1] on the occasion of the 10-year jubilee of *Bohr*'s atomic model, of the use of the adiabatic hypothesis as a heuristic aid in the discovery of the quantum conditions for complex systems, and of the special position of so-called degenerate systems which became increasingly evident in the publications of *Bohr* and others which followed the invention of *Bohr*'s atomic model. Today we may add, on the occasion of the 20-year jubilee of *Bohr*'s atomic model, that *Ehrenfest*'s adiabatic hypothesis has retained its significance in wave mechanics as well. Only the emphasis is now no longer on the validity of classical mechanics when a system undergoes adiabatic transformation (since even in the description of stationary states of the system classical mechanics has in general proved inadequate); it is rather on the fact, first demonstrated in wave mechanics by *Born*, that on transforming a system adiabatically, it always remains in one of the definite stationary states possible with fixed external parameters; (in the case of rapid non-adiabatic external actions transitions in general take place from one stationary state to others in consequence of so-called "Schüttelwirkung" or "shaking action").

Although the setting up of the adiabatic hypothesis is *Ehrenfest*'s principal achievement in the field of quantum statistics, another of *Ehrenfest*'s contributions to this field may also be discussed here, which, although less well-known, is nevertheless of the utmost importance. This is his paper written in collaboration with *V. Trkal* on the theory of the chemical constant.[2] Here *Ehrenfest*'s critical eye lit upon the circumstance, only apparently trivial, that the entropy of a double quantity of a gas is defined as double that of

---

[1] *Die Naturwissenschaften* **11**, 543 (1923).

[2] P. Ehrenfest and V. Trkal, *Koninklijke Akademie van Wetenschappen te Amsterdam. Proceedings* **23**, 162 (1920); *Annalen der Physik* **65**, 602 (1921).

the single quantity at the same density and temperature, whereas the general prescription of classical statistics for calculating the thermodynamic functions leads, when applied to ideal gases, to a different result. It was only after what was, from the standpoint of those days, an unjustifiable and arbitrary division of the probabilities concerned by $N!$ (where N denotes the number of molecules present) that there was agreement with the phenomenological convention just mentioned. *Ehrenfest* recognised correctly that this "obscure point" of dividing the thermodynamic probabilities by $N!$ is connected with the impossibility of changing a quantity of gas reversibly into the double quantity and thus determining the entropy, so that at this point there is room for a definition. He showed further that the theory of the dissociation equilibrium of gases can be established quite independently of this obscure point, by considering only reversible processes of molecular dissociation which are actually possible, and referring everything to the phase-space of the atoms (or groups of atoms), which are fixed in number. The first indication was thereby given of the significance, for the values of the chemical constants, of the symmetry numbers of a molecule – the numbers, that is, of those permutations of similar atoms in the molecule which can also be produced by rigid rotation of the molecule.

As regards the elucidation of the above obscure point, it was only by the application of wave mechanics to a system of N identical particles (e. g. the molecules of a gas enclosed in a vessel) and its stationary states that this was achieved. When the energy of the individual particles is given, there are, in the absence of interaction between the particles, $N!$ different possible eigenfunctions of the whole system in configuration space. But in nature (if for the sake of simplicity we here disregard a slight complication of the situation due to the presence of nuclear spin) only a single linear combination of these eigenfunctions occurs, either the symmetric or the antisymmetric one. Hence the number of non-degenerate states of the whole gas is $1/N!$ times less than was originally assumed, and the "obscure point" thus ceases to be obscure. As a matter of history, *Ehrenfest* made a second essential contribution to the gradual recognition of this fact. Even before the wave mechanics of configuration space had been formulated, so that it was not yet possible to speak unambiguously of stationary states of the whole gas, *Einstein*, following up an idea due to *Bose* on the entropy of cavity radiation regarded as a "gas of light quanta", had introduced a mode of counting the states of a monatomic gas which led to a new method of calculating the entropy of the ideal gas, and hence to a new theory of gas degeneracy. It turned out later that this theory was identical with that which follows from the assumption that only those states of the gas exist in nature which have eigenfunctions symmetrical in the particle coordinates. In *Bose* and *Einstein*'s first paper these authors were not by any means completely clear about the basis of their considerations, and it was *Ehrenfest* who pointed out to them that they had in their considerations implicitly abandoned the usual assumption of the statistically independent behaviour of the gas atoms.

What we have presented here should be regarded as merely exemplifying *P. Ehrenfest*'s mode of creative work and thought. It is impossible to deal exhaustively, within the limits of an essay, with all the stimulating ideas which emanated from him. We can here only mention in passing his contributions to the theory of the interference effects occurring when *Röntgen* rays are scattered by polyatomic molecules; to the theory of osmotic pressure; to the theory of the Brownian motion (in which connection one might with some justification charge him with an excessive predilection for minor paradoxes). Noteworthy also are his well-known wave-mechanical theorem on the classical motion of the centre of a wave-packet; his suggestion for an outline of the spinor calculus from the mathematical point of view; and finally his earlier contributions to the clarification of the physical foundations of the special theory of relativity, in particular the concept of "signal velocity". Mention should also be made of his inaugural address in Leiden, still worth reading today, "On the crisis in the hypothesis of a luminiferous ether", which attempts to do justice to the theory of his prematurely deceased friend *W. Ritz*, the discoverer of the combination principle for spectra – a theory not tenable in the light of experience but none the less interesting in conception.

His reflections at this time also led *Ehrenfest* to the question thrown up by the special theory of relativity, to which no answer could be given on the basis of the electrodynamics of *Maxwell* and *Lorentz* alone, the question of the "structure" of the electron and the nature and magnitude of its self-energy. (To this question he devoted a short note, concerned with the electromagnetic couple or torque acting on a moving ellipsoidal electron.) This question, after lying dormant for a long time, has now re-emerged as a live scientific issue, and discussion again centres round it. At this point I may perhaps conclude with a personal reminiscence of a critical intervention by *Ehrenfest* in a discussion. It was at the time when *Dirac* had just published his first paper on the theory of radiation, in which the electromagnetic field is quantised. *Ehrenfest* immediately pointed out that this theory must involve the difficulty of an infinite self-energy of the electron, since it makes essential use of the value of the field potentials at the position of the electron itself, and must be regarded as a re-interpretation in terms of correspondence of the classical theory of a *point*-electron. This is a difficulty which was in fact destined to prove extremely embarrassing and troublesome in the course of the subsequent development of quantum electrodynamics, and which still remains unsolved at the present time.

As we look back once more over *Ehrenfest*'s scientific activity, it appears to us as a living witness to the abiding truth that scientifically objective criticism, no matter how severe, always has a stimulating and fertilising effect, provided it is consistently thought out to a conclusion.

9. Einstein's Contribution to Quantum Theory*

Albert Einstein (1879–1955)

Photo by Trude Fleischmann (From: Carl Seelig, Albert Einstein. Eine dokumentarische Biographie, Europa Verlag, Zürich 1954)

* First published in P. A. Schilpp: *Albert Einstein: Philosopher Scientist. The Library of Living Philosophers*, volume 7. Evanston, Ill. 1949, pp. 149–160. The present version is translated from the German edition, *Albert Einstein als Philosoph und Naturforscher*, ed. P. A. Schilpp, Stuttgart (1955), pp. 74–84, which is believed to be Pauli's original wording.

If new features of the phenomena of nature are discovered that are incompatible with the system of theories assumed at that time, the question arises, which of the known principles used in the description of nature are general enough to comprehend the new situation and which have to be modified or abandoned. The attitude of different physicists on problems of this kind, which makes strong demands on the intuition and tact of a scientist, depends to a large extent on the personal temperament of the investigator. In the case of *Planck*'s discovery in 1900 of the quantum of action during the course of his famous investigations of the law of the black-body radiation, it was clear that the law of the conservation of energy and momentum and *Boltzmann*'s principle connecting entropy and probability, were two pillars sufficiently strong to stand unshaken by the development resulting from the new discovery. It was indeed the faithfulness to these principles which enabled *Planck* to introduce the new constant h, the quantum of action, into his statistical theory of the thermodynamic equilibrium of radiation.

The original investigation of *Planck*, however, had treated with a certain discretion the question whether the new "quantum-hypothesis" implied the necessity of changing the laws of microscopic phenomena themselves independent of statistical applications, or whether one had to use only an improvement of the statistical methods to enumerate equally probable states. In any case, the tendency towards a compromise between the older ideas of physics, now called the "classical" ones, and the quantum theory was always favoured by *Planck*, both in his earlier and later work on the subject, although affirmation of such a possibility was to diminish considerably the significance of his own discovery.

Such considerations formed the background of *Einstein*'s first paper on quantum theory [1],* which was preceded by his papers on the fundamentals of statistical mechanics[1] ** and accompanied, in the same year 1905, by his other fundamental papers on the theory of the Brownian movement[2] and the theory of relativity.[3] In this and subsequent papers [2, 3, 4b], *Einstein* clarified and strengthened the thermodynamical arguments underlying *Planck*'s theory so much that he was able to draw definite conclusions on the microscopic phenomena themselves. He gave to *Boltzmann*'s equation between entropy S and "probability" W,

$$S = k \log W + \text{const.} , \tag{1}$$

---

* Editors' Note: All numerals appearing in brackets [ ] in this paper refer to Einstein's papers, dealing with the quantum theory, appearing under equivalent numbers at the close of this paper.

[1] A. Einstein, *Annalen der Physik* (4) **9**, 417 (1902); **11**, 170 (1903); **14**, 354 (1904).

**Here the translation corrects the chronology of the German version.

[2] A. Einstein, *Annalen der Physik* (4) **17**, 549 (1905).

[3] A. Einstein, *Annalen der Physik* (4) **17**, 891 (1905).

a definite physical meaning by defining W for a given state, as the relative duration in which this state (which may deviate more or less from the state of thermodynamical equilibrium) is realized in a closed system with a given value of its energy. Hence, *Boltzmann's* relation is not only a definition of W, but also gives a connection between quantities which are in principle observable. For instance, one obtains for the mean square of the energy fluctuation ε of a small partial volume of a closed system, as a consequence of (1), the expression

$$\overline{\varepsilon^2} = k \left[-\left(\frac{\partial^2 S}{\partial E^2} \right)_{T,V} \right]^{-1} = kT^2 \left(\frac{\partial E}{\partial T} \right)_V , \qquad (2)$$

where T is the temperature and E the average energy (we disregard here the complication of the formula due to density fluctuations, because it is absent in the case of radiation). This relation must hold independently of the adopted theoretical model. If the energy of a system as a function of the temperature is empirically known, the model has to be in accordance with the fluctuation computed with help of equation (2) and inversely, the assumption of such a theoretical model prescribes the choice of states supposed to be equally probable in *Boltzmann's* relation (1). For the mean square of the energy fluctuation of the part of the radiation within the frequency interval $(v, v + dv)$, in the small partial volume V of a cavity filled with radiation in thermodynamical equilibrium, *Planck's* radiation formula gives, according to (2), the expression, first derived by *Einstein* [4b],

$$\overline{\varepsilon^2} = hvE + \frac{c^3}{8\pi v^2} \frac{E^2}{V dv} , \qquad (3)$$

if E is the mean energy of the radiation in V of the frequency interval in question. Whereas the second term can easily be interpreted with help of the classical wave theory as due to the interferences between the partial waves,[4] the first term is in obvious contradiction to classical electrodynamics. It can, however, be interpreted by analogy to the fluctuations of the number of molecules in ideal gases with the help of the picture that the energy of radiation stays concentrated in limited regions of space in energy amounts hv, which behave like independent particles, called "light quanta" or "photons."

As one was reluctant to apply statistical methods to the radiation itself, *Einstein* also considered the Brownian motion of a mirror which perfectly reflects radiation in the frequency interval $(v, v + dv)$, but transmits for all other frequencies [4b]. If P_v is the frictional force corresponding to the velocity v of the mirror normal to its surface, *Einstein's* general theory of the

---

[4] For a quantitative computation, see H. A. Lorentz: *Théories statistiques en thermody-namique*, Leipzig 1916, Appendix No. IX.

Brownian movement gives, for the irregular change Δ of the momentum of the mirror in the normal direction during the time interval τ, the statistical relation

$$\overline{\Delta^2} = 2Pm\overline{v^2}\tau = 2PkT\tau \;, \tag{4}$$

since $m\overline{v^2} = kT$ (m is the mass of the mirror). One first computes P according to the usual wave theory as given by

$$P = \frac{3}{2c}\left(\varrho - \frac{1}{3}v\frac{\partial\varrho}{\partial v}\right)dv \cdot f \;, \tag{5}$$

where ϱdv is the radiative energy per unit volume of the frequency interval $(v, v + dv)$ considered, and f the surface of the mirror. Inserting (5) into (4), and using *Planck*'s formula, one obtains

$$\frac{\overline{\Delta^2}}{\tau} = \frac{1}{c}\left[h v \varrho + \frac{c^3}{8\pi v^2}\varrho^2\right]dv \cdot f \;. \tag{6}$$

This formula is very closely connected with (3), since using $E = \varrho dv V$ one has

$$\frac{\overline{\Delta^2}}{\tau} = \frac{1}{c}f\frac{\overline{\varepsilon^2}}{V} \;. \tag{6a}$$

Just as in (3), it is only the last term in (6) which can be explained by the classical wave theory, whereas the first term can be interpreted with the picture of corpuscular light quanta of the energy $h v$ and the momentum $h v / c$ in the direction of their propagation.

We have to add two remarks.

1. If one starts with the simplified law of Wien for the black-body radiation, which holds for $h v \gg kT$ (or whose validity is restricted to this interval), only the first term in (3) is obtained.

2. In his first paper [1], *Einstein* computed for the region of validity of *Wien*'s law, with help of a direct application of equation (1), the probability of the rare state in which the entire radiation energy is contained in a certain partial volume, instead of considering the mean square of the energy fluctuation. Also in this case he could interpret the results with the help of the above mentioned picture of corpuscular "light quanta." In this way *Einstein* was led to his famous "light quantum hypothesis," which he immediately applied to the photoelectric effect and to *Stokes*' law for fluorescence [1], later also to the generation of secondary cathode rays by X-rays [5] and to the prediction of the high frequency limit in the *Bremsstrahlung* [9]. All this is so well known today that it is hardly necessary to go into a detailed discussion of these consequences. We are only briefly recalling that, by this early work of *Einstein*, it became clear that the existence of the quantum of action implies a radical

change in the laws governing all micro-phenomena. In the case of radiation, this change is expressed in the contrast between the use of the particle picture and the wave picture for different phenomena.

The consequences of *Planck*'s theory, that harmonic oscillators with the eigenfrequency v can only have discrete energy values, given by integral multiples of hv [2], was also successfully applied by *Einstein* to the theory of the specific heat of solids [3]. Methodically it has been pointed out that on this occasion *Einstein* for the first time applied the simpler method of the canonical ensemble to the derivation of the free energy and the mean energy of such oscillators as a function of the temperature, whereas in the earlier papers of *Planck* the entropy as a function of the energy was calculated with aid of *Boltzmann*'s method in which the microcanonic ensemble is used. Regarding the physical content of the theory, it seems obvious that the assumption of only a single value of the frequency of the oscillators in the solid body could not be correct. In connection with *Madelung*[5] and *Sutherland*'s[6] discovery of a relation between the assumed value of this frequency and the elastic properties of the solid, this problem was discussed in several subsequent papers of *Einstein* [7, 8, 9], among which *Einstein*'s report at the Solvay Congress in 1911 is most interesting, since it was given after the establishment of the empirical formula of *Nernst* and *Lindemann* for the thermal energy of solids and just before the problem was solved theoretically by *Born* and *Kármán*[7] and independently, by *Debye*.[8] It may be considered as rather strange today that these later theories were not found much earlier, all the more since the method of eigenvibrations was applied to the black-body radiation from the standpoint of the classical theory much earlier by *Rayleigh* and *Jeans*. One has to bear in mind, however, that until then no general rule for determining the discrete energy values of states had been found and also that physicists were rather hesitant to apply quantum laws to objects so widely extended in space as the eigenvibrations of a body.

Einstein's report on the constitution of radiation at the physics meeting in Salzburg [5] in 1909, where he appeared before a larger audience for the first time, can be considered as one of the landmarks in the development of theoretical physics. It deals with both special relativity and quantum theory and contains the important conclusion that the elementary process must be directed (needle radiation) not only for absorption, but also for emission of radiation, although this postulate was in open conflict with the classical idea of emission in spherical waves, which is indispensable for the understanding of the coherence properties of radiation, as they appear in interference ex-

---

[5] E. Madelung, *Physikalische Zeitschrift* **11**, 898 (1910).
[6] W. Sutherland, *Philosophical Magazine* (6) **20**, 657 (1910).
[7] M. Born and Th. von Kármán, *Physikalische Zeitschrift* **13**, 297 (1912).
[8] P. Debye, *Annalen der Physik* (4) **39**, 789 (1912).

periments. *Einstein*'s postulate of a directed emission process has been further supported by strong thermodynamical arguments in his subsequent work. In papers published with *L. Hopf* [6] (which later also caused an interesting discussion with *von Laue* [12] on the degree of disorder in the "black" radiation) he could extend the earlier work on the fluctuations of momentum of a mirror under the influence of a radiation field to the corresponding momentum fluctuations of a harmonic oscillator. In this way, it was possible, at least for this particular system which played such an important role in *Planck*'s original theory, to compute the translatory motion in equilibrium with the surrounding radiation, besides their oscillating motion which had been treated much earlier by *Planck*. The result was disappointing for those who still had the vain hope of deriving *Planck*'s radiation formula by merely changing the statistical assumptions rather than by a fundamental break with the classical ideas regarding the elementary micro-phenomena themselves: The classical computation of the fluctuation of momentum of an harmonic oscillator in its interaction with a radiation field is only compatible with the well-known value $3/2\,kT$ for its kinetic energy in thermodynamic equilibrium, if the radiation field fulfills the classical law of *Rayleigh-Jeans* instead of the law of *Planck*. If inversely the latter law is assumed, the fluctuations of momentum of the oscillators must be due to irregularities in the radiation field, which have to be much larger than the classical ones for a small density of the radiation energy.

With *Bohr*'s successful application of quantum theory to the explanation of the line spectra of the elements with help of his well-known two "fundamental postulates of quantum theory" (1913), a rapid development started, in the course of which the quantum theory was liberated from the restriction to such particular systems as *Planck*'s oscillators.

Therefore the problem arose of deriving *Planck*'s radiation formula using general assumptions holding for all atomic systems in accordance with *Bohr*'s postulates. This problem was solved by *Einstein* in 1917 in a famous paper [13] which can be considered as the peak of one stage of *Einstein*'s achievements in quantum theory (see also [10] and [11]) and as the ripe fruit of his earlier work on the Brownian movement. With the help of general statistical laws for the spontaneous and induced emission processes and for the absorption processes which are the inverse of the former, he could give a new basis to *Planck*'s radiation formula by making the assumption of the validity of two general relations between the three coefficients which determine the frequency of these processes and which, if two of these coefficients are given, permits the computation of the third. As these results of *Einstein* are today contained in all textbooks of quantum theory, it is hardly necessary to discuss here the details of this theory and its later generalization to more complicated radiation processes [15]. Besides this derivation of *Planck*'s radiation formula, the same paper discusses also the momentum exchanged between the atomic system and the radiation in a definite and very general way, using again equation (4) of the theory of the Brownian movement, which connects the mean square of the momentum exchanged in a certain time interval and the friction force P_v. The latter can be computed, using the general assumption indicated by both experience and experiment that the emission or absorption induced from pencils of radiation with different directions are independent of each other.[9] The condition (4) is then fulfilled in *Planck*'s radiation field, only if the spontaneous emission is assumed to be directed in such a way that for every elementary process of radiation an amount hv/c of momentum is emitted in a random direction and that the atomic system suffers a corresponding recoil in the opposite direction. The latter consequence was later confirmed experimentally by *Frisch*.[10]

Insufficient attention has been paid according to the author's opinion, to *Einstein*'s own critical judgement of the fundamental role ascribed to "chance" in this description of the radiation processes by statistical laws. We are therefore quoting the following passage from his paper of 1917:

"Die Schwäche der Theorie liegt einerseits darin, daß sie uns dem Anschluß an die Undulationstheorie nicht näher bringt, andererseits darin, daß sie Zeit und Richtung der Elementarprozesse dem "Zufall" überläßt; trotzdem hege ich das volle Vertrauen in die Zuverlässigkeit des eingeschlagenen Weges."*

The contrast between the interference properties of radiation, for the description of which the superposition principle of the wave theory is indispensable, and the properties of exchange of energy and momentum between radiation and matter, which can only be described with the help of the corpuscular picture, was undiminished and seemed at first to be irreconcilable. As is well known, *de Broglie* later quantitatively formulated the idea that a similar contrast will appear again with matter. *Einstein* was very much in favour of this new idea; the author remembers that, in a discussion at the physics meeting in Innsbruck in the autumn of 1924, *Einstein* proposed to search for interference and diffraction phenomena with molecular beams.[11] At the same time, in a paper of *S. N. Bose*, a derivation of *Planck*'s formula was given, in which only the corpuscular picture, but no wave-theoretical concept was used. This inspired *Einstein* to give an analogous application to

---

[9] Compare to this point the discussion between Einstein and Jordan [16].

[10] R. Frisch, *Zeitschrift für Physik* **86**, 42 (1933).

* "The weakness of the theory lies, on the one hand, in the fact that it does not bring us any closer to a merger with the undulatory theory, and, on the other hand, in the fact that it leaves the time and direction of elementary processes to 'chance'; in spite of this I harbor full confidence in the trustworthiness of the path entered upon." (Translated by the editors.)

[11] Compare in this connection also the earlier discussion by Einstein and Ehrenfest [14] of questions regarding molecular beams.

the theory of the so-called degeneration of ideal gases [17], now known to describe the thermodynamical properties of a system of particles with symmetrical wave functions (Einstein-Bose statistics). It is interesting that later an attempt was made to apply this theory to liquid helium. The fundamental difference between the statistical properties of like and unlike particles, which is also discussed in the cited papers of *Einstein*, is connected, according to wave mechanics, with the circumstance that due to *Heisenberg*'s principle of indeterminacy, which belongs to the foundations of the new theory, the possibility of distinguishing between different like particles, with help of the continuity of their motion in space and time, is getting lost. Shortly after *Einstein*'s paper appeared, the thermodynamical consequence of the other alternative of particles with antisymmetric wave functions, which applies to electrons, was discussed in the literature ("Fermi-Dirac statistics").

The formulation of quantum mechanics which soon followed the publication of *de Broglie*'s paper was not only decisive, for the first time since *Planck*'s discovery, in establishing again a self-consistent theoretical description of such phenomena in which the quantum of action plays an essential role, but it made also possible the achievement of a deeper insight into the general epistemological situation of atomic physics in connection with the point of view termed by *Bohr* "complementarity".[12] The writer belongs to those physicists who believe that the new epistemological situation underlying quantum mechanics is satisfactory, both from the standpoint of physics and from the broader standpoint of the conditions of human knowledge in general. I regret that *Einstein* seems to have a different opinion on this situation; and this all the more, because the new aspect of the description of nature, in contrast to the ideas underlying classical physics, seems to open up hopes for a future development of different branches of science towards a greater unity of the whole.

Inside physics in the proper sense we are well aware that the present edifice of quantum mechanics is still far from its final form, but, on the contrary, leaves problems open which *Einstein* considered already long ago. In his previously cited paper of 1909 [4b], he stresses the importance of *Jeans*' remark that the elementary electric charge e, with the help of the velocity of light c, determines the constant e^2/c which is of the same dimension as the quantum of action h (thus aiming at the now well known fine structure constant $2\pi e^2/hc$). He emphasized (l. c., p. 192) "that the elementary quantum of electricity e is a stranger in Maxwell-Lorentz' electrodynamics" and expressed the hope that "the same modification of the theory which contains the elementary quantum e as a consequence, will also have as a consequence

---

[12] An account of *Einstein*'s position during this development is given in the subsequent article of *N. Bohr*. [This remark refers to Bohr's contribution to the same volume of Schilpp dedicated to Einstein to which his own article was devoted; it is discarded in the German edition of Pauli's *Aufsätze*.]

the quantum structure of radiation." The reverse of this statement certainly turned out to be not true, since the new quantum theory of radiation and matter does not have the value of the elementary electric charge as a consequence, so that the latter is still a stranger in quantum mechanics, too.

The theoretical determination of the fine structure constant is certainly the most important of the unsolved problems of modern physics. We believe that any regression to the ideas of classical physics (as, for instance, to the use of the classical field concept) cannot bring us nearer to this goal. To reach it, we shall, presumably, have to pay with further revolutionary changes of the fundamental concepts of physics with a still farther digression from the concepts of the classical theories.

List of Einstein's Papers on Quantum Theory

1. "Über einen die Erzeugung und Verwandlung des Lichtes betreffenden heuristischen Gesichtspunkt." *Annalen der Physik*, Lpz. (4) **17**, 132 (1905).
2. "Zur Theorie der Lichterzeugung und Lichtsabsorption." *Annalen der Physik*, Lpz. (4) **20**, 199 (1906).
3. "Die Plancksche Theorie der Strahlung und die Theorie der spezifischen Wärme." *Annalen der Physik*, Lpz. (4) **22**, 180 and 800 (1907).
4. Discussion with W. Ritz: a) W. Ritz, *Physikalische Zeitschrift* **9**, 903 (1908) and **10**, 224 (1908); b) A. Einstein: "Zum gegenwärtigen Stand des Strahlungsproblems." *Physikalische Zeitschrift* **10**, 185 (1909); c) W. Ritz and A. Einstein: "Zur Aufklärung." *Physikalische Zeitschrift* **10**, 323 (1909).
5. "Über die Entwicklung unserer Anschauungen über das Wesen und die Konstitution der Strahlung." (Report given at the physics meeting in Salzburg, September 1909.) *Physikalische Zeitschrift* **10**, 817 (1909).
6. A. Einstein and L. Hopf: a) "Über einen Satz der Wahrscheinlichkeitsrechnung und seine Anwendung in der Strahlungstheorie." *Annalen der Physik*, Lpz. **33**, 1096 (1910). (Compare also below, reference 12). – b) "Statistische Untersuchung der Bewegung eines Resonators in einem Strahlungsfeld." *Annalen der Physik*, Lpz. **33**, 1105 (1910).
7. "Eine Beziehung zwischen dem elastischen Verhalten und der spezifischen Wärme bei festen Körpern mit einatomigem Molekül." *Annalen der Physik*, Lpz. **34**, 170 and 590 (1911).
8. "Elementare Betrachtungen über die thermische Molekularbewegung in festen Körpern." *Annalen der Physik*, Lpz. **35**, 679 (1911).
9. *La théorie du rayonnement et les quanta. Rapports et discussions de la Réunion tenue à Bruxelles, du 30 octobre au 3 novembre 1911, sous les auspices de M. E. Solvay.* Paris, 1912. – Report by Einstein: "L'état actuel du problème des chaleurs spécifiques."
10. "Thermodynamische Begründung des photochemischen Äquivalentgesetzes." *Annalen der Physik*, Lpz. **37**, 832 (1912) and **38**, 881 (1912).
11. A. Einstein and O. Stern: "Einige Argumente für die Annahme einer molekularen Agitation beim absoluten Nullpunkt." *Annalen der Physik*, Lpz. **40**, 551 (1913).
12. Discussion Einstein and v. Laue: a) M. von Laue, *Annalen der Physik*, Lpz. **47**, 853 (1915); b) A. Einstein, *Annalen der Physik*, Lpz. **47**, 879 (1915); c) M. von Laue, *Annalen der Physik*, Lpz. **48**, 668 (1915).

13. "Zur Quantentheorie der Strahlung." *Physikalische Zeitschrift* **18**, 121 (1917). [Compare also *Verhandlungen der Deutschen Physikalischen Gesellschaft*, No. 13/14, (1916).]

14. A. Einstein and P. Ehrenfest: "Quantentheoretische Bemerkungen zum Experiment von Stern und Gerlach." *Zeitschrift für Physik* **11**, 326 (1922).

15. A. Einstein and P. Ehrenfest: "Zur Quantentheorie des Strahlungsgleichgewichtes." *Zeitschrift für Physik* **19**, 301 (1923). [See also: W. Pauli, *Zeitschrift für Physik* **18**, 272 (1923).]

16. Discussion Jordan-Einstein: a) P. Jordan, *Zeitschrift für Physik* **30**, 297 (1924). b) A. Einstein, *Zeitschrift für Physik* **31**, 784 (1925).

17. "Zur Quantentheorie des einatomigen idealen Gases." *Sitzungsberichte der Berliner Akademie der Wissenschaften*, (1924), p. 261 and (1925), pp. 3 and 18. [See also: S. N. Bose, *Zeitschrift für Physik* **26**, 178 (1924) and **27**, 384 (1924).]

10. Space, Time and Causality in Modern Physics*

By means of an analysis of the role of the three universal constants of nature – c the velocity of light *in vacuo*, κ the constant of gravitation and h *Planck*'s quantum of action – in the structure of physics, it is possible to delimit certain closed domains of natural laws valid under definite approximations. These domains are: – the domain of classical physics, in which independent significance can be ascribed to space and time, and which is governed by causality in the classical sense; the domain of the special theory of relativity, in which space and time are united into a single continuum; the domain of the general theory of relativity, in which the geometric relations of the space-time continuum are dependent on matter; and finally the domain of quantum mechanics, in which the classical concept of causality breaks down and is replaced by quantum-mechanical complementarity.**

In many respects the present appears as a time of insecurity of the fundamentals, of shaky foundations. Even the development of the exact sciences has not entirely escaped this mood of insecurity, as appears, for instance, in the phrases "crisis in the foundations" in mathematics, or "revolution in our picture of the universe" in physics. Indeed many concepts apparently derived directly from intuitive forms borrowed from sense-perceptions, formerly taken as matters of course or trivial or directly obvious, appear to the modern physicist to be of limited applicability. The modern physicist regards with scepticism philosophical systems which, while imagining that they have definitively recognised the *a priori* conditions of human understanding itself, have in fact succeeded only in setting up the *a priori* conditions of the systems of mathematics and the exact sciences of a particular epoch.

But are we therefore justified in demanding that earlier results and methods of science should be completely abandoned, and that unencumbered by these we should rather look for entirely new possibilities of knowledge for the human race? A simple consideration shows that this is not so; having

---

* Expanded version of a lecture to the Philosophical Society in Zurich in November 1934. From *Scientia* **59**, 65–76 (1936).
**This abstract was omitted in the original German edition of Pauli's *Aufsätze über Physik und Erkenntnistheorie*.

just now undertaken a delimitation of the standpoint of modern physics to guard against over-conservative tendencies, we are now likewise compelled to set limits to tendencies that are too revolutionary. The astronomer in fact continues to calculate planetary orbits with considerable success by Newton's law of gravitation, unconcerned in practice with the achievements of modern physics; in the same way the engineer continues to make calculations for his machines very largely according to the laws of classical mechanics, thermodynamics and electrodynamics, regardless of what is known about the atomic constitution of matter. This fact reflects the historical continuity of the development of physics, also expressed in its logical structure.

It appears indeed that in physics the earlier stages are not simply declared null and void in consequence of later steps in the development, but merely that attention is directed to a limitation of the range of applicability of these earlier stages by their inclusion as limiting cases in the more comprehensive systems of the newer physics. Thus there arise separate domains, with multiple logical interconnections, each of which involves its own *a priori* conditions; each domain is complete, in the sense that no new laws can be added to the system of natural laws of the domain concerned without partly altering the content of those already contained in it.

Physics is at a special advantage, as compared with other disciplines such as psychology or history, in being concerned with quantitatively *measurable* objects, to a very large extent independently of human emotive values, and being therefore susceptible to exact mathematical formulation. Modern physics has in no way altered this situation; we thus see the existence of the above distinct logical domains bound up with the existence of certain *constants of nature*, whose numerical values can be exactly determined by measurements.

$$* \quad * \quad *$$

As we are here directing our special attention to space, time and causality, we shall consider particularly three fundamental natural constants of physics:

1) the velocity of light $c = 3 \times 10^{10}$ cm/sec.
2) the constant of gravitation $\kappa = 1.87 \times 10^{-27}$ cm/g.
   (Here we refer to the so-called relativistic constant of gravitation; it is connected with the usual Newtonian constant k, giving the mutual gravitational force in dynes between two masses of 1 g at a distance of 1 cm apart, by the formula $\kappa = 8\pi k/c^2$); and
3) the quantum of action (Planck's constant), $h = 6.545 \times 10^{-27}$ erg sec.

We can now characterise a particular domain of the laws of nature by the condition that all velocities of material particles can be regarded as small compared with the velocity of light, and that in addition all "actions" concerned (of dimensions energy × time or momentum × length) are very large compared with the quantum of action h. In technical terms we can describe this domain as that of the "approximation $c = \infty$, $h = 0$", since the discarded terms mean that we may put $c = \infty$, $h = 0$ in all the formulae. This is the domain of the mechanics of *Galileo* and *Newton*, in which the simultaneity of spatially distant events has an objective significance. The next general domain is that in which the finiteness of c is taken into account, while h is still put equal to 0, and all actions proportional to $\kappa = 8\pi k/c^2$ are also neglected. We are here dealing with the domain of the special theory of relativity and classical (Maxwell-Lorentz) electrodynamics and optics, in which space and time are fused into a unique four-dimensional continuum. In this continuum the "interval" Δs between two events whose coordinates are (x_i^I, t^I), (x_i^{II}, t^{II}), $(i = 1, 2, 3)$ which is defined by

$$\Delta s^2 = \sum_{i=1}^{3} \left(x_i^I - x_i^{II} \right)^2 - c^2 \left(t^I - t^{II} \right)^2 ,$$

still has an objective meaning, likewise also the laws of Euclidean geometry.

The third domain, which exhausts classical physics, is that in which we only put $h = 0$ but take into account actions proportional to κ. We are here in the domain of the general theory of relativity, according to which geometry is to be regarded as dependent on matter, and direct physical reality is ascribed only to the coincidence in space and time of things objectively defined. This idea leads in well-known fashion to the equivalence of all frames of reference; but there is *one* logical assumption of the domains previously discussed that remains intact: it is assumed that once the frame of reference is prescribed, physical phenomena run their course (and can be described) independently of how they are observed, and that the requirement of determinism (causality) is satisfied in the following special sense: From a knowledge of a certain number of physical functions of state (which may be continuous functions of position in space) at an instant of time $t = t_0$, knowledge which can, in principle, be achieved with arbitrarily high accuracy by measurements, the values of these functions of state at another (later or earlier) instant $t = t_1$ can be calculated, and thereby the results of all other possible measurements at $t = t_1$ may be accurately predicted.

We are however confronted with an entirely new epistemological situation, in regard to the last-mentioned assumptions of physics, when we take into consideration those phenomena which are embraced by Planck's quantum of action h. Since these most recent achievements of quantum physics are even less familiar to most people (and this holds particularly for philosophical circles) than the theory of relativity, although they are not inferior in significance to the latter, they will be explained somewhat more fully in the following section. Before passing on to this we summarise, in tabular form, what has so far been said about the sequence of domains of laws having approximate validity under different sets of conditions.

We see from this example that on the one hand the universal validity of the uncertainty relation is a necessary condition that quantum mechanics should be free from contradictions. On the other hand we see that it is to a certain extent a matter of choice what is reckoned as belonging to the object measured and what to the means of measurement. Indeed the demarcation of the object measured from the means of measurement, the act of making the cut, as one might say, is in quantum mechanics a much more incisive operation than in classical theory, since in the former a part of the interaction between means of measurement and object must always remain undetermined. The mathematical formalism of quantum mechanics shows that the statistical statements, to which the theory leads for different choices of the position of the cut, can never contradict each other.

We cannot enter into a detailed discussion of this situation here, and will only touch on one further question of principle. On account of the statistical character of its assertions, quantum mechanics has often been compared with the kinetic theory of gases; this has been coupled with the hope that it might be possible to supplement quantum mechanics by further assertions not contained in it, without detriment to the correctness of its statistical assertions, and thus to return to determinacy in the sense of classical physics, as is possible in the kinetic theory of gases. Such a comparison however appears to me to be completely misleading, since the fundamental state of affairs in quantum mechanics, namely that the possibility of using the results of earlier measurements to predict the results of later measurements may be lost by carrying out a measurement, has no analogue in the kinetic theory of gases. It can moreover be shown that no supplementation of the assertions of quantum mechanics by other assertions in the sense of determinacy is possible without the statistical assertions of the theory at the same time losing their validity in certain cases. In other words, quantum mechanics satisfies the logical criterion, formulated in the first section, for the completeness of a system of laws of nature. The circumstance that, in quantum mechanics, one must be satisfied with statistical laws need give no cause for lamentation for a lost paradise of causality, the more so since in consequence of the new epistemological situation, which arises from the necessity of differentiating between means of measurement and object measured, and of the partial indeterminacy of their interaction, the special concept, valid in classical physics, of the determinacy of phenomena loses its unambiguous meaning.

On the one hand it must be maintained that quantum mechanics is to be regarded as a natural logical generalisation of classical mechanics, just as the theory of relativity represents a generalisation of the mechanics of *Galileo* and *Newton*. But on the other hand a certain restriction must be made; for the system of natural laws described here as regards its fundamental assumptions corresponds, in our terminology, to the approximation $c = \infty$, $\kappa = 0$; it is valid primarily only if the velocities of all particles are small compared with the velocity of light, and gravitational actions are neglected. In what sense the setting up of a "relativistic" quantum theory is to be regarded as a hitherto unsolved problem will be briefly discussed in the following concluding section.

*   *   *

According to what has been said so far, every attempt to generalise the theory as at present known (if in the meantime we disregard gravitational phenomena for simplicity) finds itself confronted with two domains, each closed within itself, which any future theory will have to include in itself, as limiting cases – firstly the "classical" domain "c finite, $h = 0$", and secondly the quantum-mechanical domain "$c = \infty$, h finite". Although partial results belonging to the more general domain "c finite, h finite" have been obtained, we do not here have to do with a self-consistent and established system of natural laws, as in the domains hitherto considered, and are therefore on hypothetical ground. We shall accordingly add only a few remarks, of a provisional kind, about these still unsolved problems.

The quantum mechanics expounded in the previous section can be characterised by the complementarity between the laws of conservation of energy and momentum on one hand and the possibility of description of physical objects in space and time on the other. It has already become evident, in the attempt to bring electromagnetic field quantities within the scope of quantum mechanics that this type of complementarity is not the most general possible type. Moreover the examples hitherto considered have always been such that the number of material particles present was fixed and constant in time. One of the most important discoveries of experimental physicists in recent times has however been the demonstration of the production of pairs of oppositely charged particles out of radiation, as well as the converse process. Thus the interaction between measuring instrument and the object to be measured will in these cases be of such a kind that not only does an exchange of energy and momentum between them remain indeterminate, but the question of *what numbers* of material particles belong to the measuring instrument and to the object measured also remains indeterminate.

On the other hand the *law of conservation of electric charge* occupies a fundamental and equally important place side by side with the laws of conservation of energy and momentum. There are some interesting attempts at classical field theories which, by using a formally more unified representation of the connection of electromagnetic and gravitational fields, unite the law of conservation of electric charge with the laws of conservation of energy and momentum into a single structure, consisting of five equations. But so far these theories have no natural connection with quantum theory, and are unable to interpret the additional fundamental property of charge, namely

Would it now be necessary to abandon as only approximately valid the property whereby the laws of nature admit a group, or is the group of mechanics perhaps only approximately valid, and should it be replaced by a more general group, valid for both mechanical and electromagnetic processes? The decision was in favour of the second alternative. This postulate could be arrived at by two paths. Either one could investigate by pure mathematics what is the most general group of transformations under which the equations of *Maxwell* and *Lorentz* which were well known at this time, preserve their form. This path was followed by the mathematician, *H. Poincaré*. Or one could determine, by critical analysis, those physical assumptions which had led to the particular group of the mechanics of *Galileo* and *Newton*. This was the path followed by *Einstein*. He showed that, from the general standpoint of the equivalence of all coordinate systems moving with constant velocity with respect to each other, the invariance of simultaneity of spatially separated events, in the sense in which it is assumed in classical mechanics, involves the special additional supposition of the possibility of infinitely great signal velocities. If this supposition is dropped and replaced by the assumption of a finite maximal signal velocity, time is also transformed, and the group, mathematically speaking, leaves invariant an indefinite quadratic form in four dimensions, three of space and one of time. The electrodynamics of *Maxwell* and *Lorentz* did in fact turn out to be invariant under the group of transformations determined by *Einstein* on the basis of these general considerations, if the maximal signal velocity was identified with the velocity of propagation of light *in vacuo*. Both *Einstein* and *Poincaré* took their stand on the preparatory work of *H. A. Lorentz*, who had already come quite close to this result, without however quite reaching it. In the agreement between the results of the methods followed independently of each other by *Einstein* and *Poincaré* I discern a deeper significance of a harmony between the mathematical method and analysis by means of conceptual experiments (Gedankenexperimente), which rests on general features of physical experience.

These early papers of *Einstein* on the special theory of relativity already showed the success in physics of a method which does not proceed from an authoritative knowledge of what things are in and by themselves. *Einstein* has repeatedly shown us how the physicist must learn to swim in a boundless ocean of ideas without such supports, and without fixed rules – ideas to which he may be inspired by an equally boundless ocean of empirical material, but which cannot be deduced from the latter by pure logic.

The physicist is not supposed to know *a priori* what the ether is; indeed, since *Einstein*'s time, he obeys the commandment "Thou shalt not make unto thee any image of the state of motion of the ether". This fundamental proposition has been put in a fresh light in the relativistic theory of gravitation or general theory of relativity, which *Einstein* established single-handed in the years 1908 to 1916. The mathematical aids he used were a combination of *Riemann*'s theory of curvature with *Minkowski*'s four-dimensional geometrical formulation of the special theory of relativity. The latter is retained locally, as a limiting case, but in the large is generalised and replaced by a field consisting of ten continuous functions of space and time, the coefficients of the indefinite quadratic differential form of the four-dimensional space-time universe. This corresponds to the realm of ideas of the differential geometry of curved spaces, in which Euclidean geometry holds only locally. The group is extended to the general group of continuously differentiable coordinate transformations, which must however leave this quadratic differential form absolutely invariant. This mathematical structure was however the final result, not the starting point, of *Einstein*'s considerations on the general theory of relativity. His starting point was rather his principle of the equivalence of uniformly accelerated motion of an observer and his system of reference, with a uniform gravitational field. It is based on the exact equality of inertial and gravitational mass, known since *Newton*'s day, from which however no one before *Einstein* had drawn this conclusion. The principle of equivalence guarantees harmony between the mathematical structure of the metric field of the space-time universe, called the G-field for short by *Einstein*, and the physics of gravitational effects. The latter do indeed follow automatically from the simplest differential laws which are consistent with the general group of transformations. In place of the single statical *Poisson*'s differential equation of Newtonian theory, *Einstein*'s ten relativistic field equations are obtained by replacing the differential expression of *Laplace* and *Poisson* on the left-hand side by a suitably chosen combination of tensors of ten components, formed out of *Riemann*'s curvature tensor by contraction; and on the right-hand side of the equation by putting, in place of the density of matter, the tensor of energy and momentum, taking account of *Einstein*'s celebrated deduction, from the special theory of relativity, of the equivalence of mass and energy. This tensor, as well as the constant of gravitation, remains the phenomenological constituent of the general theory of relativity.

The relations of this theory to the philosophy of nature and its historical development are manifold. While in the age of *Galileo*, *Descartes* and *Newton* the suppression of the Aristotelian notion of the physical quality of the points of space and the setting up of an independent space-concept played such an essential part, *Einstein*'s G-field is just a mathematical representation of the physical qualities of points in space-time. These qualities are of course not unalterably fixed, like the place which according to *Aristotle* material bodies seek, but are themselves determined by natural laws, and are dependent on matter. However, the G-field, which according to *Einstein* is just the ether in a new form, retains its conceptual independence over against matter. *Einstein* has repeatedly stated that he would find it more satisfactory if the G-field were to vanish identically in the absence of matter. He called this fundamental principle "Mach's principle" in honour of *Ernst Mach*, who paved the way for later thought on the general theory of relativity by his critique of absolute space. Nevertheless it can be said that *Mach's* principle does not follow from the equations of the general theory of relativity alone without special additional assumptions, which are hard to justify. The existence of a non-vanishing G-field in a space-time universe free from matter remains logically possible, according to these equations. And in so far as the G-field exists, space and time are not empty.

The further development of scientific ideas of space and time and their dependence on the material substance occupying them lies in the future as an open problem, as regards both large and small dimensions. It is intimately connected with the range of validity of the now "classical" concept of field, a question in which *Einstein* had so much at heart. I myself am one of those physicists who see in the foundations of present-day quantum mechanics, postulating as it does primary probabilities, a development of the mode of thought which *Einstein* created. Specified and in some cases complementary experimental conditions here play the part of the specified states of motion of the observer in *Einstein's* theory of relativity. The finiteness of the quantum of action, which sets a limit to the divisibility of phenomena in the atomic realm, plays the part of the maximal signal velocity in *Einstein's* special theory of relativity; the group of unitary transformations of quantum mechanics, which embraces all possible specifications of the experimental conditions, plays the part of the group of coordinate transformations which in general relativity connects all possible states of motion of the observers with the assertions they make in accordance with the laws. In quantum mechanics also one discusses possible measurements with the aid of conceptual experiments (Gedankenexperimente), relying on an assumed mathematical structure of the laws of nature, statistical in this case. This is just the method which *Einstein* has used with such success in physics and thereby again made fashionable.

In spite of this, *Einstein* held firmly to the narrower concept of reality of classical physics; from this point of view a description of nature which permits single events not determined by laws was bound to appear to him "incomplete". He combined with this a regressive longing, not indeed for the old mechanistic idea of the point-mass, but for his geometrical conception of the field in the general theory of relativity. Motivating his attitude, he frankly explained that to depart from the narrower reality concept of physics before quantum mechanics seemed to him to be getting perilously close to a point of view in which it is impossible to discriminate sufficiently clearly between dream or hallucination and "reality". As against this, the objective character of the description of nature given by quantum mechanics has appeared to the rest of us to be adequately guaranteed by the circumstance that its statistical laws describe reproducible processes, and that the results of observation, which can be checked by anyone, cannot be influenced by the observer, once he has chosen his experimental arrangement.

Discussion round these questions is likely to continue for a long time to come. *Einstein* conceded that he could not prove the possibility of a pure field theory which also yields the atomic structure of matter. But he insisted that the reverse, namely the impossibility of such a theory, had not been proved neither.

Even physicists who like myself do not follow *Einstein* in his general attitude to modern quantum physics can none the less readily accept his basic view towards the various tendencies or "-isms" of traditional philosophy. He evaluated these not absolutely as true of false, but relatively to each other. In his opinion the physicist can accept something from each of these tendencies. In the volume of the "Library of living philosophers" devoted to him he says, in his "reply to criticisms" (p. 684):

"(The scientist) appears as *realist* insofar as he seeks to describe a world independent of the acts of perception; as *idealist* insofar as he looks upon the concepts and theories as the free inventions of the human spirit (not logically derivable from what is empirically given); as *positivist* insofar as he considers his concepts and theories justified *only* to the extent to which they furnish a logical representation of relations among sensory experiences. He may even appear as a *Platonist* or *Pythagorean* insofar as he considers the viewpoint of logical simplicity as an indispensable and effective tool of his research."

I find it easy to sympathise with these propositions, while thinking in "isms" is strange, indeed impossible for me.

May *Einstein*'s great power of synthesis, as a human being and as a thinker, be an example for the physics of the future, when it has to balance against each other the empirically given and the mathematico-logical structure of theory.

12. Impressions of Albert Einstein*

Pauli and Einstein during a visit in Leyden
Photo taken by Ehrenfest in autumn 1926 (Courtesy: CERN Archive, Geneva)

* *Neue Zürcher Zeitung*, 22. April 1955.

> Einsteins Tod hat mich auch persönlich erreicht. Ein mir
> so wohlgesinnter, väterlicher Freund ist nicht mehr. Nie
> werde ich die Rede vergessen, die er 1945 in Princeton über
> mich und für mich gehalten, nachdem ich den Nobel-Preis
> bekommen hatte. Es war wie ein König, der abdankt und
> mich als eine Art "Wahl-Sohn" zum Nachfolger einsetzt.
> Leider existieren keine Aufzeichnungen über diese Rede
> Einsteins (sie war improvisiert und ein Manuskript existiert
> auch nicht).
>
> Letter from Pauli to Max Born, April 24, 1955

Fifty years ago a junior employé of the Patent Office in Bern was in the habit, whenever the chief, *Haller* by name, made his rounds, of causing a batch of papers to vanish into a drawer, and quickly taking out others on which were written his reports on the patent specifications. I think it unlikely that *Haller* did not notice this. Why should he object, since he was satisfied with the employé's work? After vehement protests on the part of applicants against the reports of the office based on his work had been successfully rebutted, *Haller* would sit, of an evening, over a Swiss cigar and a mug of wine and contentedly remark to no one in particular "We'll show them who is God Almighty" ("where God Almighty sits").

It was through *Einstein*'s description of "Old Haller" as a congenial and original personality that the latter became familiar to me, much more than through occasional brief remarks of his son, the sculptor *Hermann Haller*. *Einstein* liked to recall his time in Bern, of which he spoke more often and also more positively than of Zürich. The year 1905 in Bern was a particularly fruitful one for *Einstein*. His work on the patent applications which came in left behind in him a lasting close tie with technical applications of physics. It allowed him sufficient time to write, in the same room, three fundamental papers: "On a heuristic point of view in relation to the generation and transformation of light"; "The motion of particles suspended in stationary liquids which is required by the molecular kinetic theory of heat"; and "On the electrodynamics of moving bodies". The first led him, by way of the photoelectric effect and related phenomena, to the complex of problems of the quantum theory originating in *Max Planck*'s new constant of nature, and later found to govern all ideas of the structure of the atom. The second proved to be already confirmed experimentally by the "Brownian molecular motion," already known at that time, though not yet accurately investigated; in *Einstein*'s hands it soon became a successful aid to the theoretical investigation of the riddle – as it was then – of the quantum structure of radiation. The theory developed in the third paper was later called the "special theory of relativity", a name which *Einstein* did not invent himself, but took over quite early from other physicists. Immediately after the third of the papers mentioned there followed *Einstein*'s short communication "Is the inertia of a body dependent on its energy content?" containing the deduction of the essential identity of mass and energy which has had such weighty theoretical and practical consequences.

Thus from the papers whose disappearance into the drawer of the Federal patent office was only very temporary there originated in rapid sequence a new mode of thought in physics.

Einstein's style in his papers and still more in his verbal scientific discussions has the same penetration (Eindringlichkeit) and simplicity as in his description of old times in Bern. Yet at the same time he is different from his environment, different from it in his adherence to tradition, different in his freedom from constraints, shut off from it in his own more abstract world, at rest within himself. In all the innovations he has given us in physics he has at some point remained faithful to the past: In his investigations on quantum theory he adhered firmly to *Boltzmann*'s principle of the statistical interpretation of entropy; in the special theory of relativity he maintained the foundations of the electrodynamics of *H. A. Lorentz*; in his general theory of relativity, completed in 1916, that entirely new conception of gravitation as space-time geometry, he adhered to *Faraday*'s and *Maxwell*'s concept of the field in continuum physics, which was originally thought of as a mechanical state of stress of an ether, but which since the end of last century has been conceived of in a more abstract and general way.

The characteristic feature or the new mode of thought which *Einstein* introduced into physics is the unprejudiced analysis of traditional fundamental concepts on the basis of general, and in the last resort experimentally tested principles. In the process certain assumptions turn out to be unnecessary and too narrow, and certain concepts as capable of being eliminated. In the special theory of relativity it was the time-concept of which *Einstein* revealed new facets. He showed how the impossibility of signals of arbitrarily high speed – the universal velocity of light *in vacuo* setting an upper limit to this speed – makes the simultaneity of events at different places depend on the state of motion of the observer. The observer also enters in an essential way into the description of time-order. But all possible states of motion of the observer and their statements about physical events are connected by mathematical transformations – the "group" in technical mathematical terms – as the overriding law under which all possible motions are equally privileged. This programme was carried through to completion in the general theory of relativity. The equality of gravitational and inertial mass had been known since *Newton*'s day, but it needed an *Einstein* to demand and to carry out a geometrical interpretation of the gravitational field on this basis. In this interpretation energy has got not only mass, but also gravity or weight. The state of motion of the luminiferous "ether" turned out to be a concept which could be eliminated. The situation is rather that the new field, remaining conceptually independent as contrasted with matter, is itself that "ether", representing in fact physical qualities of points in the space-time world. The fourth dimension of this world, time, became as familiar to us physicists as the first three dimensions of space, and in order to express something out of the common we would nowadays have to have recourse to a higher number of dimensions than four.

Meanwhile the quantum theory of matter in the atomic domain, which *Einstein* helped to found, has developed in a direction which generalises further the principles of the explanation of nature nowadays called "classical". Here it is not only the state of motion of the observer that enters into the laws of physics, but more generally the specific experimental conditions. The indivisibility of the quantum of action and with it of atomic phenomena leads in the domain of quantum theory to an indeterminability of the interaction between the systems observed and the instruments of observation. Here too, however, there exist mathematical transformations which connect, in comprehensive fashion, the essentially statistical statements of the laws of nature which correspond to the various possible experimental conditions. *Einstein* was unwilling to recognise this generalisation of the "classical" idea of physical reality as final and as allowable, although in a certain sense it is in line with the critical mode of thought he had himself created. Many discussions took place about this, particularly between *Einstein* and *Niels Bohr*, which have been published fully in the *Einstein* volume of the "Library of Living Philosophers" (1949). Agreement was never reached.

This is closely connected with the problem of the range of the field concept which *Einstein* had propounded. In his search for a unification of the electromagnetic field with its metrical form of the gravitational field, he aimed, in his later years, at merging atomicity as well in the geometrised field concept of continuum physics. The general reasons, completely convincing to me, which others adduced against this extreme possibility did not appear to him sufficiently cogent. At my last meeting with *Einstein* a year ago in Princeton he however admitted, with his old directness and honesty, that he had not succeeded in proving the possibility of a pure field theory of matter. He regarded the problem as still undecided.

The history of an idea progresses, becomes independent; in the end its creator no longer has it under control. In his last years there began to be something of intellectual loneliness about *Einstein* in Princeton, where, taking little notice of the more recent results of exprimental physics, and using methods which had formerly proved successful, he obstinately and inflexibly pursued the theoretical aims he had set himself.

His life, pointing into the future, will continually remind us of the ideal, under threat in our day, of intellectual contemplative man whose thoughts calmly and undeviatingly dwell on the grand problems of the structure of the cosmos.

13. Albert Einstein
and the Development of Physics*

Bust of Albert Einstein

Created by Hermann Hubacher and dedicated to the Physics Institute of the ETH in
Zurich (Courtesy: CERN Archive, Geneva)

* *Neue Zürcher Zeitung*, 12. Januar 1958.

> The sad news about Einstein yesterday impressed me very
> much, I feel that with him a certain chaptre of physics is
> leaving us. I could not well refuse to write a short article on
> him for the "Neue Zürcher Zeitung."
>
> Letter from Pauli to Léon Rosenfeld, April 19, 1955

With the likeness before us of the bust, unveiled here today,* to *Einstein*, the man himself, we are reminded of how in many a talk with him, in some Institute or out of doors, we argued out the weightier problems of physics. As we regard the expression of timelessness which the artist's work likewise conveys, we must also think of how *Einstein*'s ideas, detached from their human creator, now continue an independent existence leading to distant regions beyond our ken.

It accordingly seemed to me fitting to choose as the theme of this address "Albert Einstein and the Development of Physics". His work has often received recognition. In particular we had an opportunity at the Congress in Bern on "Fifty Years of the Theory of Relativity", of discussing in detail the significance of the theory of relativity for other sciences. His papers on quantum theory too have been reviewed by various authors in the *Einstein* volume of the "Library of Living Philosophers", especially in a long and important article by *Bohr* on his discussions with *Einstein*.

So far, however, no connected account has been given of the vicissitudes in the interplay of these two lines of research in *Einstein*'s life.

Let us begin with the first decisive year of his activity, the year 1905 in Bern, when his interpretation of the photoelectric effect, his theory of the Brownian motion, and his special theory of relativity (a name it received only later) simultaneously saw the light of day. For *Einstein Boltzmann*'s statistical interpretation of entropy, *Planck*'s theory of thermal radiation and *H. A. Lorentz*'s work on electrodynamics in the state it had reached about in 1895, that were the decisive scientific experiences.

Nowadays we speak with some justification of the "Lorentz group"; but as a matter of history it was precisely the group property of his transformations that *Lorentz* failed to recognize; this was reserved for *Poincaré* and *Einstein* independently. It is regrettable that a certain amount of dispute about priority has arisen over this. The really interesting thing is to study the difference in the method of treatment of the same problem by the mathematician *Poincaré* and by the physicist *Einstein*. *Poincaré* starts from the familiar equations of *Maxwell* and shows that they admit certain transformations. An interesting light is thrown on *Einstein*'s motives by a letter from him to

---

* Address given by the author at the occasion of the dedication to the Physics Institute of ETH of the bust of Albert Einstein created by Dr. Hermann Hubacher.

Dr. *Seelig*, which has already been quoted by *Born*. *Einstein* knew, as a result of his work on the photoelectric effect, that *Maxwell*'s theory could not be generally correct. He therefore formulated the invariance of the laws of nature with respect to *Lorentz* transformations as a general postulate which is more reliable than *Maxwell*'s equations. He established the postulate independently of these equations by kinematical considerations and conceptual experiments (Gedankenexperimente) on the compatibility of the principle of relativity for translational motions with the principle of constancy of the velocity of light, assuming the relativity of simultaneity.

The process of disengaging Maxwellian electrodynamics from mechanical models of the ether, which had already begun in *Lorentz*'s work, was completed by *Einstein*. In his own words "The emancipation of the field concept from the assumption of a material carrier is one of the most interesting processes, from a psychological point of view, in the development of physical thought". He soon came to the conclusion that the state of motion of an etherial medium must be eliminated from the concepts of physics.

The extent to which *Einstein*'s work on relativity and on quantum theory went hand in hand at this time can be seen from his lecture at the Convention of Scientists at Salzburg[1] in 1908. "Zürich" appears after his name as author; the title of the lecture is "On the development of our views on the nature and constitution of radiation". After once again expounding his celebrated deduction of the equivalence of energy and inertial mass, he passes on to the quantum structure of radiation, his main result being that the elementary process of emission of light must be directional. He looks towards a theory "which can be conceived of as fusing together undulatory and emission theory".

Here, however, he remains an adherent of the use of visualisable images based on the classical field concept, in contrast with his view on the state of motion of the ether. I may at this point quote what he said in the discussion in reply to *Planck*.

I think of a quantum as a singularity surrounded by a large vector field. By means of a large number of quanta a vector field can be built up which differs little from a field of the kind we assume in radiations. I can imagine that when rays strike a bounding surface, separation of the quanta takes place by action at the surface, possibly according to the phase of the resulting field in which the quanta reach the surface of separation. The equations for the resulting field would differ little from those of existing theory. In regard to interference phenomena, we would not, I should say, have to make much change in conceptions as they now stand. We may compare this with the process of molecularisation of the carriers of the electrostatic field. The field, thought of as produced by atomised electric particles is in essence not very different from the earlier concept, and it is not impossible that something similar will happen in radiation theory. I do not see any difficulty in principle in regard to interference effects.

---

[1] *Physikalische Zeitschrift* **10**, 817 (1909).

But the matter was not quite as simple as this. Interference phenomena are independent of the intensity of the light, even when only few light quanta are involved. *Einstein* was soon perfectly well aware of this, but somehow the view he took at this time continued to be his model for the explanation which he sought later of the riddle of the quantum.

A new and essential chapter in *Einstein*'s work was reached in 1917.

The general Theory of Relativity, completed at that time, differs from the special theory in having been built up by *Einstein* alone without simultaneous contributions from other workers; it will always remain the pattern of a theory of consummate beauty of the mathematical structure. Its application to problems of the structure of the universe in the large is unique. Here I shall merely point out briefly that experimental test of its foundations has given rise to new projects. One of these, that of *Dicke* in Princeton,* is concerned with the refined repetition of the old experiment of *Eötvös* to establish the equality of gravitational and inertial mass, i. e., the equality of the gravitational acceleration of all bodies, with an accuracy increased by many powers of ten. This equality of course constitutes a cornerstone of *Einstein*'s theory. The other project, that of *Zacharias* (Cambridge, Mass.) concerns the experimental proof of the dependence,** which was postulated by *Einstein*, of the rate of a clock on the gravitational field, by comparison of the time on an atomic clock on the Jungfraujoch† with that of another clock at normal sea level. To carry this out a considerable increase of the accuracy at present attainable would be necessary. I wanted to show you by these examples that the general theory of relativity, against which the reproach has often been brought of somewhat lacking a relation to experiment, is just recently again exerting a fertilising influence on experimental research.

It was not only in general relativity that *Einstein*'s researches reached a culmination about the years 1916–1917, but also in the realm of quantum theory. For about this time *Einstein* also published his fundamental paper on the balance of energy and momentum of radiation and atoms, deduced from the general form of the statistical laws of the various types of quantum process of emission and absorption of light. The theory again led to the result that the process of emission of light must be assumed to be directional, which was also confirmed experimentally later.

---

* Cf. R. H. Dicke, in *Relativity, Groups and Topology*, ed. C. DeWitt and B. S. DeWitt (New York, 1964), p. 167; P. G. Roll, R. Krotkov and R. H. Dicke, *Annals of Physics* (N. Y.) **26**, 442 (1967).

** Jerrold Reinach Zacharias (1905–1986) was Professor of Physics at MIT in Cambridge, Mass. His plans at the end of 1955 to test together with his collaborator Rainer Weiss the general theory of relativity using his atomic clocks never were performed because he became involved in other projects. See Jack S. Goldstein: *A Different Sort of Time. The Life of Jerrold R. Zacharias. Scientist, Engineer, Educator*. Cambridge, Massachusetts 1992, p. 149.

† Observatory in the Swiss Alps.

At the end of this paper of *Einstein*'s there is a celebrated passage on the significance of chance, which I will quote once more.

"The weakness of the theory lies on the one hand in not bringing us any closer to union with wave theory, and on the other in leaving the time and direction of elementary processes to 'chance'. None the less I have complete faith in the reliability of the road that has been taken."

Einstein would never accept *a priori* probabilities. In those days he often said: "For the rest of my life I will ponder on the question of what light is!" His success with the general theory of relativity could not fail to strengthen his belief that the classical field concept would suffice in principle to explain the whole of physics, to such an extent that he could hardly imagine any other solution.

In the subsequent development of the general theory of relativity a problem cropped up which could not be finally settled. *Ernst Mach* had suggested that inertia might be traced back entirely to the action of distant masses. If this principle of *Mach*'s were correct, *Einstein*'s G-field would have to vanish if all matter were removed. In setting up his theory *Einstein* was probably guided by this principle and regarded it as correct. But it has not been possible to deduce it from the equations of the theory. It seems to be inherent in the nature of the field concept that while the field is influenced by the distribution of mass, it nevertheless continues to exist as an independent reality even when all masses are removed. What the ultimate solution will be we do not know.

While *Einstein* was meditating on a unification of his theory of the gravitational field to embrace electromagnetism as well it soon appeared that it was not only to the structure of light that the quantum of action applied, but that it covered matter as well. When *Einstein* heard of *de Broglie*'s work on matter waves he was one of the first who were at once inclined to appreciate this idea. Shortly afterwards, in connection with a paper by *Bose*, he dealt with the statistics of a system consisting of identical particles in a new way which is now known as "Einstein-Bose statistics".

A further chapter in *Einstein*'s creative activity opened in 1927, when the structure of the new wave mechanics was being completed. I was able to be present at the great discussions on wave mechanics between *Einstein*, *Bohr* and others at the Solvay Conference in Brussels. For me it will always remain an unforgettable experience. *Einstein* of course conceded the logical consistency of the new wave mechanics; but he regarded the statistical laws of the new theory as incomplete. "One can't make a theory out of a lot of 'maybe's'" he often said, and also "deep down it is wrong, even if it is empirically and logically right". A mode of thought in terms of pairs of opposites, visualisable images depending on the choice of experimental arrangements, *a priori* probabilities – these *Einstein* could not accept.

Yet these views and concepts which he rejected are essential constituents of the so-called "Copenhagen interpretation" of quantum mechanics, founded by *Bohr*, which I also follow, in common with most theoretical physicists. *Einstein*'s opposition to it is again reflected in the papers which he published, at first in collaboration with *Rosen* and *Podolsky*, and later alone, as a critique of the concept of reality in quantum mechanics. We often discussed these questions together, and I invariably profited very greatly even when I could not agree with *Einstein*'s views. "Physics is after all the description of reality" he said to me, continuing, with a sarcastic glance in my direction "or should I perhaps say physics is the description of what one merely imagines?" This question clearly shows *Einstein*'s concern that the objective character of physics might be lost through a theory of the type of quantum mechanics, in that as a consequence of its wider conception of the objectivity of an explanation of nature the difference between physical reality and dream or hallucination might become blurred.

The objectivity of physics is however fully ensured in quantum mechanics in the following sense. Although in principle, according to the theory, it is in general only the statistics of series of experiments that is determined by laws, the observer is unable, even in the unpredictable single case, to influence the result of his observation – as for example the response of a counter at a particular instant of time. Further, personal qualities of the observer do not come into the theory in any way – the observation can be made by objective registering apparatus, the results of which are objectively available for anyone's inspection. Just as in the theory of relativity a group of mathematical transformations connects all possible coordinate systems, so in quantum mechanics a group of mathematical transformations connects the possible experimental arrangements.

Einstein however advocated a narrower form of the reality concept, which assumes a complete separation of an objectively existing physical state from any mode of its observation. Agreement was unfortunately never reached. To the end of his days he clung to the hope of an explanation of the atomic constitution of matter through the classical field concept.

From 1927 on *Einstein* was disappointed by the development of physics. Inflexibly he withdrew into his intellectual loneliness. While his subsequent papers on field theory are written with the same mathematical mastery as the earlier ones, close contact with nature seems to be lacking in them. It is doubtful whether these last theoretical formulations of *Einstein*'s have actual application in physics.

After he had withdrawn unsatisfied from the line of his research directed towards quantum theory, the other line also, directed towards field theory became physically problematical.

If we could have put before *Einstein* a synthesis of his general theory of relativity with quantum theory, discussion with him would have been much easier. But the duality between the field and the instruments for its measurement, while latent in present-day quantum mechanics, is not expressed with conceptual clarity. The relation of the applicability of the ordinary space-time concept in the small to the properties of the smallest physical objects, the so-called "elementary" particles, has not been laid bare.

Einstein's life ended with a question to physical science and with the challenge to us of a synthesis. Of this *Hubacher*'s bust shall constantly remind us as we pass by. In a remoter future, when our problems will long since have lost their significance, let this bust still stand here to be to new generations a symbol of constancy in the midst of change.

if painting them. The sought-for bridge between sense perceptions and ideas or concepts seems to be conditioned by ordering operators or factors (which in contrast to *Bernays* I am however not prepared to describe as "rational") by which this pre-conceptual layer of symbolic images is also governed. It is interesting that the word "archetype" used for instance by *Kepler* for the (Platonic) pre-existent images,[1] is now also used by *C. G. Jung* for unvisualisable ordering factors, which are supposed to manifest themselves psychically as well as physically.[2]

2. According to the conception here put forward, the *a priori* character of *Kant*'s rationally formulated ideas, laid down once for all, is thus transferred to the pre-existent images (archetypes) present and operating outside of consciousness ("in the unconscious"). We agree with *P. Bernays* in no longer regarding the special ideas, which *Kant* calls synthetic judgments *a priori*, generally as the pre-conditions of human understanding, but merely as the special pre-conditions of the exact science (and mathematics) of his age. In distinction to *Plato*, however, and in agreement with *Gonseth*'s "philosophie ouverte", we look on the pre-existent primordial images not as unalterable, but as relative to the development of the conscious standpoint. It is precisely the reaction of consciousness upon the images in the unconscious[3] – a reaction likely not to be separated from the reverse action of the images upon consciousness, in the sense of a "complementarity", that appears to me to constitute the essence of the process of development of human cognition, called "dialectical" by *F. Gonseth*.

---

[1] In a historical study which has appeared meanwhile: "Der Einfluß archetypischer Vorstellungen auf die Bildung naturwissenschaftlicher Theorien bei Kepler" (*Naturerklärung und Psyche*, Rascher Verlag, Zürich 1952; English translation in *The interpretation of Nature and the Psyche*, London, 1955) I attempt to explain more fully the situation I have briefly sketched here. [Essay 21 in this volume.]

[2] C. G. Jung, *Eranos Jahrbuch* 1946: "Der Geist der Psychologie"; English translation in *Eranos Yearbook*, London, 1954.

[3] C. G. Jung occasionally speaks of a "secular displacement of the standpoint of the unconscious" (cf. for instance *Psychologie und Alchemie*, Zürich, 1944, p. 181; English translation in *Collected Works of C. G. Jung* (Bollingen Foundation, New York, volume **12**.)

15. *Phenomenon and Physical Reality**

Without accepting or favouring a particular philosophical
"-ism", 'phenomenon' and 'reality' are analysed from the
standpoint of the professional every-day life of the physicists. The logical structure of physical theories, including
its characteristic connections with observation and exper-
imentation, is briefly indicated, with classical mechanics,
classical relativistic field theories and quantum mechanics
as examples. It is emphasised that physicists consider their
science as being in the course of a development. The problem is therefore never, whether or not the present theories
will remain as they are, but merely in which direction they
will change.**

In the following lecture I wish to give some indications as to which problems,
connected with the key-words phenomenon and reality, play an important
part in contemporary physics, without claiming anything like mastery over
this inexhaustible theme. In the course of my remarks I shall also touch on
controversial questions, for it is towards them that general interest is chiefly
directed. To give the philosophers their bearings, I may say at once that
I am not myself an adherent of any particular philosophical trend with a
name ending in "-ism". I am moreover opposed to associating particular
"-isms" with particular physical theories, such as for instance the theory of
relativity or quantum or wave mechanics, although this is occasionally done
by physicists. My general tendency is rather to hold a middle course between
extreme directions. In this sense I think it best to consider first of all how
phenomenon and reality occur in the physicist's everyday professional life.

1. Phenomenon and Reality
in the Everyday Life of the Physicist

The phenomenon, the appearance, can be elementary, or it can be highly
complex. Among directly given phenomena are the contents of conscious-

---

* *Dialectica* 11 (15 March 1957), pp. 35–48. Introduction to a Symposium on the occasion
of the International Congress of Philosophers in Zürich, 1954.
**This Abstract is not reproduced in the German edition of Pauli's *Aufsätze über Physik
und Erkenntnistheorie*.

ness. Their description as perceptions is one-sided, insofar as thoughts and ideas also arise spontaneously; in German we speak of "Einfälle" (ideas occurring to one) meaning that something falls into our consciousness. I therefore suggest that the occurrence of ideas and thoughts should also be called phenomena, just like tones, colours and tactile impressions.

Our ideas do not follow an arbitrary course, but appear in a certain order. It is the connectedness of the contents of consciousness that allows us to distinguish dreaming from waking, and to experience involuntarily, as existing, external objects as well as the consciousness of our fellow-beings. That which we come upon, which is beyond our power of choice, and with which we have to reckon, is what we designate as real. European languages have two words for this, with different derivations; one is reality (from Latin res = thing) the other actuality (from agere = to do). In German the two are represented by Realität and Wirklichkeit. The more abstract concept derived from "agere" or "wirken" is closer to the one used in science.

If we now try to formulate what the physical phenomenon is, and what physical reality is, there is at once a difference of opinion. Personally I do not see how it is possible to give a definition of the phenomenon in physics which seeks to isolate the data of perception from rational and ordering principles. It seems to me rather that a separation of this sort is itself already the result of a special critical mental effort which removes the ever-present unconscious and instinctive ingredients of thinking. Limitation to contents of consciousness which are stated, or can be stated would make life as well as science impossible. Involuntarily at first, and later consciously, man postulates that which in itself can not be noticed, one can also say that which is relatively transcendental – as for example the consciousness of others, the reverse side of the moon, a history of the earth, in part unseen by any living being – in order to derive from it something that can be noticed.

From this central position it is an equally long way to the elimination of the concept of reality on the one hand, and to the acceptance, on the other, of metaphysical, unconditionally and permanently valid ontological judgments. I believe that for the exact sciences neither of these alternatives is necessary. Man will continually have the spontaneous experience of a reality, which he will describe in terms which appear to him appropriate. But he can recognize ontological judgments *as conditioned* by the efforts, hopes, wishes – in short by the general spiritual attitude of the individual or group which makes these statements. Among such attitudes, especially in the case of the scientific investigator, are the degree of his skill and the measure of knowledge in his time. In this way a tension is produced between phenomenon and reality, which constitutes the fascination of life as it does of research.

The exact scientist has to do with special phenomena and a special reality. He must restrict himself to *what is reproducible*. I include in this anything for the reproduction of which nature herself has provided. I do not assert that the reproducible in itself is more important than the unique, but I do say that the essentially unique lies outside the range of treatment by scientific methods; the aim and purpose of these methods is after all to discover and test laws of nature, upon which alone the attention of the investigator is directed, and must remain directed.

The connected formulation of conceptual systems consisting of mathematical equations and rules whereby they may be linked with data of experience is called a physical theory; within the limits of its sphere of applicability one can then describe it as a "model of reality". As I have explained elsewhere,[1] I regard it as idle to speculate on what came first, the idea or the experiment. I hope that no one still maintains that theories are deduced by strict logical conclusions from laboratory-books, a view which was still quite fashionable in my student days. Theories come into being through an understanding inspired by empirical material, an *understanding* which we may best regard, following *Plato*, as a coming into congruence (zur Deckung kommen) of internal images with external objects and their behaviour. The possibility of understanding again demonstrates the presence of typical regulatory arrangements, to which man's inner as well as outer world is subject.

I agree with *Bohr* in the opinion that the *objectivity* of a scientific explanation of nature should be defined as liberally as possible: Every mode of looking at things which one can impart to others, which others having the necessary preliminary knowledge can understand and in turn apply, which we can talk about with others, shall be called objective. In this sense all physical theories and laws are objective. However diverse its structure, the *physical phenomenon* is not simple but complex. Usually a mass of previously acquired theoretical knowledge and experience with apparatus is already incorporated in its description. It is just this, and not the isolation of data of perception, that is useful for the physicist's purpose in his everyday life. *Bohr* defines phenomenon as "referring to observations which are obtained under specified circumstances, including a statement about the *whole* experiment".

This definition makes it possible to speak of a *new* phenomenon when a part of the experimental arrangement is altered, and to take account of the limitation concerning the divisibility of the phenomenon in the explanation of nature.

2. Logical Structure of Physical Theories

This definition of the phenomenon would appear to have far-reaching significance, extending even beyond physics. Since however it has been set up

---

[1] Theorie und Experiment, *Dialectica* **6**, 141 (1952); preceding essay.

with special regard to quantum mechanics, it is natural to pass on now to the discussion of the logical structure of various physical theories. We are here chiefly concerned with the mechanics of *Galileo* and *Newton*, which nowadays we call classical, the theory of relativity and quantum mechanics. There is an extensive literature[2] dealing with these theories and also with their epistemological content. Here I must content myself with selecting a few points somewhat arbitrarily. One of these is concerned with the concept of causality in classical mechanics. One of the most important advances made by the latter consists in the recognition that a cause cannot be found for uniform motion any more than for rest. The recognition of this fact was closely connected with the application of the mathematical group-concept in physics: classical mechanics admits the group of all uniform translational motions, nowadays called the Galilean group. Two states related by an element of the group are called *equivalent* (relative to the group considered). The description of nature must then not single out one of these states in preference to the other. This group-theoretical viewpoint has led, in *Einstein*'s hands, to results of the greatest beauty in the special and general theories of relativity. In the former, the Galilean group is modified into the *Lorentz* group, which transforms time as well, and leaves invariant an indefinite quadratic form in the four-dimensional manifold of space-time. In the general theory of relativity the group is extended to the group of all coordinate transformations. This can however be done only by taking into the theory a new physical reality, namely the gravitational field. This field appears as ten functions of space and time, which, as coefficients of the invariant quadratic form of the metric, undergo appropriate transformation in a general transformation of coordinates. It seems to me probable that the range of application of the mathematical group concept in physics has not yet been exhausted today.

We have seen that the emergence of this conception in physics was from the outset associated with a freer treatment of the idea of cause. It will be explained later that the idea of causality, criticised earlier from the empirical standpoint by *D. Hume*, has undergone a further essential generalisation in quantum mechanics.

In view of proposals to *split* the concept of causality into a "physical" and an "ontological" concept, I should like to express a general criticism of the method often employed of rescuing a concept which has begun to requite emendation by introducing two methodologically separate regions, one in which it applies, and another in which it no longer applies. Thus it appears to me to be a misuse of the word "ontological" to prefix it to the word "cause", as if to prop up something shaky.

---

[2] In this connection cf. also *Dialectica* **2**, No. 3/4, pp. 305–424 (1948); and the volume on Einstein in the *Library of Living Philosophers* series (1948).

Instead of "causal" the physicist prefers to say *deterministic*. By this he means a theory in which the state of a system at all other times, earlier and later, follows mathematically from the state at a given time. To achieve this it is necessary in mechanics to introduce the initial position and initial velocity of all masses as two independent quantities characterising the state. From this there subsequently developed in quantum mechanics a complementary pair of opposites.

Just as fundamental as classical mechanics of a point particles is classical field physics, created by *Faraday* and *Maxwell* as electrodynamics, and carried further by *Einstein* in the relativistic theory of gravitation mentioned above. Here I shall only remark that the classical field concept arises by abstraction from the conditions under which the field can be measured. A duality is thereby introduced between the field and its sources, which in my opinion involves hitherto unsolved problems. *Einstein* however still hopes[3] to be able to set up a unified classical field theory embracing the whole of physics, but concedes that he cannot prove the possibility of such a theory. It appears to me an unsatisfactory feature of the classical field concept that a single field which does not interact with other objects, and therefore stands outside the complementarity of instruments of observation and system observed and can never be measured, is nevertheless logically possible in this theory although it is physically unreal. A satisfactory theory would in my opinion allow the field and the test body serving to measure it to be thought of as complementary opposites.

I shall mention only briefly that classical field physics, like classical mechanics, is among the deterministic theories. It is of interest that *Einstein* regards this deterministic feature of classical theories as less fundamental than another more general feature, which can be designated as "realistic" in a narrower sense. He characterises it as follows:[4]

There is such a thing as the real state of a physical system, which exists objectively, independently of any observation or measurement, and can in principle be described by the methods of expression of physics.*

This requirement however merely paraphrases a special ideal which is satisfied in classical particle mechanics and electrodynamics, and also in the theory of relativity, but not in the equally objective description of nature given by quantum mechanics.

---

[3] Written in 1954.
[4] Cf. a) A. Einstein, *Memorial volume to Louis de Broglie*, Paris 1951, p. 6; b) *The Meaning of Relativity*, 4th ed., Princeton, 1953; and especially c) his essay in *Scientific Papers presented to Max Born*, New York 1953, pp. 33–40.
* This corrects the misplaced end of quotation of the German edition.

*Wissen Sie etwas von einem "Institut für europäische Ge-
schichte" in Mainz?* – Dieses hat mich angefragt (es un-
terzeichnet ein Professor Dr. Martin Göhring), ob ich im
Rahmen einer Arbeitstagung desselben im Oktober einen
Vortrag über das Thema "Die Wissenschaft und das abendländische Weltbild" halten könnte. (N.B. Das Wort "Weltbild" würde ich lieber durch "Denken" ersetzen. – Offen-
bar ist Herr von Weizsäcker von meinem Aufsatz über Kepler, den Sie kennen, und einem Brief, den ich ihm darüber
geschrieben habe, so beeindruckt, daß er mich in Deutsch-
land überall als Redner und Artikelschreiber empfiehlt.)

Das Thema lockt mich. Denn es ist die Wissenschaft
(und nicht die christliche Religion), die mich geistig ans
Abendland fesselt. Sowohl für indische Mystik wie für
Laotse habe ich gefühlsmäßig viel übrig, aber das wissen-
schaftliche Denken wird bei mir eine etwaige Konversion
zum Osten (wie beim Deutschen R. Wilhelm und beim Eng-
länder A. Huxley) mit Sicherheit verhindern.

Die *Ab*grenzung und *Be*grenzung der Wissenschaft ge-
genüber der Mystik – ich glaube, daß sie dem modernen
Abendländer als "Ost-West-Problem" erscheint – ist also
ein Thema, das mich sehr lockt; es würde zugleich implizite
die Frage beantworten, inwiefern *ich* selbst ein Abendländer
bin.

Letter from Pauli to Pascual Jordan, May 19, 1954

It is certainly a rash undertaking to speak in so short a time on a topic like
"Science and Western Thought", which could easily occupy a whole course
of lectures.

Western thought as a whole has always been influenced by the near and
far Asiatic East. It seems to be agreed, however, that science, more than anything else, is really characteristic of western civilisation. Mathematics and
natural science are specially distinguished from man's other intellectual ac-
tivities by being teachable and verifiable. Both qualities demand a lengthy
and in part critical elucidation. By teachability I mean communicability to
others of trains of thought and of results, made possible by a progressive
tradition, in which the learning of what is already known requires an intellectual effort of quite a different kind from that required for the discovery
of something new. In the latter process the creative irrational element finds
more essential expression than in the former. In science there is no general
rule for passing from the empirical material to new concepts and theories
capable of mathematical formulation. On one hand empirical results pro-
vide stimulus for trains of thought; on the other hand thoughts and ideas are
themselves phenomena, which often arise spontaneously, to undergo subse-

quent modification when brought face to face with the observational data. It is not always possible to check by experiment every separate assertion of a scientific theory, although the system of thought as a whole must, if it deserves the name of a scientific theory, contain possibilities of a check by empirical methods. This is what constitutes its verifiability.

Teachability is common to exact science and to logically provable mathematics. The possibility of mathematical proof, and the possibility of applying mathematics to nature, are fundamental experiences of humanity, which first arose in antiquity. These experiences were at once regarded as enigmatical, superhuman and divine, and contact was made with the religious atmosphere.

It is here that we meet the fundamental *problem of the relation between knowledge of salvation and scientific knowledge*. Periods of dispassionate research on critical lines are often succeeded by others in which the aim is to try to include science in a more comprehensive spiritualism involving mystical elements. In contrast to science, the mystical attitude is not characteristic of the occident (Abendland); in spite of differences in detail it is common to occident and orient. In this connection I may at this point refer the reader to an excellent book by *R. Otto*, "West-östliche Mystik" (Gotha, 1926) which makes a comparison between the mysticism of *Meister Eckhart* (1250–1327) and that of the Indian *Shankara* (about 800), the founder of the Vedanta philosophy. Mysticism seeks the unity of all external things and the unity of the inner man with them; this it does by seeking to see through the multiplicity of things as illusory and unreal. Thus there comes about, stage by stage, man's unity with the Godhead – Tao in China, Samadhi in India or Nirvana in Buddhism. The last-named states are likely to be equivalent from the western point of view to the extinction of ego-consciousness. Thoroughgoing mysticism does not ask "why?" It asks "How can man escape the evil, the suffering, of this terrible, menacing universe? How can it be recognised as appearance, how can the ultimate reality, the Brahman, the One, the Godhead (no longer personal for *Eckhart*) be seen?" It is however in keeping with the spirit of western science – in a certain sense one might say with the Greek spirit – to ask, for instance, "Why is the One mirrored in the Many? What is it that mirrors, and what is mirrored? Why has the One not remained alone? What originates the so-called illusion?" In his book, mentioned above, *Otto* pertinently speaks (on p. 126) of the "concern with salvation, which starting from certain situations of calamity, found given beforehand, seeks to alleviate them, not however to solve theoretically the problem of whence they come; and which is content to let insoluble problems lie, or cobbles them up as best it can with scanty auxiliary theories". I believe that it is the destiny of the occident continually to keep bringing into connection with each other these two fundamental attitudes, on the one hand the rational-critical, which seeks to understand, and on the other the mystic-irrational, which looks for the redeeming experience of oneness. *Both* attitudes will always reside in the human soul, and each will always carry the other already within itself as the germ of its contrary. Thus there arises a sort of dialectical process, of which we do not know whither it is leading us. I believe that as occidentals (Abendländer) we have to commit ourselves to this process, and recognise the pair of opposites as complementary. We cannot and will not completely sacrifice the ego-consciousness which observes the universe, but we can also accept intellectually the experience of oneness as a kind of limiting case or ideal limiting conception. While allowing the tension of opposites to remain, we must also recognise that on any path to knowledge or to salvation we are dependent on factors beyond our control, which religious language has always designated as Grace.

Among the attempts that have occurred in the course of history to effect a synthesis of the basic attitudes of science and of mysticism there are two which I should like particularly to stress. One of these originates with *Pythagoras* in the sixth century B. C., is then carried on by his disciples and developed further by *Plato*, appearing in late antiquity as Neo-Platonism and Neo-Pythagoreanism. Since much of this philosophy was taken over into early Christian theology, it continues thereafter in persevering association with Christianity, to blossom anew in the Renaissance. It was through the rejection of the *anima mundi*, the world-soul, and a return to *Plato's* doctrine of knowledge in *Galileo's* work, and through a partial revival of Pythagorean elements in that of *Kepler*, that the science of modernity, which we now call classical science, arises in the seventeenth century. After *Newton* it rapidly separates itself on rational-critical lines from its original mystical elements. The second attempt is that of alchemy and hermetic philosophy, which has lapsed since the seventeenth century.

Out of the long process of development in the history of thought, in which this problem of relations keeps coming up in new guise, I can select for the sake of example only a few features, which are significant for our own time as well. Recent researches have revealed the powerful influence of Babylonian mathematics and astronomy on the beginnings of science in Greece. The critical scientific spirit however reached its first culmination in classical Hellas. It was there that those contrasts and paradoxes were formulated which also concern us as problems, though in altered form: appearance and reality, being and becoming, the one and the many, sense experience and pure thought, the continuum and the integer, the rational ratio and the irrational number, necessity and purposefulness, causality and chance. It was there too that speculation about a way out of the difficulties of the relation between unity and multiplicity led, as a triumph of the rational mode of thought, to the idea of the atom of *Leucippus* (about 440 B. C.) and *Democritus* (about 420 B. C.). It would not be correct to designate these thinkers as materialists in the modern sense. Spiritual and material were not then separated to the same extent as in later ages; thus *Democritus* assumed atoms of the soul as well as of material bodies, between which fire represented a connecting link. In the century-long dispute over the question whether space devoid of matter could exist, the atomists belong to the side which admits this possibility, in that space between the atoms is supposed to be empty. *Democritus* denies chance and finalistic causes; atoms fall in empty space according to the laws of necessity. If I have understood correctly, however, an initial "swerve" of the atoms from rectilinear motion is sometimes supposed to take place, in the sense of an incipient circular motion, and only the latter can lead to the cosmogonic (world-generating) vortex. This ancient form of atomism does not contain the element of empirical verifiability, so it is not yet a scientific theory in the modern sense but, as a precursor of such a theory, yet only a philosophical speculation.

Prior to *Democritus* with his rational approach, *Pythagoras*, who has been mentioned above, was already at work (about 530 B. C.). He and his disciples founded an expressly mystical doctrine of salvation, which was most intimately tied up with mathematical thought, and was based on the earlier Babylonian number-mysticism. For him, and for the Pythagoreans, wherever number is, there also is soul, the expression of the unity which is God. Whole-number relationships, as they occur in the proportions of the frequencies of the simple musical intervals, are harmony, that is to say, they are what brings unity into contrasts. As part of mathematics number also belongs to an abstract supersensuous eternal world which can be apprehended not by the senses but only in contemplation by the intellect. Thus for the Pythagoreans mathematics and contemplative meditation (the original meaning of "theoria") are very closely connected; for them mathematical knowledge and wisdom (sophia) are inseparable. Special significance was attached to the *tetraktys*, fourfoldness, and there is a traditional oath of the Pythagoreans: "by him who has committed to our soul the *tetraktys*, original source and the root of eternal Nature."

As a reaction against the rationalism of the atomists, *Plato* (428–348 B. C.) took over into his doctrine of ideas many of the mystical elements of the Pythagoreans. He shares with them his higher valuation of contemplation as compared with ordinary sense experience, and his passionate participation in mathematics, especially in geometry, with its ideal objects. The discoveries of his friend *Theaetetus* on incommensurable intervals (proportions which cannot be represented by rational fractions) made a profound impression on him. Indeed, we have here to do with a fundamental question, which cannot be decided by sensuous apprehension but only by thought.

It is just the distinction between ideal geometric objects and the bodies apprehended by the senses that determines *Plato*'s conception of what nowadays we call matter. For him this distinction lies in a wholly passive something, difficult to grasp by thought, which he denotes by various feminine words, as for example receptacle or nurse for the ideas. Mention must

the quantum of action comes into play. In order to determine the properties of atomic objects, the observer, according to this theory, can choose freely between experimental arrangements which are in general mutually exclusive. This applies in particular to momentum and energy on the one hand, and to the spatio-temporal course of events on the other (*Heisenberg*'s uncertainty relation; *N. Bohr*'s complementarity). The position of the observer accordingly changes in quantum physics from that of a hidden spectator to that of an acting agent, whose effects on the system observed by him with appropriate instruments can no longer be compensated.

This situation of "complementarity" makes it necessary to introduce *primary probabilities* into physics, as a logical generalization of the deterministic form of the laws of nature in "classical" physics.[2] These probabilities are determined by fields in multi-dimensional spaces, which describe the *statistics* of series of measurements carried out under similar initial conditions, and which express only *possibilities* for the case of a *single* measurement. Unlike the fields of classical physics, these "probability fields", which have also been called "catalogues of expectation", cannot be measured simultaneously at different places. Making a measurement at *one* place means that we pass to a *new* phenomenon with altered initial conditions to which belongs a new set of possibilities to be expected, and accordingly a new field has to be stated *everywhere*. Thus in atomic physics phenomena have a new property of *wholeness*, in that they cannot be decomposed into partial phenomena without thereby in each case changing the whole phenomenon in an essential way.

Once the physical observer has chosen his experimental arrangement, he has no further influence on the result of the measurement, the objective record of which is universally accessible. Subjective properties of the observer or his psychic state do not enter into the laws of quantum mechanics any more than they do into those of classic physics.

Ch. de Montet, with a subtle gift for sensing psychological and physical parallels, has characterized[3] the situation in quantum physics here described as "sacrifice and choice". There is an essential difference in physics as compared with the more general psychological situation of sacrifice although there is agreement in regard to the giving up of certain values (loss of knowledge) in favour of others; in physical measurement the "gift of the sacrificing" is not a part of himself, but a portion of the external world, so that no transformation (Wandlung) of the observer takes place. After the measurement the system observed, separated once more from the observer, is left to itself.

---

[2] Cf. my article "Wahrscheinlichkeit und Physik" in *Dialectica* **8**, 112–124 (1954). [Essay 3 in this volume.]

[3] Ch. de Montet: *L'évolution vers l'essentiel*, Lausanne 1950. Unfortunately the author died soon after the book appeared, so that I never met him.

This suggests a comparison[4] between the inner process of sense-perception, or more generally every appearance of new content of consciousness, and observation in physics, in so far as physical measuring instruments can be regarded as technical extensions of the observer's sense organs. In the case of sense perception, however, new content of consciousness remains incorporated as a constituent part of the perceiving subject. Since the unconscious is not quantitatively measurable, and therefore not capable of mathematical description and since every extension of consciousness ("bringing into consciousness") must by reaction alter the unconscious, we may expect a "problem of observation" in relation to the unconscious, which, while it presents analogies with that in atomic physics, nevertheless involves considerably greater difficulties. These difficulties must manifest themselves in logical paradoxes when the attempt is made to comprehend the unconscious conceptually. For instance the dream itself, according to *Freud* a "royal road" to the unconscious, is, regarded epistemologically, already a content of consciousness as soon as it has been recollected on awakening; it is moreover a psycho-physical process, in so far as physiological processes in the brain necessarily accompany it. The mere apprehension of the dream has already, so to speak, altered the state of the unconscious, and thereby, in analogy with a measuring observation in quantum physics, created a new phenomenon. Conscious reflection on a dream must therefore result in a still more far-reaching alteration of the unconscious, to which there is no direct analogue in physics.

The following quotations are intended to show how the logic paradoxes raised by the problem of observation come to light in *Jung*'s statements[5] * about the unconscious.

He calls the contents of consciousness "conscious and unconscious at the same time, that is, conscious under one aspect and unconscious under another" and adds:

As is the way of paradoxes, this statement is not immediately comprehensible. We must, however, accustom ourselves to the thought that conscious and unconscious have no clear demarcations, the one beginning where the other leaves off. *It is rather the case that the psyche is a conscious-unconscious whole.*[6]

---

[4] Cf. in this connection also P. Jordan: *Verdrängung und Komplementarität*, Hamburg-Bergedorf 1947.

[5] C. G. Jung: *Von den Wurzeln des Bewußtseins*, Zürich 1954. The chapter VII "Theoretische Überlegungen zum Wesen des Psychischen" quoted here is a reprint from his essay entitled "Der Geist der Psychologie" first published in *Eranos Jahrbuch* **14**, 385–490 (1946).

* In the following the corresponding passages from the English translation in *The Collected Works of C. G. Jung*, volumes **6, 8, 9, 12** and **13**. New York 1953 f. are quoted.

[6] *The Collected Works of C. G. Jung*, volume **8**, p. 200.

So far I have said nothing about the concept "the psyche" which here occurs along with the pair of opposites conscious-unconscious. This concept was defined earlier by *Jung*, in agreement with the given quotation, as "the totality of all the psychic processes, conscious as well as unconscious."[7]

A few pages after the passage first quoted it is however stated that:[8]

Matter and spirit both appear in the psychic realm as distinctive qualities of conscious contents. The ultimate nature of both is transcendental, that is, irrepresentable, since the psyche and its contents are the only reality which is given to us *without a medium.*

It is not the non-intuitive character of matter and spirit that causes the logical difficulties at this point, but the assertion in the last clause that the psyche is "given to us without a medium". For how can the "totality of conscious and unconscious processes", how can a "conscious-unconscious whole (Ganzheit)" be "given without intermediary (unmittelbar)?"

To the physicist, as also to the naive understanding, it would appear that only the contents of consciousness are "given without intermediary". Beyond that, however, the physicist may doubt whether a "conscious-unconscious whole" does not perhaps go far beyond what can still be described as "psyche". Indeed he is not convinced that the range of "psyche" as a noun necessarily arises, as a meaningful question for scientific consideration, alongside "psychical" as an adjective,[9] which certainly covers passions, emotions and sensuous activity. The use of the noun "psyche", which, obviously, recalls the Platonic philosophy and its universal soul (Weltseele), involves the danger that the psychical element is herewith unwittingly imagined as too completely isolated from material happenings in nature, the atomic domain of which, like the unconscious is not ascertainable in itself, but only indirectly so.

The use of the noun-substantive psyche in psychology was intended to emphasize the contrast with the mechanistic world-picture which claimed to reduce all happenings to deterministic physics as then known. Meanwhile *Planck*'s quantum of action, which since 1900 had been an alien intruder into this limited world-picture, has brought about a revolution in physics,

---

[7] C. G. Jung: *Psychologische Typen*, Zürich, 1921. Chapter XI, *Definitions*, p. 661 s. v. "soul", from which however "psyche" is expressly distinguished. English translation by H. G. Baynes, in *The Collected Works of C. G. Jung*, volume **6**, p. 463.

[8] *Wurzeln des Bewußtseins*, p. 580. [*C. G. Jung's Collected Works*, volume **8**, p. 216.]

[9] At this occasion I would like to call attention to the logical curiosity contained in the use by *C. G. Jung* of the combination of words "psychic statement". It does not in fact concern a classification of the statements into psychic and non-psychic but the property associated to *all* statements, *independently of their content*, to be among the contents of the consciousness of the person stating, "that is, psychic" (hence also being accessible to investigation with respect to psychological conditions). From the point of view of formal logics the combination of words "psychic statement" used in this way therefore appears as a *pleonasm* such as "weiße Schimmel" (Schimmel = white horse).

which, by using, "correspondence arguments" reached a provisional conclusion in the setting up of quantum or wave mechanics in 1927. Physicists who have lived through this development either evince a regressive longing for the old state of affairs, or else they look for a development which will lead still further away from the old "classical" ideal of explanation of nature. This second category of physicists, to which I belong, is thus inclined to regard even the sphere of application of present-day atomic physics as limited, and is quite prepared to regard a process taking place in a material substratum as something not yet understood, if it involves that directedness towards an end, fitness for a purpose and wholeness which we regard as characteristic of life and living things. Thus for instance *Bohr* emphasizes a new aspect of the problem of observation in his conjecture that the additional condition that an organism should remain alive when subjected to an experiment sets a limit in principle to the verifiability and applicability to a living object of the quantum-physical laws of the inorganic realm.[10] In this way the *psychophysical interconnections* which we frequently meet in daily life seem once more to have come to occupy a central position in scientific development.[11] Ever since the seventeenth century these have been something of an embarrassment to the world-picture of "classical" physics, in that it has been necessary to postulate, just at this point, a connection of a different, "parallelistic", kind, in addition to the ordinary causal connection. Is it *only* in the association of physical and psychical processes, and not in other situations as well, that a parallelistic relation exists? And does not a relation of parallelism mean that it is justifiable to demand that that which is associated, or "corresponds" (the corresponding), should also be embraced conceptually in a unity of essence?

Now it seems to me very remarkable that the most recent tendency in the psychology of the unconscious, namely that represented by *C. G. Jung*, has developed in the direction of *recognizing the non-psychical in connection with the problem of psycho-physical unity*. The first step was when psychology en-

---

[10] *Bohr's* point of view on life phenomena, differing both from "mechanistic" and from "vitalistic" ideas, is expounded e. g. in the periodical "Erkenntnis", **14**, 293, 1936, in an article *"Kausalität und Komplementarität"* (Causality and Complementarity), which also gives references to earlier literature.

[11] In his book *Neuere Probleme der Abstammungslehre* 2nd ed., 1954, the zoologist *B. Rensch* discusses, in connection with the question of the origin of living things, a conception which he calls "hylopsychistic". According to this idea "psychical processes in some form are a property of all living things" (p. 361). Using the argument that it is in principle unlikely that the law of parallel connection "suddenly came into being at some time in the course of a gradual and invariably continuous phylogenesis" he indicates the possibility, in principle, of "ascribing to inanimate things also, and hence to the inorganic, very primitive psychical components of processes running strictly in parallel" (p. 381).

countered *alchemy*,[12] which I regard here as a genuine "symbol".[13] Alchemy was a doctrine having mystic-gnostic elements; by the use of identifications[14] which have become strange to us today, its language constantly gave new and extreme expression to psycho-physical unity, as well as to the unity of what takes place in the experimenter (the "artist", as alchemy puts it) with what takes place in the matter (correspondence between microcosmos and macrocosmos). *Jung*'s psychology thus encountered the matter, and in so far as alchemy was the precursor of later scientific chemistry also the rest of science. We are not surprised that soon after this first encounter with alchemy the psycho-physical problem, and also the problem of the inclusion of the observer in the course of nature, become relevant in this psychology. In fact, *Jung* in 1946[15] made drastic alteration in the concepts he employed, in order to take account of these fundamental problems. Moreover he does this particularly in view of the phenomena of "extra sensory perception" (ESP), to which I shall return briefly at the end of the next section.

Jung attempts to take account of the non-psychical by a special concept "psychoid",[16] and also by altering his older concept of "archetype",[17] which was originally used synonymously with "primordial image". This concept of *Jung*'s psychology, which I do not here assume to be well-known, can be briefly elucidated by the following quotations, arranged in chronological order, which also show its gradual alteration and development. It cannot be dissociated from *Jung*'s idea, mentioned earlier, of a collective-archaic layer of the unconscious, which is capable of reproducing mythological motifs spontaneously.

C. G. Jung, *Psychologische Typen* (1921), Chapter XI, *Definitions* (s. v. "Image"):*

---

[12] *C. G. Jung*'s most important writings on alchemy are *Das Geheimnis der goldenen Blüte*, in collaboration with *R. Wilhelm*, 1st ed. München 1929 [*The Collected Works of C. G. Jung*, Volume **13**, pp. 1–56]; *Psychologie und Alchemie*, 1st ed. Zürich 1944, 2nd ed. 1952 [*The Collected Works of C. G. Jung*, Volume **12**]; and in *Symbolik des Geistes*, Zürich 1948, Contribution V: "Der Geist Mercurius". [*The Collected Works of C. G. Jung*, Volume **13**, pp. 191–250].

[13] In *Psychological Types*, Chapter XI, *Definitions*, s. v. "symbol", *Jung* defines the symbolic expression as the "best possible description ... of a relatively unknown fact".

[14] The reader may be reminded of the correspondences: the seven planets, the seven metals, among which the planet mercury = Hermes = quicksilver; spirit = soul = alcohol, etc. Is it fortuitous that *Freud* hit upon the alchemist mode of expression "to sublimate"?

[15] See C. G. Jung: *Von den Wurzeln des Bewußtseins*, Zürich 1954, see footnote 5 above.

[16] *The Collected Works of C. G. Jung*, volume **8**, p. 183 f.

[17] Prof. *E. Panofsky* (Princeton) has kindly informed me that the oldest known occurrence in literature of the Greek word αρχετνποσ is in *Cicero*, Letters to Atticus, 12. 5. and 16. 3., who translates the word into Latin. *Cicero*'s Greek sources are not known to us. Through his authority the word came into common use in late antiquity.

* *The Collected Works of C. G. Jung*, volume **6**, p. 443 ff.

The primordial image, elsewhere also termed 'archetype', is always collective, i. e., it is at least common to entire peoples or epochs. ... the primordial image can be conceived as a mnemic deposit, an imprint or *engramm* (Semon), which has arisen through a condensation of countless processes of a similar kind. ... The primordial image is the precursor of the *idea* and its matrix.

Über die Energetik der Seele (Psychologische Abhandlungen, volume II, Zürich 1928), p. 198:*

Archetypes are typical modes of apprehension, and wherever we meet with uniform and regularly recurring modes of apprehension we are dealing with an archetype, no matter whether its mythological character is recognized or not.

Psychologie und Religion, Zürich 1940, p. 93:**

Even dreams are made of collective material to a very high degree, just as, in the mythology and folklore of different peoples, certain motifs repeat themselves in almost identical form. I have called these motifs "archetypes", and by this I mean forms or images of a collective nature which occur practically all over the earth as constituents of myth and at the same time as autochthonous, individual products of unconscious origin. The archetypal motifs presumably derive from patterns of the human mind that are transmitted not only by tradition and migration but also by heredity. The latter hypothesis is indispensable, since even complicated archetypal images can be reproduced spontaneously without there being any possibility of direct tradition.

Ibid., p. 186:# (We assume the existence of)

a certain unconscious condition as an inherited *a priori* factor. By this I naturally do not mean the inheritance of ideas (Vorstellungen), which would be difficult if not impossible to prove. I suppose, rather, the inherited quality to be something like the formal possibility of producing the same or similar ideas over and over again. I have called this possibility the "archetype". Accordingly, the archetype would be a structural quality or condition peculiar to a psyche that is somehow connected with the brain.

Wurzeln des Bewußtseins (1954), p. 577:##

We must, however, constantly bear in mind that what we mean by "archetype" is in itself irrepresentable (unanschaulich). but has effects which make visualizations of it possible, namely, the archetypal images and ideas (Vorstellungen).

---

* *The Collected Works of C. G. Jung*, volume **8**, p. 137 f.
** *The Collected Works of C. G. Jung*, volume **11**, p. 50.
# Ibid., p. 103 f.
The Collected Works of C. G. Jung, volume **8**, p. 214.

Ibid., p. 573:* (Archetype)

as well as being an image in its own right, is at the same time a *dynamism* which makes itself felt in the numinosity and fascinating power of the archetypal image.

Ibid., p. 579:**

Just as the "psychic infra-red", the biological instinctual psyche, gradually passes over into the physiology of the organism and thus merges with its chemical and physical conditions, so the "psychic ultraviolet", the archetype, describes a field which exhibits none of the peculiarities of the psychological and yet, in the last analysis, can no longer be regarded as psychic, although it manifests itself psychically. But physiological processes behave in the same way, without on that account being declared psychic. Although there is no form of existence that is not mediated to us psychically and only psychically, it would hardly do to say that everything is merely psychic. We must apply this argument logically to the archetypes as well.

Ibid., p. 601:#

The qualitatively rather than quantitatively definable units with which the unconscious works, namely the archetypes, therefore have a nature that *cannot with certainty be designated as psychic.*

Ibid., p. 602:## (Archetypes are)

empirically derived postulates – archetypes – whose content, if any, cannot be represented to the mind. Archetypes, so far as we can observe and experience them at all, manifest themselves only through their ability to *organize* images and ideas (Vorstellungen), and this is always an unconscious process that cannot be detected until afterwards.

Aion (1951), p. 260:† (It is a matter of)

certain complex thought-forms, the archetypes, which must be conjectured as the unconscious organizers of our ideas. The motive force that produces these configurations cannot be distinguished from the transconscious factor (Tatbestand) known as instinct. There is, therefore, no justification for visualizing the archetype as anything other than the image (Gestalt) of instinct in man.

Wurzeln des Bewußtseins (1954), p. 5:‡

'Archetype' is an explanatory paraphrase of the Platonic εἶδος.

---

*   Ibid., p. 211.
** Ibid., p. 215.
# Ibid., p. 230.
Ibid., p. 231.
† *The Collected Works of C. G. Jung*, volume **9**, pt. 2, p. 179.
‡ *The Collected Works of C. G. Jung*, volume **9**, pt. 1, p. 4.

Ibid., p. 6:*

The archetype is essentially an unconscious content that is altered by becoming conscious and by being perceived, and it takes its color from the individual consciousness in which it happens to appear.

Ibid., p. 6, footnote 4:**

One must, for the sake of accuracy, distinguish between 'archetype' and 'archetypal ideas' (Vorstellungen). The archetype as such is a hypothetical and irrepresentable (unanschaulich) model, something like the 'pattern of behavior' in biology.

These quotations may give the reader a picture of the function of the concept 'archetype' in *Jung*'s psychology, and of its transformation from the original meaning of 'primordial image' to that of an irrepresentable (unanschauliches) structural element of the unconscious, a regulator, which organizes representations (Vorstellungen). Personally I see in this the first indications of the recognition of ordering principles, which are neutral[18] in respect of the distinction psychical-physical, but which, in contrast with the concretistic psycho-physical unified language of ancient alchemy are ideal and abstract, that is, of their very nature irrepresentable (unanschaulich). Thus the great difficulties and paradoxes in the problem of observation appear clearly. These changes in the ideas of the unconscious show that while still far from having been definitively worked out from the logical side, they are the expression of a line of research in course of development. The physicist is well aware how these two things often go hand in hand, and how useless it is to tie down what is in a state of flux, whether by mere repetition or by logically elaborated axiomatisation. In such a case I think it is important to look at research from a more general standpoint than that of the special field.

2. Applications of the Ideas of the Unconscious in Quantitative Sciences

Without committing myself to quite general discussions of old philosophical problems connected with the fact that our ideas are arranged (Angeordnetsein) such as for instance the coincidence of thought-forms with forms of being, I should like here to discuss some applications of the ideas of the unconscious to quantitative sciences. For this purpose mathematics and bi-

---

* Ibid., p. 5.
** Ibid., p. 5.
[18] Cf. also in this connection C. G. Jung, *Aion* (1951), pp. 372, 373.

of teleology. The latter then must be replaced in some way by the introducing of "chance".

As a physicist I should like at this point to voice my misgivings in the criticism[24] that so far this model is not supported by any positive probabilistic consideration. Such a consideration would have to consist of a comparison between the theoretical *time-scale* of evolution which follows from the model and its empirical time-scale: *It would have to be shown that on the basis of the assumed model anything fit for a purpose (Zweckmäßiges) which is in fact present had a sufficient chance of arising within the empirically known time-scale. A consideration of this sort has however nowhere been attempted.*[25,26] Instead, attention is deflected from this cardinal question by the remark that anything not fit for its purpose (Unzweckmäßiges) will certainly perish or that certain old "vitalistic" concepts (whose names usually terminate with "-force") break down.

While in the case of the firmly established results of genetics[27] we are concerned, as in atomic physics, with statistical laws, which have been discovered and verified by series of experiments on frequently occurring reproducible events, *rare or even unique events* are specially important for biological evolution.[28] I must content myself, as an outsider, with pointing out this fundamental difference, and confirming my impression that the phenomena before us, which are certainly highly complex, have not as yet been analysed and understood.

In conclusion, I should like to discuss briefly the controversial question of "extra-sensory perception" (ESP), which constitutes a borderland between physics and psychology, and can just as well be called "parapsychology" as "biophysics". We already have quantitative experiments in this field, carried

---

[24] I know that several mathematicians and physicists agree with this criticism. I believe however that it is the problems themselves, and not the physicists, that are responsible for the difficulties.

[25] This criticism also applies to the book by *Rensch* already quoted (footnote 11, this essay) in which this model is accepted. The model would have to be supported by a positive consideration of this kind, especially in regard to the time-scale of the "anagenesis" (higher development) defined and established in this book.

[26] In the reflections of G. Wald (*Scientific American* **191**, 45, 1954) on the origin of life, which is wrapped in still greater obscurity, statements such as "one has only to wait: time itself performs the miracles" also play an essential part, without an estimate ever being made of *how long* a time would be required.

[27] The ancient Pythagoreans, with their reverence for the number four, would have taken particular pleasure in the *quaternary* chemical structure, built up on two pairs of opposites, of a nucleic acid (denoted DNA for short) which is essential for the processes of heredity and reproduction (J. D. Watson and F. H. C. Crick, *Nature* **171**, 964, 1953).

[28] Cf. also P. Jordan: "Der Begriff der Wahrscheinlichkeit in der Phylogenie" in *Scientific Papers presented to Max Born*, Edinburgh, 1953.

out by scientific methods, and employing modern mathematical statistics.[29] Usually it is a matter of guessing figures or pictures on cards. This borderland has already excited much interest among physicists, and also a good deal of rejection. Some speak of experimental or mathematical errors; others, with more caution, say that they "feel ill at ease" with these matters. To the first I would say that as far as I know errors have not actually been detected in the carefully conducted experiments. Of course it is always *relatively rare* phenomena that are involved, to some extent associated with a special gift possessed by the experimental subject. To the second I would point out that epistemological *a priori* grounds probably do not suffice to reject the existence of ESP out of hand. Even so thorough critical a philosopher as *Schopenhauer* has regarded parapsychological effects as not only possible, but as supporting his philosophy, which is indeed going far beyond what has been established by scientific empiricism.[30] The question of the existence of ESP must therefore be decided by critical empiricism.

More recent investigations of such phenomena give fresh actuality to the old question of how the psychic state of the persons taking part in the experiment fits into the course of external events. Can the phenomena of ESP be artificially influenced, positively or negatively? Results so far agree in showing the so-called "fatigue (decline) effect", which points to the importance of the *emotional factor* in the experimental subject.

Schopenhauer speaks metaphysically of the "will", which breaks through space and time, the "principium individuationis" as he calls them, and contrasts the "nexus metaphysicus" with the ordinary "nexus physicus". *Jung*[31] employs a psychological-scientific terminology instead of the philosophical-metaphysical. He attempts to generalize parallelistic connections to such *relatively rare "borderline phenomena"*,[32] and speaks in this case of a "connection (nexus) through identity of kind or 'meaning' ". Following his psychological intuition he links this up with the time-concept, by introducing for it the term "synchronicity". We have here a first attempt to penetrate into a completely new field. So far *Jung*'s idea has not been tested to any extent by detailed comparison with experimental results on ESP.

*   *   *

[29] Cf. especially S. G. Soal and F. Bateman: *Modern Experiments in Telepathy*, Faber and Faber, London 1954. In this reference an account is also given of the earlier experiments of Rhine and others.

[30] Cf. *A. Schopenhauer*'s essay "Animalischer Magnetismus und Magie" in vol. **4**, *Naturphilosophie und Ethik* of his Works.

[31] C. G. Jung: "Synchronizität als Prinzip akausaler Zusammenhänge" in *Naturerklärung und Psyche*, Zürich 1952. [English translation in *The Interpretation of Nature and the Psyche*, London 1955.]

[32] I should like to raise the question whether the most primitive psychical components (see footnote 11, this essay) assumed by *Rensch*, and ascribed to the inorganic also, do not manifest themselves in just such borderline phenomena.

Summarizing, I might point out that in this article I have allowed myself to be guided outside my more limited special field by just that agreement of the *meaning* of ideas coming up more or less simultaneously in different branches of knowledge – their meaningful coincidence: "Correspondence (Entsprechung)", "complementary pairs of opposites" and "wholeness" occur independently both in physics and in the ideas of the unconscious. The "unconscious" itself has a certain analogy with the "field" in physics, and both are brought into the realm of the irrepresentable (Unanschauliche) and paradoxical through a problem of observation. In physics however we do not speak of self-reproducing "archetypes", but of "statistical laws of nature involving primary probabilities"; but both formulations meet in their tendency to extend the old narrower idea of "causality (deteminism) to a more general form of "connections" in nature, a conclusion to which the psycho-physical problem also points. This way of looking at things leads me to expect that the further development of the ideas of the unconscious will not take place within the narrow framework of their therapeutic applications, but will be determined by their assimilation to the main stream of natural science as applied to vital phenomena.

18. Exclusion Principle
and Quantum Mechanics*

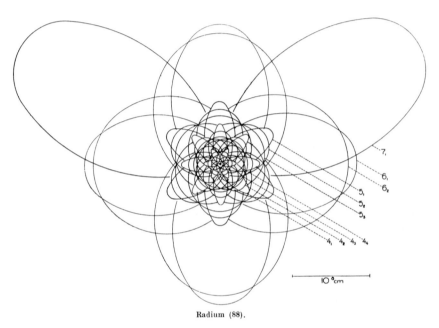

Radium (88).

Pictorial representation of the Radium atom by Hendrik Anthony Kramers
according to Bohr's atomic theory

These colored pictorial representations of the atom ("bunte Bilderbücher") before the
formulation of the *exclusion principle* and the advent of the new *quantum mechanics* were
sharply criticized by Pauli [From *Die Naturwissenschaften* **11** (1923)]

* Nobel Lecture in English, delivered at Stockholm on December 13, 1946 (Stockholm
  1948).

> The preparations for my trip to Europe are going well according to plan and I shall leave in about 4 weeks. – My first station will probably be Dublin. – Do you know anything about it whether the lecture in Stockholm which is incumbent on any Nobel-prize-winner is supposed to be a technical one (that means really for theoretical physicists) or something more popular? I would prefer the first.
>
> Letter from Pauli to Lamek Hulthén, January 30, 1946

> I have now decided to maintain my professorship in Zürich and to postpone for a while my trip to the United States. Moreover, I have proposed to Waller and to Westgren (the secretary of the Royal Swedish Academy) to deliver my Nobel-lecture on December 10th of this year.
>
> Letter from Pauli to Torsten Gustafson, August 4, 1946

The history of the discovery of the exclusion principle, for which I have received the honor of the Nobel Prize award in the year 1945, goes back to my student days in Munich. While, in school in Vienna, I had already obtained some knowledge of classical physics and the then new *Einstein* relativity theory, it was at the University of Munich that I was introduced by *Sommerfeld* to the structure of the atom – somewhat strange from the point of view of classical physics. I was not spared the shock which every physicist, accustomed to the classical way of thinking, experienced when he came to know of *Bohr*'s 'Basic postulate of quantum theory' for the first time. At that time there were two approaches to the difficult problems connected with the quantum of action. One was an effort to bring abstract order to the new ideas by looking for a key to translate classical mechanics and electrodynamics into quantum language which would form a logical generalization of these. This was the direction which was taken by *Bohr*'s Correspondence Principle. *Sommerfeld*, however, preferred, in view of the difficulties which blocked the use of the concepts of kinematical models, a direct interpretation as independent of models as possible, of the laws of spectra in terms of integral numbers, following, as *Kepler* once did in his investigation of the planetary system, an inner feeling for harmony. Both methods, which did not appear to me irreconcilable, influenced me. The series of whole numbers 2, 8, 18, 32 ... giving the lengths of the periods in the natural system of chemical elements, was zealously discussed in Munich, including the remark of the Swedish physicist, *Rydberg*, that these numbers are of the simple form $2p^2$, if 'n' takes on all integer values. *Sommerfeld* tried especially to connect the number 8 and the number of corners of a cube.

A new phase of my scientific life began when I met *Niels Bohr* personally for the first time. This was in 1922, when he gave a series of guest lectures at Göttingen, in which he reported on his theoretical investigations on the periodic system of elements. I shall recall only briefly that the essential progress made by *Bohr*'s considerations at that time was in explaining, by means of the spherical symmetric atomic model, the formation of the intermediate shells of the atom and the general properties of the rare earth's. The question, as to why all electrons for an atom in its ground state were not bound in the innermost shell, had already been emphasized by *Bohr* as a fundamental problem in his earlier works. In his Göttingen lectures he treated particularly the closing of this innermost K-shell in the helium atom and its essential connection with the two non-combining spectra of helium, the ortho- and parahelium spectra. However, no convincing explanation for this phenomenon could be given on the basis of classical mechanics. It made a strong impression on me that *Bohr* at that time and in later discussions was looking for a *general* explanation which should hold for the closing of *every* electron shell and in which the number 2 was considered to be as essential as 8 in contrast to *Sommerfeld*'s approach.

Following *Bohr*'s invitation, I went to Copenhagen in the autumn of 1922, where I made a serious effort to explain the so-called 'anomalous Zeeman effect', as the spectroscopists called a type of splitting of the spectral lines in a magnetic field which is different from the normal triplet. On the one hand, the anomalous type of splitting exhibited beautiful and simple laws and *Landé*[1] had already succeeded to find the simpler splitting of the spectroscopic terms from the observed splitting of the lines. The most fundamental of his results thereby was the use of half-integers as magnetic quantum numbers for the doublet-spectra of the alkali metals. On the other hand, the anomalous splitting was hardly understandable from the standpoint of the mechanical model of the atom, since very general assumptions concerning the electron, using classical theory as well as quantum theory, always led to the same triplet. A closer investigation of this problem left me with the feeling that it was even more unapproachable. We know now that at that time one was confronted with two logically different difficulties simultaneously. One was the absence of a general key to translate a given mechanical model into quantum theory which one tried in vain by using classical mechanics to describe the stationary quantum states themselves. The second difficulty was our ignorance concerning the proper classical model itself which could be suited to derive at all an anomalous splitting of spectral lines emitted by an atom in an external magnetic field. It is therefore not surprising that I could not find a satisfactory solution of the problem at that time. I succeeded, how-

---

[1] A. Landé, *Zeitschrift für Physik* **5**, 231 (1921) and **7**, 398 (1921); *Physikalische Zeitschrift* **22**, 417 (1921).

ever, in generalizing *Landé*'s term analysis for very strong magnetic fields,[2] a case which, as a result of the magneto-optic transformation (Paschen-Back-effect), is in many respects simpler. This early work was of decisive importance for the finding of the exclusion principle.

Very soon after my return to the University of Hamburg, in 1923, I gave there my inaugural lecture as Privatdozent on the periodic system of elements. The contents of this lecture appeared very unsatisfactory to me, since the problem of the closing of the electronic shells had been clarified no further. The only thing that was clear was that a closer relation of this problem to the theory of multiplet structure must exist. I therefore tried to examine again critically the simplest case, the doublet structure of the alkali spectra. According to the point of view then orthodox, which was also taken over by *Bohr* in his already mentioned lectures in Göttingen, a non-vanishing angular momentum of the atomic core was supposed to be the cause of this doublet structure.

In the autumn of 1924 I published some arguments against this point of view, which I definitely rejected as incorrect and proposed instead of it the assumption of a new quantum-theoretic property of the electron, which I called a 'two-valuedness not describable classically'.[3] At this time a paper of the English physicist, *Stoner*, appeared[4] which contained, besides improvements in the classification of electrons in subgroups, the following essential remark: For a given value of the principle quantum number is the number of energy levels of a single electron in the alkali metal spectra in an external magnetic field the same as the number of electrons in the closed shell of the rare gases which corresponds to this principal quantum number. On the basis of my earlier results on the classification of spectral terms in a strong magnetic field the general formulation of the exclusion principle became clear to me. The fundamental idea can be stated in the following way: The complicated numbers of electrons in closed subgroups are reduced to the simple number *one* if the division of the groups by giving the values of the 4 quantum numbers of an electron is carried so far that every degeneracy is removed. An entirely non degenerate energy level is already 'closed', if it is occupied by a single electron; states in contradiction with this postulate have to be excluded. The exposition of this general formulation of the exclusion principle was made in Hamburg in the spring of 1925,[5] after I was able to verify some additional conclusions concerning the anomalous *Zeeman* effect of more complicated atoms during a visit to Tübingen with the help of the spectroscopic material assembled there.

[2] W. Pauli, *Zeitschrift für Physik* **16**, 155 (1923).
[3] W. Pauli, *Zeitschrift für Physik* **31**, 373 (1925).
[4] E. C. Stoner, *Philosophical Magazine* **48**, 719 (1924).
[5] W. Pauli, *Zeitschrift für Physik* **31**, 765 (1925).

With the exception of experts on the classification of spectral terms, the physicists found it difficult to understand the exclusion principle, since no meaning in terms of a model was given to the fourth degree of freedom of the electron. The gap was filled by *Uhlenbeck* and *Goudsmit*'s idea of electron spin,[6] which made it possible to understand the anomalous *Zeeman* effect simply by assuming that the spin quantum number of one electron is equal to 1/2 and that the quotient of the magnetic moment to the mechanical angular moment has for the spin a value twice as large as for the ordinary orbit of the electron. Since that time, the exclusion principle has been closely connected with the idea of spin. Although at first I strongly doubted the correctness of this idea because of its classical mechanical character, I was finally converted to it by *Thomas*' calculations[7] on the magnitude of doublet splitting. On the other hand, my earlier doubts as well as the cautious expression 'classically non-describable two-valuedness' experienced a certain verification during later developments, since *Bohr* was able to show on the basis of wave mechanics that the electron spin cannot be measured by classically describable experiments (as, for instance, deflection of molecular beams in external electromagnetic fields) and must therefore be considered as an essentially quantum mechanical property of the electron.[8,9]

* * *

The subsequent developments were determined by the occurrence of the new quantum mechanics. In 1925, the same year in which I published my paper on the exclusion-principle, *De Broglie* formulated his idea of matter waves and *Heisenberg* the new matrix-mechanics, after which in the next year *Schrödinger*'s wave mechanics quickly followed. It is at present unnecessary to stress the importance and the fundamental character of these discoveries, all the more as these physicists have themselves explained, here in Stockholm, the meaning of their leading ideas.[10] Nor does time permit me to illustrate in detail the general epistemological significance of the new discipline of quantum mechanics, which has been done, among others, in a number of articles by *Bohr*, using hereby the idea of 'complementarity' as a new central

6   S. Goudsmit and G. Uhlenbeck, *Die Naturwissenschaften* **13**, 953 (1925). *Nature* **117**, 264 (1926).

7   L. H. Thomas, *Nature* **117**, 514 (1926) and *Philosophical Magazine* **3**, 1 (1927). Compare also J. Frenkel, *Zeitschrift für Physik* **37**, 243 (1926).

8   Compare *Rapport du Sixième Conseil Solvey de Physique*, Paris 1932, pp. 217–225.

9   For this earlier stage of the history of the exclusion principle compare also the author's note in *Science* **103**, 213 (1946), which partly coincides with the first part of the present lecture.

10 The Nobel-lectures of W. Heisenberg, E. Schrödinger and P. A. M. Dirac are collected in *Die moderne Atomtheorie*, Leipzig 1934.

concept.[11] I shall only recall that the statements of quantum mechanics are dealing only with possibilities, not with actualities. They have the form 'This is not possible' or 'Either this or that is possible', but they can never say 'that will actually happen then and there'. The actual observation appears as an event outside the range of a description by physical laws and brings forth in general a discontinuous selection out of the several possibilities foreseen by the statistical laws of the new theory. Only this renouncement concerning the old claims for an objective description of the physical phenomena, independent of the way in which they are observed, made it possible to reach again the selfconsistency of quantum theory, which actually had been lost since *Planck*'s discovery of the quantum of action. Without discussing further the change of the attitude of modern physics to such concepts as 'causality' and 'physical reality' in comparison with the older classical physics I shall discuss more particularly in the following the position of the exclusion principle on the new quantum mechanics.

As it was first shown by *Heisenberg*,[12] wave mechanics leads to qualitatively different conclusions for particles of the same kind (for instance for electrons) than for particles of different kinds. As a consequence of the impossibility to distinguish one of several like particles from the other, the wave functions describing an ensemble of a given number of like particles in the configuration space are sharply separated into different classes of symmetry which can never be transformed into each other by external perturbations. In the term 'configuration space' we are including here the spin degree of freedom, which is described in the wave function of a single particle by an index with only a finite number of possible values. For electrons this number is equal to two; the configuration space of N electrons has therefore $3N$ space dimensions and N indices of 'two-valuedness'. Among the different classes of symmetry, the most important ones (which moreover for two particles are the only ones) are the symmetrical class, in which the wave function does not change its value when the space and spin coordinates of two particles are permuted, and the antisymmetrical class, in which for such a permutation the wave function changes its sign. At this stage of the theory three different hypotheses turned out to be logically possible concerning the actual ensemble of several like particles in Nature:

I. This ensemble is a mixture of all symmetry classes.
II. Only the symmetrical class occurs.
III. Only the antisymmetrical class occurs.

---

[11] The articles of *N. Bohr* are collected in *Atomic theory and the description of nature* (Cambridge University Press, 1934). See also his article "Light and Life", *Nature* **131**, 421 and 457 (1933).
[12] W. Heisenberg, *Zeitschrift für Physik* **38**, 411 (1926) and **39**, 499 (1926).

As we shall see, the first assumption is never realized in nature. Moreover, it is only the third assumption that is in accordance with the exclusion principle, since an antisymmetrical function containing two particles in the same state is identically zero. The assumption III can therefore be considered as the correct and general wave mechanical formulation of the exclusion principle. It is this possibility which actually holds for electrons.

This situation appeared to me as disappointing in an important respect. Already in my original paper I stressed the circumstance that I was unable to give a logical reason for the exclusion principle or to deduce it from more general assumptions. I had always the feeling and I still have it today, that this is a deficiency. Of course in the beginning I hoped that the new quantum mechanics, with the help of which it was possible to deduce so many half-empirical formal rules in use at that time, will also rigorously deduce the exclusion principle. Instead of it there was for electrons still an exclusion: not of particular states any longer, but of whole classes of states, namely the exclusion of all classes different from the antisymmetrical one. The impression that the shadow of some incompleteness fell here on the bright light of success of the new quantum mechanics seems to me unavoidable. We shall resume this problem when we discuss relativistic quantum mechanics but wish to give first an account of further results of the application of wave mechanics to systems of several like particles.

In the paper of *Heisenberg*, which we are discussing, he was also able to give a simple explanation of the existence of the two non-combining spectra of helium which I mentioned in the beginning of this lecture. Indeed, besides the rigorous separation of the wave functions into symmetry-classes with respect to space-coordinates and spin-indices together, there exists an approximate separation into symmetry classes with respect to space-coordinates alone. The latter holds only so long as an interaction between the spin and the orbital motion of the electron can be neglected. In this way the para- and ortho-helium spectra could be interpreted as belonging to the class of symmetrical and antisymmetrical wave functions respectively in the space-coordinates alone. It became clear that the energy difference between corresponding levels of the two classes has nothing to do with magnetic interactions but is of a new type of much larger order of magnitude, which one called exchange energy.

Of more fundamental significance is the connection of the symmetry classes with general problems of the statistical theory of heat. As is well known, this theory leads to the result that the entropy of a system is (apart from a constant factor) given by the logarithm of the number of quantum states of the whole system on a socalled energy shell. One might first expect that this number should be equal to the corresponding volume of the multidimensional phase space divided by h^f, where h is *Planck*'s constant and f the number of degrees of freedom of the whole system. However, it

at this low temperature the thermal equilibrium between the two modifications of the hydrogen molecule (ortho-H_2: odd rotational quantum numbers, parallel proton spins; para-H_2: even rotational quantum numbers, antiparallel spins) was not yet reached. As you know, this hypothesis was later confirmed by the experiments of *Bonhoeffer* and *Harteck* and of *Eucken*, which showed the theoretically predicted slow transformation of one modification into the other.

Among the symmetry classes for other nuclei those with a different parity of their mass numbers M and their charge number Z are of a particular interest. If we consider a compound system consisting of numbers A_1, A_2, ... of different constituents, each of which is fulfilling the exclusion principle, and a number S of constituents with symmetrical states, one has to expect symmetrical or antisymmetrical states if the sum $A_1 + A_2 + ...$ is even or odd. This holds regardless of the parity of S. Earlier one tried the assumption that nuclei consist of protons and electrons, so that M is the number of protons, $M - Z$ the number of electrons in the nucleus. It had to be expected then that the parity of Z determines the symmetry class of the whole nucleus. Already for some time the counter-example of nitrogen has been known to have the spin 1 and symmetrical states.[18] After the discovery of the neutron, the nuclei have been considered, however, as composed of protons and neutrons in such a way that a nucleus with mass number M and charge number Z should consist of Z protons and $M - Z$ neutrons. In case the neutrons would have symmetrical states, one should again expect that the parity of the charge number Z determines the symmetry class of the nuclei. If, however, the neutrons fulfill the exclusion principle, it has to be expected that the parity of M determines the symmetry class: For an even M, one should always have symmetrical states, for an odd M, antisymmetrical ones. It was the latter rule that was confirmed by experiment without exception, thus proving that the neutrons fulfill the exclusion principle.

The most important and most simple crucial example for a nucleus with a different parity of M and Z is the heavy hydrogen or deuteron with $M = 2$ and $Z = 1$ which has symmetrical states and the spin $I = 1$, as could be proved by the investigation of the band spectra of a molecule with two deuterons.[19] From the spin value 1 of the deuteron can be concluded that the neutron must have a half-integer spin. The simplest possible assumption that this spin of the neutron is equal to 1/2, just as the spin of the proton and of the electron, turned out to be correct.

There is hope, that further experiments with light nuclei, especially with protons, neutrons and deuterons will give us further information about the

---

[18] R. de Laer Kronig, *Die Naturwissenschaften* **16**, 335 (1928). W. Heitler und G. Herzberg, *Die Naturwissenschaften* **17**, 673 (1929).

[19] G. N. Lewis and M. F. Ashley, *Physical Review* **43**, 837 (1933). G. M. Murphy and H. Johnston, *Physical Review* **45**, 550 (1934) and **46**, 95 (1934).

nature of the forces between the constituents of the nuclei, which, at present, is not yet sufficiently clear. Already now we can say, however, that these interactions are fundamentally different from electromagnetic interactions. The comparison between neutron-proton scattering and proton-proton scattering even showed that the forces between these particles are in good approximation the same, that means independent of their electric charge. If one had only to take into account the magnitude of the interaction energy, one should therefore expect a stable di-proton or $_2\mathrm{He}^2$ ($M = 2$, $Z = 2$) with nearly the same binding energy as the deuteron. Such a state is, however, forbidden by the exclusion principle in accordance with experience, because this state would acquire a wave function symmetric with respect to the two protons. This is only the simplest example of the application of the exclusion principle to the structure of compound nuclei, for the understanding of which this principle is indispensable, because the constituents of these heavier nuclei, the protons and the neutrons, fulfil it.

In order to prepare for the discussion of more fundamental questions, we want to stress here a law of nature which is generally valid, namely, the connection between spin and symmetry class. *A half-integer value of the spin quantum number is always connected with antisymmetrical states (exclusion principle), an integer spin with symmetrical states.* This law holds not only for protons and neutrons but also for photons and electrons. Moreover, it can easily be seen that it holds for compound systems, if it holds for all of its constituents. If we search for a theoretical explanation of this law, we must pass to the discussion of relativistic wave mechanics, since we saw that it can certainly not be explained by non relativistic wave mechanics.

* * *

We first consider classical fields,[20] which, like scalars, vectors and tensors, transform with respect to rotations in the ordinary space according to a one-valued representation of the rotation group. We may, in the following, call such fields briefly 'one-valued' fields. So long as interactions of different kinds of field are not taken into account, we can assume that all field components will satisfy a second order wave equation, permitting a superposition of plane waves as a general solution. Frequency and wave-number of these plane waves are connected by a law which, in accordance with *De Broglie*'s fundamental assumption, can be obtained from the relation between energy and momentum of a particle claimed in relativistic mechanics by division with the constant factor $\hbar$ equal to *Planck*'s constant divided by 2π. Therefore, there will appear in the classical field equations, in general,

---

[20] Compare for the following the author's report in *Reviews of Modern Physics* **13**, 203 (1941), where older literature is given. See also W. Pauli and V. Weisskopf, *Helvetica Physica Acta* **7**, 709 (1934).

a new constant μ with the dimension of a reciprocal length, with which the restmass m in the particle picture is connected by $m = \hbar\mu/c$, where c is the vacuum-velocity of light. From the assumed property of one-valuedness of the field it can be concluded, that the number of possible plane waves for a given frequency, wave number and direction of propagation, is for a non-vanishing μ always odd. Without going into details of the general definition of spin, we can consider this property of the polarization of plane waves as characteristic for fields which, as a result of their quantization, give rise to integer spin values.

The simplest cases of one-valued fields are the scalar field and a field consisting of a four vector and an antisymmetric tensor like the potentials and field strengths in *Maxwell*'s theory. While the scalar field is simply fulfilling the usual wave equation of the second order in which the term proportional to μ^2 has to be included, the other field has to fulfil equations due to *Proca* which are a generalization of *Maxwell*'s equations which follow* in the particular case $\mu = 0$. It is satisfactory that for these simplest cases of one-valued fields the energy density is a positive definite quadratic form of the field quantities and their first derivatives at a certain point. For the general case of one valued fields it can at least be achieved that the total energy after integration over space is always positive.

The field components can be assumed to be either real or complex. For a complex field, in addition to energy and momentum of the field, a four-vector can be defined which satisfies the continuity equation and can be interpreted as the four-vector of the electric current. Its fourth component determines the electric charge density and can assume both positive and negative values. It is possible that the charged mesons observed in cosmic rays have integral spins and thus can be described by such a complex field. In the particular case of real fields this four-vector of current vanishes identically.

Especially in view of the properties of the radiation in the thermodynamical equilibrium in which specific properties of the field sources do not play any role, it seemed to be justified first to disregard in the formal process of field quantization the interaction of the field with the sources. Dealing with this problem, one tried indeed to apply the same mathematical method of passing from a classical system to a corresponding system governed by the laws of quantum mechanics which had been so successful in passing from classical point mechanics to wave mechanics. It should not be forgotten, however, that a field can only be observed with help of its interaction with test bodies which are themselves again sources of the field.

The results of the formal process of field quantization were partly very encouraging. The quantized wave fields can be characterized by a wave function which depends on an infinite sequence of (non negative) integers as

---

* Correction of the original.

variables. As the total energy and the total momentum of the field and, in case of complex fields, also its total electric charge turn out to be linear functions of these numbers, they can be interpreted as the number of particles present in a specified state of a single particle. By using a sequence of configuration spaces with a different number of dimensions corresponding to the different possible values of the total number of particles present, it could easily be shown that this description of our system by a wave function depending on integers is equivalent to an ensemble of particles with wave functions symmetrical in their configuration spaces.

Moreover *Bohr* and *Rosenfeld*[21] proved in the case of the electromagnetic field that the uncertainty relations which result for the average values of the field strengths over finite space-time regions from the formal commutation rules of this theory have a direct physical meaning so long as the sources can be treated classically and their atomistic structure can be disregarded. We emphasize the following property of these commutation rules: All physical quantities in two world points, for which the four-vector of their joining straight line is space-like commute with each other. This is indeed necessary for physical reasons because any disturbance by measurements in a world point P_1 can only reach such points P_2 for which the vector $P_1 P_2$ is time-like, that is, for which $c(t_1 - t_2) > r_{12}$. The points P_2 with a space-like vector $P_1 P_2$ for which $c(t_1 - t_2) < r_{12}$ cannot be reached by this disturbance and measurements in P_1 and P_2 can then never influence each other.

This consequence made it possible to investigate the logical possibility of particles with integer spin which would obey the exclusion principle. Such particles could be described by a sequence of configuration spaces with different dimensions and wave functions antisymmetrical in the coordinates of these spaces or also by a wave function depending on integers again to be interpreted as the number of particles present in a specified states which now can only assume the values 0 or 1. *Wigner* and *Jordan*[22] proved that also in this case operators can be defined which are functions of the ordinary space-time coordinates and which can be applied to such a wave function. These operators do not fulfil any longer commutation rules: instead of the difference the *sum* of the two possible products of two operators, which are distinguished by the different order of its factors, is now fixed by the mathematical conditions the operators have to satisfy. The simple change of the sign in these conditions changes entirely the physical meaning of the formalism. In the case of the exclusion principle there can never exist a limiting case where such operators can be replaced by a classical field. Using this formalism of *Wigner* and *Jordan* I could prove under very general assumptions

---

[21] N. Bohr and L. Rosenfeld, *Kongelige Danske Videnskabernes Selskabs, matematisk-fysiske Meddelelser* **XII**, No. 8 (1933).

[22] P. Jordan and E. Wigner, *Zeitschrift für Physik* **47**, 631 (1928). Compare also V. Fock, *Zeitschrift für Physik* **75**, 622 (1932).

that a relativistic invariant theory describing systems of like particles with integer spin obeying the exclusion principle would always lead to the non commutability of physical quantities joined by a space-like vector.[23] This would violate a reasonable physical principle which holds good for particles with symmetrical states. In this way, by combination of the claims of relativistic invariance and the properties of field quantization, one step in the direction of an understanding of the connection of spin and symmetry class could be made.

The quantization of one-valued complex fields with a non-vanishing four-vector of the electric current gives the further result that particles both with positive and negative electric charge should exist and that they can be annihilated and generated in external electromagnetic fields.[24] This pair-generation and annihilation claimed by the theory makes it necessary to distinguish clearly the concept of charge density and of particle density. The latter concept does not occur in a relativistic wave theory either for fields carrying an electric charge or for neutral fields. This is satisfactory since the use of the particle picture and the uncertainty relations (for instance by analyzing imaginative experiments of the type of the γ-ray microscope) gives also the result that a localization of the particle is only possible with limited accuracy.[25] This holds both for the particles with integer and with half-integer spins. In a state with a mean value E of its energy, described by a wave packet with a mean frequency $\nu = E/h$, a particle can only be localized with an error $\Delta x > hc/E$ or $\Delta x > c/\nu$. For photons, it follows that the limit for the localization is the wave-length; for a particle with a finite rest-mass m and a characteristic length $\mu^{-1} = h/mc$, this limit is, in the rest system of the center of the wave packet that describes the state of the particles, given by $\Delta x > h/mc$ or $\Delta x > \mu^{-1}$.

Until now I have mentioned only those results of the application of quantum mechanics to classical fields which are satisfactory. We saw that the statements of this theory about averages of field-strength over finite space-time regions have a direct meaning while this is not so for the values of the field-strength at a certain point. Unfortunately in the classical expression of the energy of the field there enter averages of the squares of the field-strengths over such regions which cannot be expressed by the averages of the field-strengths themselves. This has the consequence that the zero-point energy of the vacuum derived from the quantized field becomes infinite, a result which is directly connected with the fact that the system considered has an infinite number of degrees of freedom. It is clear that this zero-point energy

---

[23] W. Pauli, *Annales de l'Institut Henri Poincaré* **6**, 137 (1936) and *Physical Review* **58**, 716 (1940).

[24] See Ref. 20.

[25] L. Landau and R. Peierls, *Zeitschrift für Physik* **69**, 56 (1931). Compare also the author's article in *Handbuch der Physik* **24**, Part 1, 1933, Chapter A, §2.

has no physical reality, for instance it is not the source of a gravitational field. Formally it is easy to subtract constant infinite terms which are independent of the state considered and never change; nevertheless it seems to me that already this result is an indication that a fundamental change in the concepts underlying the present theory of quantized fields will be necessary.

In order to clarify certain aspects of relativistic quantum theory I have discussed here, different from the historical order of events, the one-valued fields first. Already earlier *Dirac*[26] had formulated his relativistic wave equations corresponding to material particles with spin 1/2 using a pair of so-called spinors with two components each. He applied these equations to the problem of one electron in an electromagnetic field. In spite of the great success of this theory in the quantitative explanation of the fine structure of the energy levels of the hydrogen atom and in the computation of the scattering cross section of one photon by a free electron, there was one consequence of the theory which was obviously in contradiction with experience. The energy of the electron should have, according to this theory, both positive and negative values, and, in external electromagnetic fields, transitions should occur from states with one sign of energy to states with the other sign. On the other hand there exists in this theory a four-vector satisfying the continuity equation with a fourth component corresponding to a density which is definitely positive.

It can be shown that there is a similar situation for all fields, which, like the spinors, transform for rotations in ordinary space according to two-valued representations, thus changing their sign for a full rotation. We shall call briefly such quantities 'two-valued'. From the relativistic wave equations of such quantities one can always derive a four-vector bilinear in the field components which satisfies the continuity equation and for which the fourth component, at least after integration over the space, gives an essentially positive quantity. On the other hand, the expression for the total energy can have both the positive and the negative sign.

Is there any means to shift the minus sign from the energy back to the density of the four-vector? Then the latter could again be interpreted as charge density in contrast to particle density and the energy would become positive as it ought to be. You know that *Dirac*'s answer was that this could actually be achieved by application of the exclusion principle. In his lecture delivered here in Stockholm[27] he himself explained his proposal of a new interpretation of his theory, according to which in the actual vacuum all the states of negative energy should be occupied and only deviations of this state of smallest energy, namely holes in the sea of these occupied states are assumed to be observable. It is the exclusion principle which guarantees the stability of the

---

[26] P. A. M. Dirac, *Proceedings of the Royal Society* A, **117**, 610 (1928).
[27] See footnote 10.

vacuum, in which all states of negative energy are occupied. Furthermore the holes have all properties of particles with positive energy and positive electric charge, which in external electromagnetic fields can be produced and annihilated in pairs. These predicted positrons, the exact mirror images of the electrons, have been actually discovered experimentally.

The new interpretation of the theory obviously abandons in principle the standpoint of the one-body problem and considers a many-body problem from the beginning. It cannot any longer be claimed that *Dirac*'s relativistic wave equations are the only possible ones, but if one wants to have relativistic field equations corresponding to particles, for which the value 1/2 of their spin is known, one has certainly to assume the *Dirac* equations. Although it is logically possible to quantize these equations like classical fields, which would give symmetrical states of a system consisting of many such particles, this would be in contradiction with the postulate that the energy of the system has actually to be positive. This postulate is fulfilled on the other hand if we apply the exclusion principle and *Dirac*'s interpretation of the vacuum and the holes, which at the same time substitutes the physical concept of charge density with values of both signs for the mathematical fiction of a positive particle density. A similar conclusion holds for all relativistic wave equations with two-valued quantities as field components. This is the other step (historically the earlier one) in the direction of an understanding of the connection between spin and symmetry class.

I can only shortly note that *Dirac*'s new interpretation of empty and occupied states of negative energy can be formulated very elegantly with help of the formalism of *Jordan* and *Wigner* mentioned before. The transition from the old to the new interpretation of the theory can indeed be carried through simply by interchanging the meaning of one of the operators with that of its hermitean conjugate if they are applied to states originally of negative energy. The infinite 'zero charge' of the occupied states of negative energy is then formally analogous to the infinite zero-point energy of the quantized one-valued fields. The former has no physical reality either and is not the source of an electromagnetic field.

In spite of the formal analogy between the quantization of the one-valued fields leading to ensembles of like particles with symmetrical states and to particles fulfilling the exclusion principle described by two-valued operator quantities, depending on space and time coordinates, there is of course the fundamental difference that for the latter there is no limiting case, where the mathematical operators can be treated like classical fields. On the other hand we can expect that the possibilities and the limitations for the applications of the concepts of space and time, which find their expression in the different concepts of charge density and particle density, will be the same for charged particles with integer and with half integer spins.

The difficulties of the present theory become much worse, if the interaction of the electromagnetic field with matter is taken into consideration, since the well-known infinities regarding the energy of an electron in its own field, the so-called selfenergy, then occur as a result of the application of the usual perturbation formalism to this problem. The root of this difficulty seems to be the circumstance that the formalism of field quantization has only a direct meaning so long as the sources of the field can be treated as continuously distributed, obeying the laws of classical physics, and so long as only averages of field quantities over finite space-time regions are used. The electrons themselves, however, are essentially non-classical field sources.

At the end of this lecture I may express my critical opinion, that a correct theory should neither lead to infinite zero-point energies nor to infinite zero charges, that it should not use mathematical tricks to subtract infinities or singularities, nor should it invent a 'hypothetical world' which is only a mathematical fiction before it is able to formulate the correct interpretation of the actual world of physics.

From the point of view of logic, my report on 'Exclusion principle and quantum mechanics' has no conclusion. I believe that it will only be possible to write the conclusion if a theory will be established which will determine the value of the fine structure constant and will thus explain the atomistic structure of electricity, which is such an essential quality of all atomic sources of electric fields actually occurring in nature.

19. The Violation of Reflection Symmetries in the Laws of Atomic Physics*

Tsung-Dao Lee (∗ 1926) and Chang Ning Yang (∗ 1922)

In their office at the *Institute for Advanced Study* in Princeton. Photo by Alan W. Richard
(Courtesy: American Institute of Physics / Emilio Segrè Visual Archives)

* From *Experientia* **14**, 1–5 (1958).

The reflections of charge (C), space-coordinates (P) and time (T) and, particularly in connection with the space reflection, the distinction between polar vector and axial vector, scalar and pseudoscalar products are explained. The three different kinds of strong, medium (electromagnetic) and weak interactions are introduced. While the first two of them fulfil all reflection invariances mentioned separately, *Lee* and *Yang* showed (1956) that for the weak interactions no sufficient empirical evidence existed for the reflection invariances, and they also suggested experiments for checking them.

The qualitative aspect of the experimental results available in November 1957, which show the violation of the C and the P invariance for weak interactions, is reviewed. The methods here applied are beta-decay of oriented nuclei, polarisation of emitted electrons in beta-decay, beta-gamma correlation, asymmetry in the decay of μ-mesons generated by π-meson-decay. The solution of the θ-τ-puzzle by the assumption of a single particle (K-meson) without defined parity is mentioned.

In the concluding section some aspects of the unsolved theoretical problems of the deeper reasons for the symmetry violations of the weak interactions are briefly discussed which will possibly also lead into open cosmological questions.*

I. Categories of Interaction.
The Symmetries C, P and T

In discussing the degrees of symmetry of physical laws, it is useful to divide the interactions of physics into three categories: strong interactions, which include those between nucleons and between nucleons and mesons; electromagnetic interactions, of medium strength, which are also responsible for the outer shell of the atom; and weak interactions, to which category belong all the phenomena of beta-radioactivity associated with the emission or absorption of neutrinos, as well as the decay of Λ- and K-mesons, in which neutrinos are not involved.

Strong interactions have an even higher degree of symmetry than electromagnetic interactions; but for the purpose of this review it is not necessary to go into this in greater detail. It will suffice here to point out that these first two categories – as follows with great accuracy from the empirical material – are *separately invariant* with respect to the three following symmetry oper-

---

* This Summary in English appended to the original version is not reproduced in the German Edition of Pauli's *Aufsätze über Physik und Erkenntnistheorie*.

ations. Each of these operations associates with any possible physical state or process another one, which is likewise consistent with the laws of nature considered.

1. Particle-antiparticle Conjugation (Charge Symmetry) C^1

It is a general feature of the laws of nature governing the various "elementary particles" and their interaction that to each particle there belongs an antiparticle. If they are electrically charged this charge has opposite sign for particle and antiparticle. Conversely it is not necessary that every similar particle with opposite charge should actually be the antiparticle. Moreover, even in the case of neutral particles there can be antiparticles which are different from them. Thus the antineutron, whose existence has now also been experimentally established, has a magnetic moment directed oppositely to that of the neutron when the spins are in the same direction. It is still an open question whether the antineutrino corresponding to the neutrino is distinguishable from it experimentally, by the use of a conservation law for the difference between the total number of "light particles" (leptons) and the total number of "light antiparticles". A conservation law of this kind holds for the corresponding difference of "heavy particles" (baryons = nucleons and hyperons).

2. Space Reflection or Parity Symmetry P

This changes the sign of all three space-coordinates, thus assigning to every right-handed screw a left-handed screw. Technically this spatial operation of reflection distinguishes so-called "axial" vectors from "polar" vectors. It is only the latter that are properly characterised by a *length with direction*; the former are characterised by an *area with a sense of circulation*. Axial vectors, also called pseudovectors, do not change sign on reflection, polar vectors on the other hand do. A velocity is a polar vector, an angular momentum, in particular every "spin", is an axial vector.

The association of a direction with a pseudovector is therefore not invariant on reflection; in defining the association a left-handed screw has always preferential meaning before a right-handed one. The association of the normal to the area with a sense of circulation, which represents the axial vector, is invariant under rotations. Which of the two directions is to be chosen for this normal is however a matter of convention. To make it definite, *Ampère*'s float rules can be used, or equivalent prescriptions such as the following: let the surface be the horizontal plane of the paper; then if the sense of circulation is anticlockwise the associated normal direction is to point upwards towards the reader, and conversely downwards if the circulation is clock-

---

[1] The letter C denotes "charge".

wise. Expressions such as "spin direction" are always to be understood in this conventional sense.

While it is possible to form, from two ordinary (polar) vectors the P-invariant scalar (product of the lengths of the vectors into the cosine of the angle between them) it is possible, given a polar and an axial vector, to define only a *pseudoscalar* as their product, which is invariant for rotations of the coordinate system, but changes sign on spatial reflection. For in order to be able to form this pseudoscalar product, including its sign, one must assign to the axial vector (area with sense of circulation) a direction of the normal, by means of the above-mentioned convention. The pseudoscalar product is then the product of the magnitude of the area, the length of the polar vector and the cosine of the angle between its direction and the conventionally chosen direction of the normal to the area of the axial vector – a direction which is not invariant under reflections.

The laws of nature in a theory which is invariant under spatial reflections (P-invariant) must therefore not change their form when these pseudoscalars change their sign; in such a theory there corresponds to every process another equivalent process in which the pseudoscalars have the opposite sign.

The word *parity* (German Parität, French parité) in connection with an integer denotes the distinction of even and odd. The application of this concept to spatial reflections arises from the circumstance that in the case of invariance of all interactions under spatial reflections, the eigenstates, according to wave mechanics, are divided into "even" and "odd", in such a way that the wave functions of the even states remain unchanged when the signs of all the spatial coordinates are changed (reflection), while the wave functions of the odd states change sign. The sign thus defined, $+1$ for even and -1 for odd states is called the *parity* of the state.

For interactions that are not P-invariant there does not have to be a parity of the energy states, since in this case the wave functions do not necessarily behave in such a simple way under spatial reflection.

According to the usual conception (convention) electric charge does not change its sign under the operation P, so that electric field-strength is a polar, and magnetic field-strength an axial vector.

3. Time-reversal T

This is defined in such a way that the spatial coordinates and likewise the electric charge retain their sign. One can therefore define this operation T more precisely as *"reversal of the direction of motion"* of all processes. For example, the motion of a charged particle in an external magnetic field is T-invariant only if at the same time the external magnetic field-strength changes sign.

An important consequence of T-invariance is the vanishing of the electric dipole moment of nucleons (which is analogous to the vanishing of the electric moment of molecules in a particular energy state of rotation). It turns out that weak interactions are practically negligible in this connection.

The question of the scope of the symmetry of the laws of nature has once more come into the foreground of interest through recent experimental and theoretical investigations. The achievement of *Lee* and *Yang*,[2] for which the 1957 Nobel Prize for physics was awarded, was to point out and emphasise *that in the case of weak interactions (3rd category) the experimental evidence for the validity of these three symmetry operations was completely inadequate. They also described experiments by means of which this symmetry could be tested just for these weak interactions.*

These and similar experiments have meanwhile been repeatedly performed, and have definitely established a violation of C and P symmetry for weak interactions. This will be explained in more detail in the following section II. Here we may at once remark that the question of the validity of T-invariance for weak interactions is still undecided experimentally. Theoretically this is equivalent to the question of the validity of the combined operation CP (or in reverse order PC). For the so-called CPT-theorem holds under very general and well-established assumptions, including the Lorentz invariance characteristic of the special theory of relativity. This theorem states that on the basis of these general assumptions the invariance of the theory already follows for the combination (product) of all three operations C, P and T (in any order). The reader is referred to the literature for details.[3]

One consequence of this is that the masses of particles and antiparticles (more generally the energy values of a system of particles and those of the particles C-conjugate to them) must be equal to each other.

---

[2] T. D. Lee and C. N. Yang, *Physical Review* **104**, 254 (1956).

[3] The CPT-theorem was first clearly recognised by G. Lüders, *Det Kongelige Danske Videnskabernes Selskabs, matematisk-fysiske Meddelelser* **28**, No. 5 (1954). See also *Annals of Physics* (New York) **2**, 1 (1957). Further references: J. Schwinger, *Physical Review* **82**, 914 (1951); W. Pauli in *Niels Bohr and the Development of Physics* (Pergamon Press, London 1955), p. 30; for non-local theories a condition equivalent to the CPT-theorem, which is satisfied identically for local theories, has been given by R. Jost, *Helvetica Physica Acta* **30**, 409 (1957); for further applications see T. D. Lee, R. Oehme and C. N. Yang, *Physical Review* **106**, 340 (1957).

II. Experimental Evidence for the Violation
of Left-right Symmetry (P) and Charge Symmetry (C)

Here we can give only a brief report on the qualitative side of the experiments, and must refer the reader to the literature for quantitative questions, which are still in a state of flux.

The first, though by no means the simplest experiment consists in the orientation of the spins of radioactive nuclei, for which a highly-developed special technique employing magnetic fields at low temperatures was already available. One then investigates the question whether there is an asymmetry in the direction of emission of electrons (negatons e_- or positons e_+) relative to the plane (invariant under reflections) of the nuclear spin, to which the vector I is conventionally perpendicular. In other words one investigates the distribution of the pseudoscalar $(I \cdot p_e) = Ip_e \cos\theta$, where p_e is the momentum vector of the emitted electrons, and θ denotes the angle between I and p_e. If the theory is invariant with respect to reflection, this distribution should be symmetric with respect to 0; that is, relative to the plane of the spin, as many electrons should go in a forward direction θ as in a backward direction $\pi - \theta$. Experiments[4] performed with Co^{60} (e_-) and with Co^{58} (e_+) gave a marked asymmetry; on the average

$$(I \cdot p_e) < 0 \text{ for } e_-\text{-decay},$$
$$(I \cdot p_e) > 0 \text{ for } e_+\text{-decay}.$$

More detailed discussion[5] shows that this already implies a violation of C-symmetry. For in a C-invariant theory this effect must vanish, as long as the Coulomb interaction between the nucleus and emitted electron is neglected. Moreover at a nuclear charge number of 27 for Co the influence of the Coulomb interaction is still far too small to be capable of explaining by itself the observed asymmetry effect.

A related simpler experiment is the measurement of the polarisation of electrons emitted in a given direction in beta-decay. Here the polarisation is determined by the plane, with sense of circulation, (defined in the system in which the electron is at rest) of the electron spin; the associated conventional

---

[4]   C. S. Wu, E. Ambler, R. W. Hayward, D. D. Hoppes and R. P. Hudson, *Physical Review* **105**, 1413 (1957): Co^{60}; H. Postma, W. J. Huiskamp, A. R. Miedema, M. J. Steenland, H. A. Tolhoek and C. J. Gorter, *Physica* **23**, 259 (1957): Co^{58}; E. Ambler, R. W. Hayward, D. D. Hoppes, R. P. Hudson and C. S. Wu, *Physical Review* **106**, 1361 (1957): Co^{60}, Co^{58}; analogous experiment with polarised neutrons: M. T. Burgy, R. J. Epstein, V. E. Krohn, T. B. Novey, S. Raboy, G. R. Ringo and V. L. Telegdi, *Physical Review* **107**, 1731 (1957).
[5]   T. D. Lee and C. N. Yang, *Physical Review* **104**, 254 (1956); T. D. Lee, R. Oehme and C. N. Yang, *Physical Review* **106**, 340 (1957).

direction of the vector σ_e forms with this plane a right-handed screw, seen from the particle; and one measures the pseudoscalar $(\sigma_e \cdot p_e)$.

The experiments[6] showed strong polarisation, in the sense that for e_--decay, on the average $(\sigma_e \cdot p_e) < 0$, i.e., axial vector σ_e and p_e form a left-handed screw; for e_+-decay, on the average $(\sigma_e \cdot p_e) > 0$, i.e., the axial vector σ_e and p_e form a right-handed screw.

Of a similar nature is the measurement of the sense of the circular polarisation of photons whose emission in a second process follows the emission of electrons (beta-decay in the excited nucleus). In this case the pseudoscalar $(p_e \cdot \sigma_\gamma)$ is measured. The result of this experiment was also positive.[7]

We now come to the important experiment, also carried out at the instigation of *Lee* and *Yang*, on the decay of the μ-meson, which yielded a positive result[8] at about the same time as the first experiment with directed nuclear spins.

Consider π-mesons which decay into a μ-meson and a neutrino, in accordance with

$$\pi \to \mu + \nu$$

whereupon the μ-meson subsequently decays into two neutrinos (more precisely into a neutrino ν and an antineutrino $\bar{\nu}$) as well as an electron:

$$\mu \to e + \bar{\nu} + \nu \, .$$

The first reaction is the polariser of the μ-meson, the second the analyser. The observed asymmetry of the electron emission relative to the plane perpendicular to the direction of motion of the μ-mesons proves that reflection symmetry is violated in both reactions. As a subsidiary result of the strong polarisation with respect to their direction of motion of the μ-mesons produced, the possibility arose of an accurate measurement of their magnetic

---

[6] First carried out by H. Frauenfelder, R. Bobone, E. von Goeler, N. Levine, H. R. Lewis, R. N. Peacock, A. Rossi and G. de Pasquali, *Physical Review* **106**, 386 (1957): Co^{60}; afterwards by M. Goldhaber, L. Grodzins and A. W. Sunyar, *Physical Review* **106**, 826 (1957): Bremsstrahlung; S. S. Hanna and R. S. Preston, *Physical Review* **106**, 1363 (1957): Cu^{64}; H. Frauenfelder, A. O. Hanson, N. Levine, A. Rossi and G. de Pasquali, *Physical Review* **107**, 643 (1957): Møller scattering; M. Deutsch, B. Gittelmann, R. W. Bauer, L. Grodzins and A. W. Sunyar, *Physical Review* **107**, 1733 (1957): Ga^{66}, Cl^{34}; A. de Shalit, S. Kuperman, H. J. Lipkin and T. Rothem, *Physical Review* **107**, 1459 (1957): double scattering; F. Boehm, T. B. Novey, C. A. Barnes and B. Stech, *Physical Review* **108**, 1497 (1957): N^{13}.

[7] H. Schopper, *Philosophical Magazine* **2**, 710 (1957); H. Appel and H. Schopper, *Zeitschrift für Physik* **149**, 103 (1957); F. Boehm and A. H. Wapstra, *Physical Review* **106**, 1364 (1957); **107**, 1202 and 1462 (1957).

[8] R. L. Garwin, L. M. Ledermann and M. Weinrich, *Physical Review* **105**, 1415 (1957): cyclotron; J. I. Friedman and V. L. Telegdi, *Physical Review* **105**, 1681 (1957): photographic plates; see also D. Berley, T. Coffin, R. L. Garwin, L. M. Ledermann and M. Weinrich, *Physical Review* **106**, 835 (1957).

moment. Further experiments to determine the sign of the pseudoscalar $(\sigma_\mu \cdot p_\mu)$ are in progress.

All the experiments cited here are in agreement with a *special model* of the neutrino, which has been proposed independently by several authors.[9] It is usually described, somewhat inaccurately, as the "two component theory", but I should like to call it in its two variants "*R*-model" and "*L*-model" for short. The characteristic feature of the "*R*-model" is that only the neutrino whose spin and direction of motion form a right-handed screw can exist, as well as the associated antineutrino whose spin and momentum will then *per contra* necessarily form a left-handed screw. This means therefore that in the case of the neutrino it is only for $(\sigma_\nu \cdot p_\nu) > 0$ or in the case of the antineutrino only for $(\sigma_\nu \cdot p_\nu) < 0$ that any interaction takes place with other particles. For such a model *C*- and *P*-invariance are necessarily violated, *CP*- and *T*-invariance are possible but not necessary, and a conservation law holds for the difference between particle and antiparticle numbers for leptons. The experiments so far do not however suffice to establish with certainty the correctness of this special model. For in order to determine the constants in the most general interaction of beta-decay without *P*- and *C*-symmetry further experiments are necessary, which in themselves have nothing to do with parity, and determine the directional correlation of electron and neutrino on emission. One cannot measure this directly; but the recoil of the heavy particles produced (the nuclei, or in the case of decay of the free neutron, the protons) is susceptible to measurement. From these the direction and magnitude of the neutrino's momentum can then be deduced by the law of conservation of momentum. Although these measurements have now been significantly facilitated by the powerful radioactive sources available in uranium reactors, they are still in a confused, mutually contradictory state, and their further development must be awaited.

Even if the special *R*-model and *L*-model respectively of the neutrino should prove correct for all its reactions, this would scarcely give a sufficient explanation for the violation of *P*-symmetry in the case of weak interactions in general. For as *Lee* and *Yang* already remarked in their first paper,[10] there are almost certainly also interactions violating parity, in which the neutrino does not take part at all. In the so-called "θ-τ puzzle" the assumption of *P*-invariance (conservation of parity in the reactions involved) leads to the necessity of assuming several particles having approximately equal masses and lifetimes.[11] No explanation with any degree of plausibility has been found

[9]   A. Salam, *Nuovo Cimento* **5**, 229 (1957); T. D. Lee and C. N. Yang, *Physical Review* **105**, 1671 (1957); L. Landau, *Nuclear Physics* **3**, 127 (1957).

[10] See footnote 2.

[11] See in this connection R. Dalitz, *Philosophical Magazine* **44**, 1068 (1953); E. Fabri, *Nuovo Cimento* **11**, 479 (1954); also Proceedings of the sixth Rochester Conference (1956).

for this. If parity violation is accepted, it is however sufficient to assume one and the same particle (K-meson) in these various decay reactions, which then does not necessarily have a parity.

III. Survey of Theoretical Problems

The deeper unsolved difficulties of quantised field theories, which manifest themselves in mathematical divergencies, do not come to light in the case of weak interactions, in which one can be satisfied with the lowest approximations of perturbation theory. Nor does the fact that a theoretical derivation and interpretation of the mass- and spin-values of the particles in nature does not exist, make itself directly felt if a purely phenomenological standpoint is adopted for the theory in regard to the new phenomena. At the present stage of the theory there appears to be an abundance of formal possibilities rather than a formal inexplicability in regard to the empirical violation of the C- and P-symmetries.

Although it has turned out on this occasion also to be methodologically correct first of all to put the question as to the how, and to postpone the more profound question as to the why, yet the latter question is there, unanswered, and is likely to become more insistent in the future. I think it is a mistake to take refuge from it in what appears to me to be a superficial opportunist "hush-hush philosophy" ("Beschwichtigungsphilosophie"[12]), or in overly simple "patent solutions".

From this point one can proceed in two directions. First the question of why weak interactions violate the C- and P-symmetries can be replaced by the different question of why these symmetries are present in strong and in electromagnetic interactions. One can try to reduce these symmetries to other more special properties of these interactions.

Secondly one can try to discover and to justify a connection between symmetry violations in the small and properties of the universe in the large.[13] But this goes beyond the possibilities of theories of gravitation as now known. Gravitational actions, which are not included in the three categories of interaction introduced at the beginning, must of course be characterized as still much weaker than the "weak interactions". However, according to *Einstein*'s theory of gravitation, which is contradicted by no known phenomena, gravitational actions satisfy all the symmetries C, P and T. Moreover direct

---

[12] Expression due to *Paul Ehrenfest*.

[13] T. D. Lee: "Weak Interaction", in *Proceedings of the seventh Rochester Conference* (1957), Section on *Mach's principle*; for the general discussion see also E. P. Wigner, *Reviews of Modern Physics* **29**, 255 (1957).

influences of the gravitational field on the atomic phenomena under discussion are completely negligible in practice.

In order to achieve anything beyond vague speculations in the question of the connection between the small and the large some essential new ideas are still lacking. This is not, however, to assert definitely the impossibility of such a connection.

Thus the new empirical results discussed here lead us to problems whose solution perhaps still lies in the remote future.

*   *   *

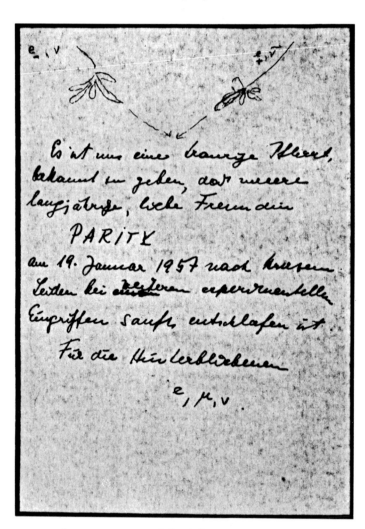

Announcement of the fall of parity by Pauli

20. On the Earlier and More Recent History of the Neutrino *

Pauli and Chien-Shiung Wu (∗ 1912)

Photo taken in Rehovot, Israel, in September 1957 (Courtesy: American Institute of
Physics / Emilio Segrè Visual Archives)

---

* Extended and (especially in Section 5) supplemented version (September 1958) of a lecture to the *Zürcher Naturforschende Gesellschaft* on 21st January, 1957 (immediately
after the announcement of the first experiments on parity violation). – An independent
translation of this essay is contained in Klaus Winter, ed.: *Neutrino Physics*. (Cambridge University Press, Cambridge, 1991), pp. 1–24. It was done before the existence
of Schlapp's translation was known (see the Preface by C. P. Enz).

Mit vielen anderen Physikern sehe ich mit Freude Ihrem 80. Geburtstag am 7. November dieses Jahres entgegen. Noch ist es wohl zu früh, Ihnen zu gratulieren, doch dürfte es nicht zu früh sein, Ihnen schon jetzt ein Geschenk zu machen. Es war mir nicht möglich, zu diesem Termin etwas fertig zum Druck zu haben. Doch konnte ich rechtzeitig ein getyptes Manuskript einer erweiterten Fassung meines Vortrages über die Geschichte des Neutrinos fertigstellen, das ich hier für Sie persönlich beilege. (Natürlich ist es die Idee, daß Sie es behalten mögen.)

Sie sind die erste, die dieses Manuskript erhält und ich bin sehr gespannt, ob Sie an meiner Darstellung, insbesondere der älteren Geschichte, etwas auszusetzen haben. Ich habe wesentlich mehr gelesen, als das, was im Manuskript zitiert ist. Doch scheint mir das Angeführte für die heutigen Leser genügend. Auch die ältere Geschichte findet heute vielfach Interesse, insbesondere hat Herr Reines (Los Alamos) mich um eine Kopie gebeten. Sobald eine englische Übersetzung vorliegen wird, werde ich sie ihm schicken.

Letter from Pauli to Lise Meitner, October 3, 1958

I. Problems of Interpretation
of the Continuous Energy Spectrum of Beta Rays

The continuous energy spectrum of beta rays, discovered by *J. Chadwick* in 1914,[1] immediately raised difficult problems of theoretical interpretation. Was it to be ascribed directly to the primary electrons emitted by the radioactive nucleus, or to secondary processes? The first view, which turned out to be the correct one, was advocated by *C. D. Ellis*,[2] the second by *L. Meitner*.[3] The latter appealed to the fact, known from alpha and gamma rays, that nuclei possess discrete energy levels. She focused the discussion on the discrete energies of the electrons which are likewise observed in many beta-radioactive nuclei. *Ellis* was able to interpret these as electrons ejected from the outer shells by monochromatic nuclear gamma rays by internal conversion, and to relate them to the observed X-ray lines. According to *L. Meitner*'s theory however, at least one of the electrons of discrete energy was a genuine primary electron from the nucleus, which could then likewise eject other secondary

---

[1] J. Chadwick, *Verhandlungen der Deutschen Physikalischen Gesellschaft* **16**, 383 (1914).
[2] C. D. Ellis, *Proceedings of the Royal Society* (London) A **101**, 1 (1922).
[3] L. Meitner, *Zeitschrift für Physik* **9**, 131 and 145 (1922); **11**, 35 (1922).

electrons of lower energies from the outer shells.[4] This postulated primary electron of discrete energy could however never be detected. Moreover there are beta-radioactive nuclei, such as RaE, which do not emit gamma rays and in which moreover the electrons of discrete energy are completely absent. In the controversy which arose between *Ellis* and *L. Meitner*, *Ellis*[5] in 1922 summarised his position as follows:

Frl. *Meitner's* theory is a very interesting attempt to give a simple explanation of β-decay. The experimental facts do not however fit into the framework of this theory, and it looks very much as if the simple analogy between α- and β-decay cannot be maintained. β-decay is a much more complicated process and the general indications I have given about it appear to me at the moment to involve a minimum of constraint."

The question which had been raised of the interpretation of the continuous beta spectrum was obviously not brought any nearer to being answered by this statement, and discussion continued on whether it was primary (*Ellis*) or whether an originally discrete energy was broadened out into a continuum by subsequent secondary processes (*L. Meitner*). This controversy however finally came to an end in an experiment: *the absolute measurement of the heat of absorption of the beta electrons*. It was known as a result of counting experiments that *one* electron is emitted from the nucleus per decay. In the event of subsequent secondary processes the heat measured in the calorimeter per decay should correspond to the upper limit of the beta spectrum; in the event of a primary process, however, to its mean energy. The measurement was carried out with RaE by *C. D. Ellis* and *W. A. Wooster*.[6] The result was a quantity of heat per decay whose value, converted into volts, was 344,000 volts $\pm$ 10%, which was in good agreement with the mean energy of the beta spectrum. The upper limit of the beta spectrum on the other hand would have corresponded to about a million volts, which was completely excluded by the experiments. *Ellis* emphasised that his experiment still left open the possibility that the energy balance was produced by a continuous gamma spectrum which would not have been absorbed in the calorimeter and would have escaped observation.

  L. Meitner was not yet convinced by this experiment and immediately resolved to repeat it with improved apparatus. For this purpose *W. Orthmann*, a co-worker of *Nernst*, constructed a special differential calorimeter. With its aid the heat measurement of the beta-electrons of RaE was now repeated

---

[4] In a later paper (*Zeitschrift für Physik* **34**, 807 (1925)) *L. Meitner* showed experimentally that, contrary to an earlier view of *Ellis*, the γ-rays are emitted by the nucleus produced *after* the emission of the α- or β-particles.

[5] C. D. Ellis, *Zeitschrift für Physik* **10**, 303 (1922).

[6] C. D. Ellis and W. A. Wooster, *Proceedings of the Royal Society* (London) A **117**, 109 (1927).

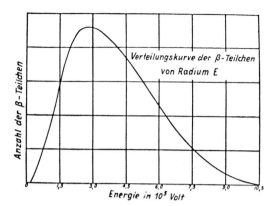

Fig. 1. Continuous beta spectrum of RaE

with greater accuracy.[7] The result, 337,000 volts ± 6%, completely confirmed *Ellis* and *Wooster*'s result.

Going still further, *L. Meitner* showed, by special experiments with counters, that the continuous gamma spectrum considered by *Ellis* was not present.

According to these experimental results only two theoretical possibilities remained for the *interpretation of the continuous beta spectrum.*

1) Energy conservation holds only statistically in those interactions which are responsible for beta-radioactivity.
2) The energy law is strictly valid for each primary individual process, but in this process another very penetrating radiation, consisting of *new neutral particles*, is emitted along with the electrons.

The first possibility was advocated by *Bohr*, the second by myself. Before we go into the history of these further questions, which finally gave a verdict in favour of the second possibility, we must briefly sketch the development of our ideas on nuclear structure.

2. Neutrino and Nuclear Structure

After *Rutherford*'s first experiments on artificial nuclear transmutations the generally accepted idea about the structure of nuclei was that they consisted of protons and electrons. It was from this point of view that nuclear structure

---

[7]   L. Meitner and W. Orthmann, *Zeitschrift für Physik* **60**, 143 (1930).

was discussed by *Rutherford* himself in his celebrated Bakerian Lecture.[8] This included among others the hypothesis of the existence of a nucleus of charge 0 and its possible properties. It soon became known[9] that *Rutherford* had proposed the name *neutron* for this new hypothetical particle. He thought of it as a combination, of nuclear dimensions, of a proton and an electron. Accordingly he set experiments on foot in his laboratory to search for this neutron in hydrogen discharges, a search which was bound to prove fruitless.

The idea that nuclei consist of protons and electrons was abandoned only very reluctantly and slowly. In this connection the quantum or wave mechanics set up in 1927 was finally decisive. According to this there are two kinds of particles, the antisymmetric fermions and the symmetric bosons. Composite particles are fermions or bosons according as the number of fermions they contain is odd or even. Corresponding results hold for spin, fermions always having half-integral and bosons integral spin. Since it soon turned out that electrons and protons are fermions, the idea that these are the sole building-stones of all nuclei led to the conclusion that the parity of the charge number should determine the symmetry character of the nucleus. This conclusion was however not found to hold in practice. The first counter example was the "nitrogen anomaly" as we called it at the time; for it was shown by *R. Kronig*[10] and by *W. Heitler* and *G. Herzberg*[11] from band spectra that nitrogen with charge number 7 and mass number 14 has spin 1 and Bose statistics. Other analogous cases followed later, such as Li 6 (charge 3, mass 6) and the deuteron (charge 1, mass 2), both likewise having spin 1 and *Bose* statistics. The final result was that it is the parity of the mass number, not that of the charge number, that determines the symmetry character of the nuclei.

I now tried to link up this problem of spin and statistics of the nuclei with the other problem of the continuous beta spectrum, without giving up the energy law, by the idea of a new neutral particle. In December 1930, when the heavy neutron had not yet been found experimentally, I sent a letter on this subject to a conference of physicists in Tübingen, at which *Geiger* and *L. Meitner* were present.[12]

---

[8] E. Rutherford, *Proceedings of the Royal Society* (London) A **97**, 374 (1920); for the neutral nucleus see p. 396.
[9] Cf. for example J. L. Glasson, *Philosophical Magazine* **42**, 596 (1921).
[10] R. Kronig, *Die Naturwissenschaften* **16**, 335, 1928.
[11] W. Heitler and G. Herzberg, *Die Naturwissenschaften* **17**, 673 (1929).
[12] I am greatly indebted to *L. Meitner* for letting me have a copy of this letter, which she had kept.

Open Letter to the Group of Radioactive Persons
at the Conference of the District Society in Tübingen

Physical Institute of the *Federal Institute of Technology*, Zürich

Zürich, 4 December 1930
Gloriastr.

Dear Radioactive Ladies and Gentlemen,
As the bearer of these lines, for whom I pray the favour of a hearing will explain in more detail, I have, in connection with the "wrong" statistics of the N and Li 6-nuclei as well as the continuous β-spectrum, hit upon a desperate remedy for rescuing the "alternation law"[13] of statistics and the energy law. This is the possibility that there might exist in the nuclei electrically neutral particles, which I shall call neutrons, which have spin 1/2, obey the exclusion principle and moreover differ from light quanta in not travelling with the velocity of light. The mass of the neutrons would have to be of the same order as the electronic mass and in any case not greater than 0.01 proton masses. – The continuous β-spectrum would then be understandable on the assumption that in β-decay, along with the electron a neutron is emitted as well, in such a way that the sum of the energies of neutron and electron is constant.
There is now the further question of what forces act on the neutrons. The most likely model for the neutron seems to me, on wave-mechanical grounds, (the bearer of these lines knows more about this) to be that the stationary neutron is a magnetic dipole with a certain moment μ. The experiments of course require that the ionising action of such a neutron cannot be greater than that of a γ-ray, and then μ could very likely not be greater than $e \times 10^{-13}$ cm.
I do not in the meantime trust myself to publish anything about this idea, and in the first place turn confidently to you, dear radioactive folk, with the question – how would things stand with regard to the experimental detection of such a neutron if it possessed an equal or perhaps ten times greater penetrating power than a γ-ray?
I admit that my remedy may perhaps appear unlikely from the start, since one probably would long ago have seen the neutrons if they existed. But 'nothing venture, nothing win', and the gravity of the situation with regard to the continuous β-spectrum is illuminated by a pronouncement of my respected predecessor in office, Herr Debye, who recently said to me in Brussels "Oh, it's best not to think about it at all – like the new taxes". One ought therefore to discuss seriously every avenue of rescue. – So, dear radioactive folk, put it to the test and judge. – Unfortunately I cannot appear personally in Tübingen, since on account of a dance which takes place in Zürich on the night of 6 to 7 December I cannot get away from here.
With many greetings to you, likewise also to Herr Back.

Your most humble servant,   W. Pauli

You see how modest were the figures I still had in mind at that time. Actually the penetrating power of the particles nowadays called neutrinos is about 100 light-years Pb instead of 10 cm, the factor as compared with gamma-rays 10^{16} or 10^{17} instead of 10, while the rest mass and the magnetic

---

[13] Its enunciation is: Exclusion Principle (*Fermi* statistics) and half-integral spin if the total number of particles is odd, *Bose* statistics and integral spin if the total number is even.

moment are theoretically 0, and the experimental upper limits are 0.002 electron masses and 10^{-9} *Bohr* magnetons.[14]

Soon there came a letter from *Geiger* in reply to mine. He had discussed my question with the others in Tübingen as well, especially with *L. Meitner*. Unfortunately I no longer have this letter, but I remember that his reply was positive and encouraging: from the experimental point of view my new particles were quite possible.

I had soon given up again the idea that the neutral particles emitted in beta-decay are at the same time constituents of the nuclei, on account of the empirical values of the nuclear masses.

In a lecture in Pasadena in June 1931 on the occasion of a meeting of the American Physical Society, I gave the first public report on my idea of new highly penetrating neutral particles in beta decay. I no longer regarded them as building stones of the nucleus, and for this reason I no longer called them neutrons on this occasion, but used no special name for them. However, the matter still seemed to me very uncertain, and I did not have my lecture printed.

That same year, 1931, I travelled direct from U.S.A. to Rome, where a great international congress on nuclear physics took place in October. There I met *Fermi* in particular, who at once showed lively interest in my idea, and a very positive attitude to my new neutral particles; and also *Bohr*, who in complete contrast defended his idea that in beta decay energy was conserved only statistically. Soon afterwards he published this idea in his Faraday Lecture.[15] To give you a notion of his ideas at this time I quote the following passage.[16]

"At the present stage of atomic theory, however, we may say that we have no argument, either empirical or theoretical, for upholding the energy principle in the case of β-ray disintegrations, and are even led to complications and difficulties in trying to do so. Of course, a radical departure from this principle would imply strange consequences, in case such a process could be reversed. Indeed, if, in a collision process, an electron could attach itself to a nucleus with loss of its mechanical individuality, and subsequently be recreated as a β-ray, we should find that the energy of this β-ray would generally differ from that of the original electron. Still, just as the account of those aspects of atomic constitution essential for the explanation of the ordinary physical and chemical properties of matter implies a renunciation of the classical idea of causality, the features of atomic stability, still deeper-lying, responsible for the existence and the properties of atomic nuclei, may force us to renounce the very idea of energy balance. I shall not enter further into such speculations and their possible bearing on the much debated question of the source of stellar energy. I have touched upon them here mainly to emphasise that in atomic theory, notwithstanding all the recent progress, we must still be prepared for new surprises."

---

[14] C. L. Cowan jr. and F. Reines, *Physical Review* **107**, 528 (1957).
[15] N. Bohr, Faraday Lecture, "Chemistry and the Quantum theory of Atomic Constitution." *Journal of the Chemical Society* (London) 1932, pp. 349–384.
[16] N. Bohr, l. c., p. 383.

In regard to the more general possibility of surprises in the case of the interactions we now call "weak", *Bohr* was, in a different context, to be right in the end. However his idea of a merely statistical validity of the energy law for these interactions did not appear acceptable either to me or to *Fermi*. We had many private discussions about this in Rome in 1931. I saw no theoretical reason for regarding the law of conservation of energy as less certain than, for example, the law of conservation of electric charge. From the empirical point of view the decisive factor seemed to me to be whether the beta spectra of the electrons exhibit a sharp upper limit, or whether they exhibit a Poisson distribution extending to infinity. In the first case my idea of new particles would in my opinion be assured.[17] At this time the question was not yet experimentally decided, but *Ellis*, who was also present in Rome, already had plans for a renewed attack on this experimental problem.

The following year, 1932, *Chadwick* discovered the long-sought neutron of charge number 0 and mass number 1, by bombarding light nuclei with alpha particles. *Fermi*, in seminars in Rome, thereupon named my new particle, which is emitted in beta decay, *neutrino*, to distinguish it from the heavy neutron;[18] this Italian name was soon in general use. Thereafter the new idea of nuclear structure developed rapidly, according to which the nuclei consist of protons and neutrons; these are nowadays called "nucleons", and both are fermions with spin 1/2. The idea was originated independently by several authors; in Italy it was advocated by *Majorana*, with *Fermi*'s support.

Thus, a general clarification followed at the Solvay Conference on atomic nuclei in Brussels in October 1933, where among other speakers *Joliot* and *Chadwick* reported on their experimental discoveries of positron decay and of the neutron, and *Heisenberg* reported on nuclear structure. *Fermi* and *Bohr* too were again present. It was now evident that on the basis of this idea of nuclear structure the neutrinos, as they were now called, must be fermions, in order that the statistics may be conserved in beta decay. Furthermore, *Ellis* gave a report on new experiments by his pupil *W. J. Henderson*,[19] which confirmed the sharp upper limit of the beta spectrum and its interpretation.

On this basis of the new situation my earlier caution in postponing publication now seemed superfluous.

After *Heisenberg*'s report I gave my ideas on the neutrino (as it was now called) in the discussion; this also appeared in print in the Report of the Conference[20] and is reproduced here.

---

[17] For the theoretical interpretation of the upper limit of the spectrum see also C. D. Ellis and N. F. Mott, *Proceedings of the Royal Society* (London) A **141**, 502 (1933).

[18] I owe this information to Sig. *E. Amaldi*.

[19] W. J. Henderson, *Proceedings of the Royal Society* (London) A **147**, 572 (1934).

[20] *Septième Conseil de Physique Solvay* 1933: *Noyaux Atomiques*. Paris 1934, p. 324f.

La difficulté provenant de l'existence du spectre continu des rayons β consiste, comme on sait, en ce que la durée moyenne de vie des noyaux qui émettent ces rayons, comme celle des noyaux des corps radioactifs qui en résultent, possède des valeurs bien déterminées. On en conclut nécessairement que l'état, ainsi que l'énergie et la masse du noyau qui reste après l'expulsion de la particule β sont aussi bien déterminés. Je n'insiste pas sur les efforts qu'on pourrait tenter pour échapper à cette conclusion, mais je crois, conformément à l'opinion de M. *Bohr*, qu'on se heurtera toujours à des difficultés insurmontables dans l'explication des faits expérimentaux.

Dans cet ordre d'idées, deux interprétations des expériences se présentent. Celle que défend M. *Bohr* admet que les lois de la conservation de l'énergie et de l'impulsion sont en défaut quand il s'agit d'un processus nucléaire où des particules légères jouent un role essentiel. Cette hypothèse ne me paraît pas satisfaisante, ni même plausible. D'abord, la charge électrique est conservée dans le processus, et je ne vois pas pourquoi la conservation de la charge serait plus fondamentale que celle de l'énergie et de l'impulsion. Ensuite, ce sont précisément des relations énergétiques qui règlent plusieurs propriétés caractéristiques des spectres β (existence d'une limite supérieure et rapport avec les spectres γ, critère de stabilité de *Heisenberg*). Si les lois de conservation n'étaient pas valables, il faudrait bien conclure de ces relations qu'une désintégration β est toujours accompagnée d'une perte d'énergie et jamais d'un gain; cette conclusion implique une irréversibilité des processus à l'égard du temps, qui ne me paraît guère acceptable.

En juin 1931, à l'occasion d'une conférence à Pasadena, j'ai proposé l'interprétation suivante: les lois de conservation restent valables, l'expulsion des particules β étant accompagnée d'une radiation très pénétrante de particules neutres, qui n'a pas été observée jusqu'ici. La somme des énergies de la particule β et de la particule neutre (ou des particules neutres, puisqu'on ne sait pas s'il n'y en a qu'une ou s'il y en a plusieurs) émises par le noyau dans un seul processus, sera égale à l'énergie qui correspond à la limite supérieure du spectre β. Il va sans dire que nous n'admettons pas seulement la conservation de l'énergie, mais aussi celle de l'impulsion, celle de l'impulsion angulaire et celle du caractère de la statistique dans tous les processus élémentaires.

Quant aux propriétés de ces particules neutres, les poids atomiques des éléments radioactifs nous apprennent tout d'abord que leur masse ne peut pas dépasser beaucoup celle de l'électron. Pour les distinguer des neutrons lourds, M. *Fermi* a proposé le nom «neutrino». Il est possible que la masse propre des neutrinos soit égale à zéro, de sorte qu'ils devraient se propager avec la vitesse de la lumière, comme les photons. Toutefois leur pouvoir pénétrant dépasserait de beaucoup celui des photons de même énergie. Il me paraît admissible que les neutrinos possèdent un spin 1/2 et qu'ils obéissent à la statistique de *Fermi*, bien que les expériences ne nous fournissent aucune preuve directe de cette hypothèse. Nous ne savons rien de l'interaction des neutrinos avec les autres particules matérielles et avec les photons: l'hypothèse qu'ils possèdent un moment magnétique, comme je l'avais proposé autrefois (la théorie de *Dirac* conduit à prévoir la possibilité de l'existence de particules neutres magnétiques), ne me paraît du tout fondée.

Dans cet ordre d'idées, l'étude expérimentale du bilan de l'impulsion dans les désintégrations β constitue un problème de la plus haute importance; on peut prévoir que les difficultés seront très grandes à cause de la petitesse de l'énergie du noyau de recul.

The difficulty of the recoil measurements emphasised here has only quite recently been finally overcome.

Following on this *Chadwick* reported on the first unsuccessful attempts to detect absorption of neutrinos experimentally; these experiments gave an upper limit of 0.001 magnetons for the magnetic moment of the neutrino. *Bohr*'s opposition had become appreciably weaker as compared with his Faraday lecture. Having become very cautious about asserting the non-validity of the energy law, he confined himself to his much more general proposition that no one knew what surprises might still be in store for us in this field.

Incidentally it was not until 1936[21] that he completely accepted the validity of the energy law in beta decay and the neutrino, by which time *Fermi*'s theory had already been successfully developed.

3. The Creation of a Theory of Beta Decay

Stimulated by the discussions of the Solvay Conference, *Fermi*[22] developed his theory of beta decay soon afterwards. Part of *Fermi*'s conclusions relating to the form of the beta spectrum and the deduction of the rest mass of the neutrino were also drawn independently and simultaneously by *F. Perrin*,[23] who was likewise present at the Solvay Conference. Indeed, for this purpose a complete theory of the interaction is not necessary, if one confines oneself to so-called "allowed" transitions, in which the non-relativistic approximation for the nucleons in the nucleus is sufficient. Apart from the corrections, of importance only for larger nuclear charges, due to the Coulomb interaction of nucleus and electron, the shape of the beta spectrum is completely determined for these transitions by the statistical weight factor $\varrho(E_e)$ of the density of states in phase space. This factor, which is very sensitive to the value of the rest mass m_ν of the neutrino, is given by

$$\varrho(E_e)dE_e = p_e^2 dp_e p_\nu^2 \frac{dp_\nu}{dE_\nu} = p_e E_e p_\nu E_\nu dE_e \ . \tag{1}$$

Here the natural units $\hbar = c = 1$ have been used, the indices e, ν refer to electrons and neutrinos respectively, and energy E and momentum p are related by $E^2 = p^2 + m^2$, so that $dE/dp = p/E$.

If ΔE is the energy difference of the nucleus in the initial and final states of the decay, the energy law requires that

$$E_\nu = \Delta E - E_e \ . \tag{2}$$

Since m_ν is the minimal energy of the neutrino, the upper limit E_0 of the electron energy in the spectrum satisfies

$$E_0 = \Delta E - m_\nu \ , \tag{3}$$

---

[21] N. Bohr, *Nature* **138**, 25 (1936).
[22] E. Fermi, *Ricerca Scientifica* **2**, Part 12 (1933). *Zeitschrift für Physik* **88**, 161 (1934).
[23] F. Perrin, *Comptes Rendus* **197**, 1625 (1933).

that is,

$$E_\nu = E_0 - E_e + m_\nu \qquad (4)$$

and

$$\varrho(E_e)dE_e = p_e E_e(E_0 - E_e + m_\nu)\sqrt{(E_0 - E_e)(E_0 - E_e + 2m_\nu)}dE_e . \quad (5)$$

In the case $m_\nu \neq 0$ the behaviour of E_ν in the neighbourhood of the upper limit E_0, namely for $E_0 - E_e \ll m_\nu$ is quite different from its behaviour for $m_\nu = 0$, viz.

$$\varrho(E_e)dE_e = p_e E_e(E_0 - E_e)^2, \quad \text{for } m_\nu = 0 . \qquad (6)$$

By comparison with the empirical form of the spectrum *Fermi* and *Perrin* came to the conclusion, as early as 1933, that $m_\nu = 0$.

The most accurate estimate of the upper limit for the rest mass m_ν of the neutrino, following from the beta spectrum of tritium (H^3) measured accurately by *L. M. Langer* and *R. J. D. Moffat*,[24] is obtained by the same principle.[25]

The result is[26]

$$m_\nu < 250 \text{ eV} = 0.002 \, m_e .$$

We shall thus always presuppose $m_\nu = 0$ in what follows.

The Kurie plot of the allowed transitions shows that (apart from a factor $F(Z, E_e)$ of the Coulomb correction) the statistical density factor $\varrho(E_e)$ alone determines the shape of the beta spectrum. A rather long development of experimental technique was needed before this result could be confirmed.[27]
In the *Kurie* plot

$$\sqrt{\frac{N(E_e)}{F(Z, E_e)p_e E_e}} = K(x) \qquad (7)$$

---

[24] L. M. Langer and R. J. D. Moffat, *Physical Review* **88**, 689 (1952).

[25] In addition to the statistical factor ϱ a further correction comes in here for $m_\nu \neq 0$, first noted by J. R. Pruett, *Physical Review* **73**, 1219 (1948). This depends on a factor which can in general lie between -1 and 1. For the most general expression of this factor in terms of the coupling constants see C. P. Enz, *Nuovo Cimento* **6**, 250 (1957). For the form of the interaction assumed nowadays, this correction however vanishes.

[26] Cf. also in this connection discussions by L. Friedman and L. G. Smith, *Physical Review* **109**, 2214 (1958); J. J. Sakurai, *Physical Review Letters* **1**, 40 (1958); L. Friedman, ibid, **1**, 101 (1958).

[27] An example of a forbidden transition is the decay of RaE, which has played such an important role in the history of the interpretation of the continuous electron spectrum. The shape of the RaE spectrum is not determined solely by the factor ϱ of the density of states, on which account it is even today still of interest as an object of investigation. See W. Bühring and J. Heintze, *Physical Review Letters* **1**, 176 (1958) and *Zeitschrift für Physik* **153**, 237 (1958).

This does not however admit of experimental test in this form, since no reactors exist as neutrino source with emission of positons. We can, however, consider the reaction corresponding to the process inverse to (15),

$$Cl^{37} + \bar{\nu} \rightarrow A^{37} + e_- \tag{18}$$

with antineutrinos $\bar{\nu}$ instead of neutrinos ν, which corresponds to

$$n + \bar{\nu} \rightarrow p + e_- \tag{18a}$$

for neutrons bound in the Cl^{37} nucleus. This reaction should be impossible according to the idea of the two reflection-symmetric sorts of neutrinos.

This can be formulated more concisely by means of a *"lepton charge"*, *whose sum is to be conserved in all possible reactions.* Without having any direct connection with electromagnetism, it can, like electric charge, take both signs. A common sign of the lepton charge for all leptons is purely conventional; on the other hand the sign of the quotient of lepton charge and electromagnetic charge for various particles must be fixed by experiment. For example it is not a matter of convention whether the muon (μ-meson) μ_+ and e_+, and similarly μ_- and e_- have the same or opposite lepton charge. The values of the lepton charge for e, μ and ν accepted at the present time are

$$+1 \text{ for } \mu_-, e_-, \nu_- , \qquad -1 \text{ for } \mu_+, e_+, \bar{\nu} . \tag{19}$$

We shall return to the muon later. For heavy particles (baryons) such as n and p and for bosons such as π the lepton charge is supposed to be zero. We see that this assignment leads to the result that, *on the assumption of a conservation law for lepton charge, the reactions* (16), (16a), (17) *are allowed, and reactions* (18) *and* (18a) *are forbidden.*

The reaction (18) has actually been investigated by R. Davis[39] with a negative result, with an upper limit of 0.9×10^{-45} cm^2 for the reaction cross-section. The experimental accuracy, limited by background effects of cosmic radiation, is not very great for theoretical requirements. For the theoretically possible maximum for this cross-section is itself only 2.6×10^{-45} and theories are conceivable in which this maximum value is multiplied by some factor between 0 and 1.

The reaction (18a) combined with (16) would give *emission of two electrons e without neutrino emission*, two neutrons being at the same time turned into protons. This reaction, which obviously does not satisfy a law of conservation of lepton charge has often been looked for directly, but in vain, as

---

[39] R. Davis, *Physical Review* **97**, 766 (1955); *Bulletin of the American Physical Society*, Washington Meeting, 1956, p. 219.

"double beta decay". The most accurate negative result known concerns the absence of a transition Nd^{150} $(Z = 60) \rightarrow Sm^{150}$ $(Z = 62)$.[40] The lifetime of Nd came out greater than 4.4×10^{18} years. It should be said that here the theoretical estimate is uncertain, since it involves unknown matrix elements. It leads, as a maximum, to the plausible half-life for Nd of 4×10^{15} years, which could however be pushed up to 1.9×10^{18} years.

Summarizing, we can say that the quantitative empirical verification of a law so fundamental as that of conservation of lepton charge indeed leaves much to be desired. On the other hand all known experiments are in harmony with the assumption of this conservation law. In what follows it will be assumed to be correct.

5. Violation of Parity. Law of Weak Interaction

Two years ago a critical discussion of the reflection symmetries of weak interactions inaugurated a new development of this wider field of physics, of which the properties of the neutrino dealt with in this lecture are only a special case. The so-called "$\theta - \tau$ puzzle" of the decay of K-mesons led T. D. Lee and C. N. Yang[41] to investigate more closely in the case of weak interactions the empirical evidence for the validity of charge symmetry C (more generally C means interchange of particle and antiparticle) as well as of space reflection P (of parity; in this the sign of the charge is unchanged, by definition). They found this evidence inadequate, and indicated experiments by which it could be tested.

To the great surprise of many physicists, including myself, the first time some of these experiments were carried out, they gave the result announced in January 1957 that in beta decay[42] as well as in production and decay of μ-mesons[43] the symmetry operations C as well as P can *not* be satisfied separately.

For the significance in principle of questions of symmetry I can refer to another of my essays, in which also the three categories of interaction, strong,

---

[40] C. L. Cowan, jr., F. B. Harrison, L. M. Langer and F. Reines, *Nuovo Cimento* **3**, 649 (1956); *Physical Review* **106** (L), 825 (1957).

[41] T. D. Lee and C. N. Yang, *Physical Review* **104**, 254 (1956).

[42] C. S. Wu, E. Ambler, R. W. Hayward, D. D. Hoppes and R. P. Hudson, *Physical Review* **105**, 1413 (1957): directed nuclear spins of Co 60.

[43] R. L. Garwin, L. M. Lederman and M. Weinrich, *Physical Review* **105**, 1415 (1957): Cyclotron; J. L. Friedman and V. L. Telegdi, *Physical Review* **105**, 1681 (1957): Photographic plates.

electromagnetic and weak – are explained more fully.[44] Here I shall therefore make only the following short remarks about it. Besides the symmetry operations C and P there is also time-reversal T (by definition without change of sign of the charge). The so-called CPT-theorem ensures that under very general assumptions invariance with respect to the product of the three discrete operations C, P, T (in any order) already follows from the invariance with respect to the continuous Lorentz group. Moreover the experiments[45] which have hitherto been carried out for this purpose have given the result of *compatibility with symmetry T or with the equivalent symmetry CP*.

I am now fain to apply *Bohr*'s warning, mentioned earlier, that in the case of weak interactions (as they are called nowadays) one must "be prepared for surprises", to the violation of C- and P-symmetries separately. While his special idea, which he abandoned later, of a violation of the energy law in these interactions would have concerned the *continuous* group of translations in space and time (contained in the inhomogeneous Lorentz group); our actual surprise, however, is with reference to the lowering of symmetry in the *discrete* groups of reflections in the case of weak interactions. This surprise would certainly not have occurred if *all* laws of nature exhibited *only* the low CP- or T-symmetries. So one can also say that the problem consists in understanding *why strong and electromagnetic interactions exhibit the higher symmetry of C or P separately*. This problem is still unsolved. While in electromagnetism the higher reflection symmetry could have some connection with the special form of the interaction, the situation in strong interactions is more complex. Moreover the question arises here, to be decided empirically, whether this higher reflection symmetry is actually present in *all* strong interactions, or only in pion-nucleon and nucleon-nucleon interactions. The answer to these questions must be left to the future.

The lower reflection symmetry of weak interactions is not confined to the neutrino, and can therefore not be attributed exclusively to special properties of the neutrino. It is for instance established with certainty in the decay of the neutral hyperon Λ^0 into a proton p and a negative pion π^-.

For the neutrino there is a special possibility, the discussion of which was adumbrated in Sect. 3: the so-called "*two-component model*". According to this, either *the two R-components alone* or *the two L-components alone*

---

[44] W. Pauli, *Experientia* **14**/1, 1958, p. 1; this volume, Essay 19. In this article further references are given to experiments up to the end of 1957.

[45] For the present situation (September 1958) of the experiments we refer to the Report by M. Goldhaber, in *Proceedings of the Eighth Annual International Conference on High Energy Physics*, Geneva, 1958, p. 233.

(see equations (11), (12) above) occur in Nature.[46] After *Lee* and *Yang's* first paper several authors independently suggested applying this model to the neutrino.[47] Then in fact the free neutrino already has only the reflection symmetry denoted here by *CP* or *T* since space-reflection (reversal of direction of motion relative to spin direction) is at the same time combined with transition from neutrino to antineutrino. *The two-component model of the neutrino has so far held good in the light of all experimental results.*

For a time my attitude towards this special model was somewhat sceptical[48] since it seemed to me to lay too much stress on an exceptional position for the neutrino. It has however turned out that it is capable of an interesting generalisation in regard to the form of the interaction energy in all weak interactions, in continuation of the line of thought of *Stech* and *Jensen* (see Sect. 3 above).

In the first place the experiments on the polarisation of the electron in beta decay as well as those on the angular distribution of the electrons with directed nuclear spin were compatible with the following alternative: one has either *only A and V interaction with an L-model* or *only S- and T-interaction with an R-model of the neutrino.*

For the decay of μ-mesons it was possible at once to discriminate, on the basis of the two-component model, between the two possibilities

$$\mu \to e + \nu + \nu \text{ (or } \mu \to e + \bar{\nu} + \bar{\nu}) \quad \text{and} \quad \mu \to e + \nu + \bar{\nu} \qquad (20)$$

in favour of the second possibility. It is only for this possibility that the shape of the energy spectrum of the electrons (so-called "Michel parameter" $\varrho = 3/4$) is in agreement with experience. The measurement of the direction of flight in space of the electrons relative to the direction of motion of the μ-mesons, which are produced in the process

$$\pi^+ \to \mu^+ + \nu \quad \text{or} \quad \pi^- \to \mu^- + \bar{\nu} \qquad (21)$$

then gave the result that *the interactions of V and A type only remaining* according to the two-component theory, for the case (20) must here be *present*

---

[46] For particles of zero rest mass the "two-component theory" was first given by H. Weyl, *Zeitschrift für Physik* **56**, 330 (1929). In my article in the *Handbuch der Physik* (*Principles of Wave Mechanics*, Berlin 1933) especially on p. 226 a critical discussion is given. This was *before Dirac* put forward his theory of holes, so that the reflection symmetry of the model (*CP* or *T*) on passing from particle to antiparticle remained unnoticed.

[47] A. Salam, *Nuovo Cimento* **5**, 299 (1957); T. D. Lee and C. N. Yang, *Physical Review* **105**, 1671 (1957); L. Landau, *Nuclear Physics* **3**, 127 (1957).

[48] See footnote 46.

at equal strength. Regarding the μ-meson we may mention also that the weak interaction between (p, n) and (μ, ν) must likewise be present, as the capture of μ-mesons by nuclei shows.

The reaction

$$\pi^+ \to e^+ + \nu \quad \text{or} \quad \pi^- \to e^- + \bar{\nu} \tag{22}$$

has been searched for long but in vain; recently, however, the attempt to show its presence has succeeded.[49] At the moment, however, it is still rather premature to discuss the quantitative question of the relative frequency of the two reactions (22) and (21) by comparison between experiment and theory. The order of magnitude of the quotient of the cross-sections of the electron decay and meson decay of the pion is 10^{-5} to 10^{-4}.

More difficult was the decision of the alternative S-, T- versus V-, A-interaction in beta decay. For a long time there was a hold-up here on account of wrongly evaluated recoil measurements in He^6. The first *correct indication in favour of the alternative (V, A)* was given by the angular correlation between electron and neutrino in A^{35},[50] determined by recoiled experiments. In agreement with this there was also the result of an elegant experiment by *M. Goldhaber, L. Grodzins and A. W. Sunyar*.[51] This experiment enables the screw direction of the emitted neutrino to be deduced directly from the sense of the circular polarization of the gamma rays emitted after capture of an electron from the inner atomic shells, by means of resonance scattering of the gamma rays at daughter nuclei. *The experiment with Eu^{152} gave an L-neutrino*. According to the results of the other experiments, already mentioned, this corresponds to the *alternative (V, A)*.

Further confirmation[52] was soon forthcoming for this (e. g. by new recoil experiments on He^6) so that it can now be regarded as well assured.

For the theoretical interpretation the following postulate seemed appropriate, on the basis of the transformation of *Stech* and *Jensen*, taken together with the two-component model of the neutrino: *the energy of every weak 4-fermion interaction must involve "universally" either only R- or only L-components of the participating fermions*.[53] An equivalent formulation of this

---

[49] T. Fazzini, G. Fidecaro, A. W. Merrison, H. Paul and A. V. Tollestrup, *Physical Review Letters* **1**, 247 (1958) as well as G. Impeduglia, P. Plano, A. Prodell, N. Samios, M. Schwartz and J. Steinberger, *Physical Review Letters* **1**, 249 (1958). For earlier negative experiments and the theoretical estimates see for example S. Lokanathan and J. Steinberger, *Nuovo Cimento*, Supplemento to volume **2**, 151 (1955). Also H. L. Anderson and C. M. G. Lattes, *Nuovo Cimento* **6**, 1356 (1957).

[50] W. B. Hermannsfeldt, D. R. Maxson, P. Stähelin and J. S. Allen, *Physical Review* **107** (L), 641 (1957).

[51] M. Goldhaber, L. Grodzins and A. W. Sunyar, *Physical Review* **109**, 1015 (1958).

[52] See footnote 45.

[53] This is held to include the condition that this interaction must not involve the derivatives of these spinor components explicitly. For particles of non-vanishing rest mass the R

requirement is that in the transformation $\psi' = \gamma_5\psi$ *for each participating particle separately* the density of the interaction energy must "universally" either remain unchanged or change its sign.[54]

The Stech-Jensen transformation referred to a pair of the particles simultaneously, while the two-component model of the neutrino is equivalent to the validity of the result of the transformation for the neutrino alone. *The postulate* in question *of the extended Stech-Jensen transformation is therefore a natural generalization of the two-component model for the neutrino.*

As can readily be seen, this postulate leads to the unique (automatically *CP*- or *T*-invariant) interaction law

$$
\begin{aligned}
&\left[\overline{\psi}_1\gamma_\mu(1 \pm \gamma_5)\psi_2\right]\left[\overline{\psi}_3\gamma_\mu(1 \pm \gamma_5)\psi_4\right] \\
&\equiv \left[\overline{\psi}_1\gamma_\mu(1 \pm \gamma_5)\psi_4\right]\left[\overline{\psi}_3\gamma_\mu(1 \pm \gamma_5)\psi_2\right] .
\end{aligned}
\tag{23}
$$

The identity of the two expressions is purely a matter of algebra. The sign of γ_5 must be "universally" the same. Its choice depends on the convention as to what is regarded as particle and what as antiparticle. As usual, $\overline{\psi} = \psi^*\gamma_4$, and ψ^* denotes the hermitian conjugate operator to ψ. The coupling constant is not written explicitly in (23). The postulate in the form used here does *not* require that it should be the same for the interaction of different particles.

The postulate of the "universal" weak *R*- or *L*-interactions would in general demand *equality of the strength of the V and the A interactions. This is however not empirically correct in this form for the nucleons in beta decay.* The empirical result can now[55] be summarized as follows. The interaction for beta decay is

$$
\frac{1}{\sqrt{2}}C\left[\overline{p}\gamma_\mu(1 + \lambda\gamma_5)n\right]\left[\overline{e}\gamma_\mu(1 + \gamma_5)\nu\right] + \text{herm. conj.}
\tag{24}
$$

For this more general expression for the interaction *CP*- or *T*-invariance is

---

components can be expressed in terms of the first derivatives of the *L* components and vice-versa.

[54] This postulate, or one equivalent to it, was suggested by several authors independently: E. C. G. Sudarshan and R. E. Marshak, *Physical Review* **109** (L), 1860 (1958); J. J. Sakurai, *Nuovo Cimento* **7**, 649 (1958); R. P. Feynman and M. Gell-Mann, *Physical Review* **109**, 193 (1958).

[55] See footnote 45. Here essential use has been made of a new measurement by the Russian authors *A. N. Sosnovskij, P. E. Spivak, Yu. A. Prokofiev, I. E. Kutikov* and *Yu. P. Dobrynin* of the half life of the free neutron, namely 11.7 ± 0.3 min.

equivalent to the statement that the constant λ is real, which is well supported by experiment.[56] The numerical values of the constants are

$$\lambda = 1.25 \pm 0.04 , \quad C = (1.410 \pm 0.009) \times 10^{-49} \text{ erg cm}^{-3} .$$

For the decay of the μ-meson the following expression for the interaction energy is adequate:

$$\frac{1}{\sqrt{2}} C \left[\bar{\nu} \gamma_\mu (1 + \gamma_5) \mu \right] \left[\bar{e} \gamma_\mu (1 + \gamma_5) \nu \right] + \text{herm. conj.}$$
$$\equiv \frac{1}{\sqrt{2}} C \left[\bar{\nu} \gamma_\mu (1 + \gamma_5) \nu \right] \left[\bar{e} \gamma_\mu (1 + \gamma_5) \mu \right] + \text{herm. conj.}$$
(25)

The two constants C for nucleon and for meson decay are to a good approximation empirically equal.

To interpret the departure of the constant λ from unity, *Feynman* and *Gell-Mann*[57] have proposed an interesting hypothesis. In (24) $[\bar{p} \gamma_\mu (1 + \gamma_5) n]$ should be replaced by the appropriate component of the total isotopic spin current including the π-mesons, so that the law of interaction is now

$$C \left\{ \frac{1}{\sqrt{2}} \left(\bar{p} \gamma_\mu (1 + \gamma_5) n \right) - \left(\pi_0 \frac{\partial \pi^*}{\partial x_\mu} - \pi^* \frac{\partial \pi_0}{\partial x_\mu} \right) \right\} \left[\bar{e} \gamma_\mu (1 + \gamma_5) \nu \right]$$
$$+ \text{herm. conj.}$$
(24a)

and the postulate of the "universal" weak L-interaction is restored. Here the field $\pi_0(x)$ corresponds to the neutral π-meson the (complex) field $\pi(x)$ to the charged π-meson. To explain λ the concept of "renormalisation of the coupling constants" is invoked. The conservation of the total isospin in (strong) pion-nucleon coupling ensures that this will change only the coupling constant of the axial (A) part of the interaction, while the V-coupling constant remains unchanged.

By way of criticism it should be said that only a calculation of λ from other empirical data of pion-nucleon interaction will transform the still incomplete formal scheme of "renormalisation" into a proper theory. Such a theory is at present not available, however. The proposed direct interaction of pions with electron and neutrino gives rise to possibilities of experimental test which must be awaited.

* * *

---

[56] See footnote 45.
[57] See footnote 54. Cf. also S. S. Gershtein and Ia. B. Zel'dovich *Soviet Physics JETP* **2**, 576 (1956) and M. Gell-Mann, *Physical Review* **111**, 362 (1958), where possible experimental tests of the new expression are discussed.

We have now followed the history of the neutrino part of the way, and have seen how the original ideas and concepts have proved valid later. A point now appears to have been reached when the physics of the neutrino merges with the more general physics of elementary particles. Nowadays we still describe each of these particles by its own field and each type of interaction by its own coupling constants.

What, for example, is the significance of the small numerical value of the constant of the *Fermi* interaction, of the dimension of a cross-section, compared with other atomic cross-sections? The next step, the suppression of the phenomenological physics of individual fields and coupling constants in favour of a unified conception is likely to be much more difficult than what has so far been achieved.

Title page of Robert Fludd's *Utrisque cosmi maioris scilicet et minoris metaphysica, physica atque technica historia*

Oppenheim, 1617–1621

21. The Influence of Archetypal Ideas on the Scientific Theories of Kepler*

Inzwischen habe ich meinen Ausflug ins 17. Jahrhundert weiter fortgesetzt. Daß Newton Raum und Zeit quasi zur rechten Hand Gottes gesetzt hat und zwar auf den leer gewordenen Platz des von ihm von dort vertriebenen Gottessohnes, ist eine besondere Pikanterie der Geistesgeschichte, die mir erst durch Lektüre Ihres Newton-Vortrages bekannt geworden ist. Bekanntlich hat es dann einer ganz außerordentlichen Anstrengung bedurft, um Raum und Zeit aus diesem Olymp wieder herunterzuholen. Diese Arbeit wurde noch künstlich erschwert durch Kants philosophischen Versuch, den Zugang zu diesem Olymp für die menschliche Vernunft zu sperren.

Deshalb ist für mich die Zeit besonders interessant, wo Raum und Zeit *noch nicht* dort oben waren und zwar der Moment gerade *vor* dieser verhängnisvollen Operation. Daher mein Studium von Kepler. Ich habe C. A. Meier versprochen, im psychologischen Club einen Vortrag zu halten über "Den Einfluß archetypischer Vorstellungen auf die Bildung naturwissenschaftlicher Theorien bei Kepler." Kepler benützt das Wort "Archetypen" und auch "archetypisch" in einer Weise, die genügend ähnlich ist dem Gebrauch, den Jung von diesen Begriffen macht, so daß es nicht notwendig ist, einen speziellen Unterschied zu betonen. (Sie benützen wohl auch beide dieselben antiken Quellen.) Sodann glaube ich einen vielleicht nicht uninteressanten Zusammenhang aus Keplers Schriften nachweisen zu können zwischen seinem sphärischen Trinitatssymbol, das sich durch fast alle seine Schriften hindurchzieht, und seinem leidenschaftlichen heliozentrischen Glauben (in dieser Hinsicht sind Keplers Ausführungen in dem Optikbuch "Paralipomena ad Vitellionem" besonders lehrreich).

Letter from Pauli to Markus Fierz, Dezember 29, 1947

* First published in German under the title "Der Einfluß archetypischer Vorstellungen auf die Bildung naturwissenschaftlicher Theorien bei Kepler", in *Naturerklärung und Psyche*, Rascher Verlag, Zürich, 1952. English translation by *Priscilla Silz* published in *The Interpretation of Nature and the Psyche*, Bollingen Series **LI**, Pantheon Books, New York, 1955.

Prefatory Note*

It is my pleasant duty to express my warmest thanks to all those who have given me assistance and encouragement in the writing and publication of this essay.

In particular I owe a debt of gratitude to Professor *Erwin Panofsky*, of the Institute for Advanced Study, at Princeton, for many discussions of the problems here concerned in the light of the history of ideas, also for his procurement and critical appraisal of original texts and for several translations from the Latin; to Professor *C. G. Jung* and Dr. *C. A. Meier* for detailed and essential discussions connected with the psychological aspect of the formation of scientific concepts and their archetypal basis; and to Dr. *M.-L. von Franz* for her translations from the Latin, the most numerous and most important in the essay, as well as for a painstaking and often wearisome examination of different original texts. In the English edition, her translations have been revised by Professor *Panofsky*. I may add that the English edition embodies a few minor corrections.

1

Although the subject of this study is an historical one, its purpose is not merely to enumerate facts concerning scientific history or even primarily to present an appraisal of a great scientist, but rather to illustrate particular views on the origin and development of concepts and theories of natural science in the light of one historic example. In so doing we shall also have occasion to discuss the significance for modern science of the problems which arose in the period under consideration, the seventeenth century.

In contrast to the purely empirical conception according to which natural laws can with virtual certainty, be derived from the material of experience alone, many physicists have recently emphasized anew the fact that intuition and the direction of attention play a considerable role in the development of the concepts and ideas, generally far transcending mere experience, that are necessary for the erection of a system of natural laws (that is, a scientific theory). From the standpoint of this not purely empiristic conception, which we also accept, there arises the question, What is the nature of the bridge between the sense perceptions and the concepts? All logical thinkers have arrived at the conclusion that pure logic is fundamentally incapable of constructing such a link. It seems most satisfactory to introduce at this point the postulate of a cosmic order independent of our choice and distinct from the world of phenomena. Whether one speaks of the "participation of natural things in ideas" or of a "behavior of metaphysical things – those, that

---

* This Note figures as postcriptum in the German original.

is, which are in themselves real," the relation between sense perception and idea remains predicated upon the fact that both the soul of the perceiver and that which is recognized by perception are subject to an order thought to be objective.

Every partial recognition of this order in nature leads to the formulation of statements that, on the one hand, concern the world of phenomena and, on the other, transcend it by employing, "idealizingly," general logical concepts. The process of understanding nature as well as the happiness that man feels in understanding, that is, in the conscious realization of new knowledge, seems thus to be based on a correspondence, a "matching" of inner images pre-existent in the human psyche with external objects and their behavior. This interpretation of scientific knowledge, of course, goes back to *Plato* and is, as we shall see, very clearly advocated by *Kepler*. He speaks in fact of ideas that are pre-existent in the mind of God and were implanted in the soul, the image of God, at the time of creation. These primary images which the soul can perceive with the aid of an innate "instinct" are called by *Kepler* archetypal ("archetypalis"). Their agreement with the "primordial images" or *archetypes* introduced into modern psychology by *C. G. Jung* and functioning as "instincts of imagination" is very extensive. When modern psychology brings proof to show that all understanding is a long-drawn-out process initiated by processes in the unconscious long before the content of consciousness can be rationally formulated, it has directed attention again to the preconscious, archaic level of cognition. On this level the place of clear concepts is taken by images with strong emotional content, not thought out but beheld, as it were, while being painted. Inasmuch as these images are an "expression of a dimly suspected but still unknown state of affairs" they can also be termed symbolical, in accordance with the definition of the symbol proposed by *C. G. Jung*. As *ordering* operators and image-formers in this world of symbolical images, the archetypes thus function as the sought-for bridge between the sense perceptions and the ideas and are, accordingly, a necessary presupposition even for evolving a scientific theory of nature. However, one must guard against transferring this *a priori* of knowledge into the conscious mind and relating it to definite ideas capable of rational formulation.

2

As a consequence of the rationalistic attitude of scientists since the eighteenth century, the background processes that accompany the development of the natural sciences, although present as always and of decisive effect, remained to a large extent unheeded, that is to say, confined to the unconscious. On the other hand, in the Middle Ages down to the beginning of modern times, we have no natural science in the present-day sense but merely that pre-scientific stage, just mentioned, of a magical-symbolical description of nature. This, of course, is also to be found in alchemy, the psychological significance of which has been the subject of intensive investigation by *C. G. Jung.* My attention was therefore directed especially to the seventeenth century, when, as the fruit of a great intellectual effort, a truly scientific way of thinking, quite new at the time, grew out of the nourishing soil of a magical-animistic conception of nature. For the purpose of illustrating the relationship between archetypal ideas and scientific theories of nature *Johannes Kepler* (1571–1630) seemed to me especially suitable, since his ideas represent a remarkable intermediary stage between the earlier, magical-symbolical and the modern, quantitative-mathematical descriptions of nature.[1]

In that age many things that, later on, were to be divided by a critical effort were still closely interrelated: the view of the universe was not as yet split into a religious one and a scientific one. Religious meditations, an almost mathematical symbol of the Trinity, modern optical theorems, essential discoveries in the theory of vision and the physiology of the eye (such as the proof that the retina is the sensitive organ of the eye), are all to be found in the same book, *Ad Vitellionem paralipomena. Kepler* is a passionate adherent of the Copernican heliocentric system, on which he wrote the first coherent text-book (*Epitome astronomiae Copernicanae*). The connection of his heliocentric creed – as I should like to call it, in intentional allusion to religious creeds – with the particular form of his Protestant-Christian religion in general and with his archetypal ideas and symbols in particular will be examined in detail on the following pages.

On the basis of the heliocentric conception, *Kepler* discovered his three famous laws of planetary motion: 1. Revolution in ellipses, the sun being located in one of the foci, in *De motibus stellae Martis.* 2. Radius vector of each planet covering equal areas in equal time, in *De motibus stellae Martis.* 3. Time of revolution τ proportional to $a^{3/2}$, a being half the major axis, in *Harmonices mundi*, Book V. Not very long after their discovery, these laws that today have a place in all text-books were to become one of the pillars

---

[1] The chief writings of *Kepler* are:

Mysterium cosmographicum (Tübingen, 1st edition, 1596; 2nd edition, 1621).

Ad Vitellionem paralipomena, quibus astronomiae pars optica traditur (Frankfort on the Main, 1604).

De stella nova in pede serpentarii (Prague, 1606).

De motibus stellae Martis (Prague, 1609).

Tertius interveniens (Frankfort on the Main, 1610).

Dioptrice (Augsburg, 1611).

Harmonices mundi (in five books, Augsburg, 1619).

Epitome astronomiae Copernicanae (Linz and Frankfort on the Main, 1618–21).

It should be noted that Newton's chief work, *Philosophiae Naturalis Principia Mathematica*, appeared in 1687.

upon which *Newton*[2] based his theory of gravitation, namely, the law of the diminution of the force of gravitation in inverse proportion to the square of the distance of the heavy masses from each other.

But these laws that *Kepler* discovered – the third after years of effort – are not what he was originally seeking. He was fascinated by the old Pythagorean idea of the music of the spheres (which, incidentally, also played no small part in contemporary alchemy) and was trying to find in the movement of the planets the same proportions that appear in the harmonious sounds of tones and in the regular polyhedra. For him, a true spiritual descendant of the Pythagoreans, all beauty lies in the correct proportion, for "Geometria est archetypus pulchritudinis mundi" (Geometry is the archetype of the beauty of the world). This axiom of his is at once his strenght and his limitation: his ideas on regular bodies and harmonious proportions did, after all, not quite work out in the planetary system, and a trend of research, like that of his contemporary *Galileo*, which directed attention to the constant acceleration of freely falling bodies, was quite foreign to *Kepler*'s attitude, since for such a trend the de-animation of the physical world, which was to be completed only with *Newton*'s *Principia*, had not as yet progressed far enough. In *Kepler*'s view the planets are still living entities endowed with individual souls. Since the earth had lost its unique position among the planets he had to postulate also an *anima terrae*. We shall see how the souls of the heavenly bodies play an essential role in *Kepler*'s particular views on astrology. Yet the de-animation of the physical world had already begun to operate in *Kepler*'s thought. He does, to be sure, occasionally mention the alchemical world-soul, the *anima mundi*, that sleeps in matter, is made responsible for the origin of a new star (*De stella nova*, Ch. 24), and is said to have its seat – that is, its special concentration – in the sun. But it can be seen clearly that the *anima mundi* is no more than a kind of relic in *Kepler*'s mind and plays a subordinate role compared to the individual souls of the various heavenly bodies. Although *Kepler*'s ideas reveal quite unmistakably the influence of *Paracelsus* and his pupils, the contrast between his scientific method of approach and the magical-symbolical attitude of alchemy was nevertheless so strong that *Fludd*, in his day a famous alchemist and Rosicrucian, composed a violent polemic against *Kepler*'s chief work, *Harmonices mundi*. In Section 6 we shall revert to this polemic, in which two opposing intellectual worlds collided.

Before I go into detail regarding *Kepler*'s ideas, I shall furnish some brief biographical data to illuminate the historical background of his life. *Kepler* was born in 1571 in the town of Weil in Württemberg. He was brought up in the Protestant faith; indeed, his parents originally intended him for the clergy. But early, because of his profession of the Copernican doctrine, he came into

---

[2] *Principia.*

human mind is to the Mind Divine, that
is to say, as the line is to the surface; but
both, to be sure, are circular. To the plane
in which it is contained the circle is related
as is the curve to the straight line, these
two being mutually incompatible and incommensurable, and the circle beautifully
fits into the intersecting plane (of which it
is the circumscribing limit) as well as into
the intersected sphere by way of a reciprocal coincidence of both, just as the mind
is both inherent in the body, informing it
and connected with corporeal form, and
sustained by God, an irradiation as it were,
that flows into the body from the divine
countenance; whence it [the mind] derives
its nobler nature. As this situation estab-
lishes the circle as the underlying principle
of the harmonious proportions and the
source of their determinants, so does it demand the highest possible degree of abstraction because the image of the Mind of
God dwells neither in a circle of any given
size nor in an imperfect one such as are
material and perceptible circles; and, what
is the chief thing, because the circle must
be kept as free (abstracted) from all that
which is material and perceptible as the
formulae of the curved line, the symbol of
the mind, are separated and, as it were, abstracted from the straight, the simulacrum
of the bodies. Thus we are sufficiently prepared for our task of deriving the determinants of the harmonious proportions,
subject to the mind alone, from abstract
quantities.

icum, ut est mens humana ad
divinam, linea scilicet ad superfi-
ciem, utraque tamen circularis, ad
planum vero, in quo et inest, se
habet ut curvum ad rectum, quae
sunt incommunicabilia et incom-
mensurabilia, inestque pulchre
circulus tam in plano secante,
circumscribens illud, quam in
sphaerico secto, mutuo utriusque
concursu, sicut animus et in cor-
pore inest, informans illud con-
nexusque formae corporeae, et in
Deo sustentatur, veluti quaedam
ex vultu divino in corpus derivata
irradiatio, trahens inde nobliorem
naturam. Quae causa sicut sta-
bilit proportionibus harmonicis circulum pro subiecto et ter-
minorum fonte, sic vel maxime
abstractionem commendat, cum
neque in certae quantitatis circulo, neque in imperfecto, ut sunt
materiales et sensiles, insit divini-
tatis animi adumbratio, et quod
caput est, tantum a corporeis et
sensilibus deceat esse abstractum
circulum, quantum curvi rationes,
animi symbolum, a recto, corporum umbra, secretae et velut
abstractae sunt. Satis igitur muniti
sumus ad hoc, ut harmonicis proportionibus, animi solus obiectis,
terminos ex abstractis potissimum
quantitatibus petamus.[4]

This picture of the relationship between the human mind and the Mind
Divine fits in very well with the interpretation of knowledge, already touched
upon, as a "matching" of external impressions with pre-existent inner images. *Kepler* formulates this idea very clearly, adducing his favourite author,
Proclus, in support of his views.

For, to know is to compare that which is
externally perceived with inner ideas and
to judge that it agrees with them, a process
which *Proclus* expressed very beautifully
by the word "awakening," as from sleep.

Nam agnoscere est, externum sen-
sile cum ideis internis conferre
eisque congruum judicare. Quod
pulchre exprimit Proclus vocabulo
suscitandi, velut e sommo. Sicut

---

[4] *Harmonices mundi*, Book V (*Frisch*, Vol. V, p. 223).

For, as the perceptible things which appear in the outside world make us remember what we knew before, so do sensory experiences, when consciously realized, call forth intellectual notions that were already present inwardly; so that that which formerly was hidden in the soul, as under the veil of potentiality, now shines therein in actuality. How, then, did they [the intellectual notions] find ingress? I answer: All ideas or formal concepts of the harmonies, as I have just discussed them, lie in those beings that possess the faculty of rational cognition, and they are not at all received within by discursive reasoning; rather they are derived from a natural instinct and are inborn in those beings as the number (an intellectual thing) of petals in a flower or the number of seed cells in a fruit is innate in the forms of the plants.

enim sensilia foris occurentia faciunt nos recordari eorum, quae antea cognoveramus, sic mathemata sensilia, si agnoscuntur, eliciunt igitur intellectualia ante intus praesentia, ut nunc actu reluceant in anima, quae prius veluti sub velo potentiae latebant in ea. Quomodo igitur irruperunt intro? Respondeo, omnino ideas seu formales rationes harmonicarum, ut de iis supra disserebamus, inesse iis, quae hac agnoscendi facultate pollent, sed non demum introrsum recipi per discursum, quin potius ex instinctu naturali dependere iisque connasci, ut formis plantarum connascitur numerus (res intellectualis) foliorum in flore et cellularum in pomo.[5]

We shall return to *Kepler*'s special views on the morphology of plants. The concept of *instinctus*, which occurs here, is always used by him in the sense of a faculty of perception, whereby he thinks of geometrical forms quantitatively determined. To him, geometry is in fact a value of the highest rank. "The traces of geometry are expressed in the world so that geometry is, so to speak, a kind of archetype of the world."[6] "The geometrical – that is to say, quantitative – figures are rational entities. Reason is eternal. Therefore the geometrical figures are eternal; and in the Mind of God it has been true from all eternity that, for example, the square of the side of a square equals half the square of the diagonal. Therefore, the quantities are the archetype of the world."[7] " … the Mind of God, whose copy is here [on earth] the human mind that from its archetype retains the imprint of the geometrical data from the very beginnings of mankind."[8]

---

[5] L.c., Book IV (*Frisch*, V, p. 224).

[6] *De stella nova*, Chapter IX (*Frisch*, II, p. 642 f.). " … geometriae vestigia in mundo expressa, sic ut geometria sit quidam quasi mundi archetypus."

[7] Letter of *Kepler* to *Hegulontius* (*Frisch*, I, p. 372). "Nobis constat, creatum mundum et quantum factum; geometricae figurae (h. e. quantitativae) sunt entia rationis. Ratio aeterna. Ergo figurae geometricae sunt aeternae, nempe ab aeterno verum erat in mente Dei, lateris tetragonici quadratum, e. gr., esse dimidium de quadrato diametri. Ergo quanta sunt mundi archetypus."

[8] *Apologia contra Fludd* (*Frisch*, V, p. 429). " … in mente divina, cujus exemplar hic est humana, characterem rerum geometricarum inde ab ortu hominis ex archetypo suo retinens."

this example it can be seen that in *Kepler* the symbolical picture precedes the conscious formulation of a natural law. The symbolical images and archetypal conceptions are what cause him to seek natural laws. For this reason we also regard *Kepler*'s view of the correspondence between the sun with its surrounding planets and his abstract spherical picture of the Trinity as primary: *because he looks at the sun and the planets with this archetypal image in the background he believes with religious fervour in the heliocentric system* – by no means the other way around, as a rationalistic view might cause one erroneously to assume. This heliocentric belief, to which *Kepler* remained faithful from early youth, impels him to search for the true laws of the proportion of planetary motion as the true expression of the beauty of creation. At first this search went in a wrong direction, which was later corrected by the results of actual measurement.

Kepler's conception of the sun with the planets as the image of the Trinity is also very clearly revealed in the following quotation from his treatise, *Tertius interveniens*, written in German. We shall dwell later on the significance of the title and the other contents of the book. The passage in question is taken from Section 126, which bears the title "A Philosophical Discourse *de signaturis rerum.*" It runs thus:

And as the heavenly *corpora* (*orbes*) are *vel quasi* signified and depicted in the geometrical *corporibus* and *contra*: So also will the heavenly movements that take place in a *circulo* correspond to the geometrical *planis circulo inscriptis*. (See above, num 59.)

Indeed, the most holy Trinity is depicted in a *sphaerico concavo*, and this in the world, and *prima persona, fons Deitatis, in centro*; the *centrum*, however, is depicted in the sun, *qui est in centro mundi*; for it, too, is a source of all light, movement, and life in the world. Thus is *anima movens* represented *in circulo potentiali* which is *in puncto distincto*: thus a physical thing, a *materia corporea*, is represented in *tertia quantitatis specie trium dimensionum*: thus is *cuiusque materia forma* represented *in superficie*. For as a *materia* is informed by its *forma*, so is a geometrical *corpus* shaped by its external facets and *superficies*: of which things many more could be adduced.

Now, as the Creator played, so he also taught Nature, as His image, to play; and to play the very same game that He played for her first. . . .

From these words of simple beauty it appears that *Kepler* connects the Trinity with the three-dimensionality of space and that the sun with the planets is regarded as a less perfect image of the abstract spherical symbol. By means of this conception, which is related to the idea of correspondences, *Kepler* avoids a pagan worship of Helios and remains true to Christian belief. In this connection I should also like to mention the "Epilogus de Sole conjecturalis" with which *Kepler* concludes his chief work, the *Harmonices mundi*, and in which, among other things, he defines, from his Christian point of view, his attitude toward the pagan hymn to the sun by his favourite author, *Proclus*. *Kepler*'s notion of a playful activity established ever since the creation of the world and replayed by nature in imitation of the original is also in accord with the idea of the "signature".

With regard to the concept "anima movens" I should like to remark that *Kepler*'s views on the cause of movement are vacillating. In one passage in his treatise on the new star he says:

Finally, those motive powers of the stars share in some way in the capacity of thought so that as it were they understand, imagine, and aim at their path, not of course by means of ratiocination (reflection and logical conclusion) like us human beings but by an innate impulse implanted in them from the beginning of Creation; just so do the animal faculties of natural things acquire, though without ratiocination, some knowledge of their goal to which they direct all their actions.	Denique ut facultates illae stellarum motrices sunt mentis quodammodo participes, ut suum iter quasi intelligant, imaginentur, affectent, non ratiocinando quidem, ut nos homines, sed ingenita vi et quae in prima creatione ipsis est instincta: sic facultates animales rerum naturalium obtinent quendam intellectum finis sui (sine quidem ratiocinatione) in quem omnes suas actiones dirigunt.[14]

Here *Kepler* adopts the animistic point of view. But elsewhere he says:

The sun in the midst of the movable stars, itself at rest and yet the source of motion, bears the image of God the Father, the Creator. For what creation is to God motion is to the sun; it moves, however, within the fixed stars as the Father creates in the Son. For if the fixed stars did not create space by means of their state of immobility, nothing could move. The sun, however, distributes its motive force through the medium in which the movable things exist, just as the Father creates through the Holy Ghost or through the power of the Holy Ghost.	Sol in medio mobilium quietus ipse et tamen fons motus, gerit imaginem Dei patris creatoris. Nam quod est Deo creatio, hoc est Soli motus, movet autem in fixis, ut Pater in Filio creat. Fixae enim nisi locum praeberent sua quiete, nihil moveri posset. Dispertitur autem Sol virtutem motus per medium, in quo sunt mobilia, sicut Pater per Spiritum vel virtute Spiritus sui creat.[15]

This conception has much in common with modern physics of fields. As a matter of fact *Kepler* thought of the gravitation emanating from the sun as similar to light and yet differing from it. He also compares this gravitation to the effect of magnets, with reference to *Gilbert*'s experiments.

In view of *Kepler*'s conflict with *Fludd*, the representative of traditional alchemy, a conflict which we shall discuss later, it is important that *Kepler*'s symbol – of a type designated by *C. G. Jung* as a mandala because of its spherical form – contains no hint of the number four or quaternity. This is all the more significant since *Kepler* had an excellent knowledge of the

---

[14] *De stella nova*, Chapter XXVIII (*Frisch*, II, p. 719).
[15] *Epistola ad Maestlinum* (*Frisch*, I, p. 11).

sublunary nature and also the sensitive nature [in man] – is a slight image of *that*,
to wit, the principal [faculty], the human
mind: just so is *that* logical reasoning an
image of *these* actions or operations of the
soul, and either is a circle.

haec illius, natura dico sublunaris
aut etiam sensitiva, mentis hu-
manae principis tenuis quaedam
imago, sicut ille discursus rationis
harum actionum aut operationum
animae imago est, utraque circulus.

In so far, then, as the souls are percep-
tive of the celestial radiations and are thus
moved by them, as it were, with an inward,
self-contained movement, we must regard
them as points; but in so far as they in
turn cause movement, that is to say, trans-
fer the harmonies of the radiations which
they have perceived into their operations
and are stimulated to action by them, they
ought to be considered as circles. It follows
that, in so far as the soul takes cognizance
of the harmonies of the rays, it must chiefly
concern itself with the central figure; but in
so far as it acts, provoking meteoric phenomena (or what corresponds to these in
human beings) it must devote itself to the
circumferential figure. In an aspect, however, the effectiveness* is of greater interest
to us than the manner in which the aspect
may be perceived by the operating soul;
therefore the consideration of the circumferential figure is more important to us
than that of the central figure.

Quatenus igitur animae per-
cipiunt radiationes coelestes et
sic iis quasi moventur secum ip-
sae intus, nobis puncta sunto,
quatenus vero vicissim movent,
hoc est quatenus perceptas radi-
ationum harmonias transferunt
in opera sua iisque stimulantur
ad agendum, considerari debent
ut circulus. Sequitur igitur, ut in
quantum cognoscit harmonias radiorum, occupetur potissimum
circa centralem figuram; in quantum vero operatur, ciens meteora
(et quae similia in homine), cir-
cumferentiali sese accomodet. Et
vero in aspectu prior est nobis
cura efficaciae quam modi, quo
is percipiatur ab anima operante,
prior igitur et circumferentialis
quam centralis figurae respectus.[27]

So much for the inner and the outer figure of the aspects; the greater importance attributed to the outer figure by *Kepler* seems to indicate once more
a predominantly extravert attitude. Since the *anima terrae* causes the weather
and, like everything partaking of the nature of the soul, has the faculty of
reacting to the aspects, the weather must be sensitive to these aspects. *Kepler*
is convinced that he has proved this in numerous reports on the weather, and
he then, conversely, regards this as proof of the existence of the *anima terrae*.
The animistic conception of the cause of planetary movement, of which we
have already spoken, leads *Kepler* to the assumption of a universal connection between the phenomena of the heavens and the receptive faculties of the
individual souls.

---

* As defined in Book IV, Ch. 5 (*Frisch*, V, p. 235).
[27] *Harmonices mundi*, Book IV, Proposition VI (*Frisch*, V, p. 238).

Nothing exists or happens in the visible heavens the significance of which is not extended further, by way of some occult principle, to the earth and the faculties of the natural things; and thus these animal faculties are affected here on earth exactly as the heavens themselves are affected.	Nihil esse vel fieri in coelo visibili, cuius sensus non occulta quadam ratione in Terram inque facultates rerum naturalium porrigatur: easque facultates animales sic affici hic in Terris, ut coelum ipsum afficitur.[28]

It is interesting that *Kepler* tries to supplement the passive, receptive manifestation of the *vis formatrix* by an active effect of the same vis formatrix in making it responsible for the morphology of the plants. Whatever is sensitive to harmonious forms can also produce harmonious forms, such as, for example, the blossoms of plants with their regular number of petals, and vice versa. He therefore raises the question as to whether the vegetative soul of plants, too, has the ability to react to the proportions of the planetary rays but leaves it unanswered because he will not make any assertions without having performed experiments of his own.

It is apparent from what has been said above that in *Kepler*'s theoretical ideas astrology has been completely integrated with scientific-causal thinking; in strongly emphasizing the role of the light rays he made it a part of physics and, indeed, of optics. The astrological effectiveness of directions that are geometrically defined in relation to the sphere of the fixed stars but do not coincide with light rays (as, for example, the direction from the earth to the vernal point) is expressly rejected by *Kepler*. Furthermore, he stresses again and again the fact that in his view astrological effects are not caused by the celestial bodies but rather by the individual souls with their specifically selective reactability to certain proportions. Since this power of reacting, on the one hand, receives influences from the corporeal world and, on the other hand, is based on the image relation to God, these individual souls (the *anima terrae* and the *anima hominis*) become for *Kepler* essential exponents of cosmic harmony (*harmonia mundi*).

Kepler's peculiar conception of astrology met with no recognition. In fact, if one proceeds on this basis it hardly appears possible to avoid the empirically untenable conclusion that artificial sources of light would also be able to produce astrological effects. In general, I should like to remark in criticism of astrology that, in consequence of the vague character of its pronouncements (including the famous horoscope that *Kepler* drew up for *Wallenstein*), I see no reason to concede to horoscopes any objective significance independent of the subjective psychology of the astrologer.[29]

---

[28] *De stella nova*, Chapter 28 (*Frisch*, II, p. 719).

[29] On this point, cf. also the negative result of the statistical experiment described by *C. G. Jung* in Chapter 2 of his contribution to *The Interpretation of Nature and Psyche*.

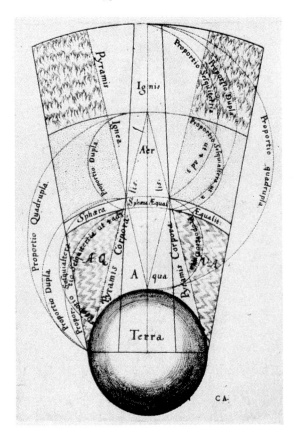

The interpenetration of the material and formal pyramids: 3.
Fludd, Utriusque Cosmi etc., p. 97

PLATE IV

ignates as "hieroglyphic figures" or "aenigmata". Plates II to IV serve as examples of this.

In agreement with old Pythagorean ideas *Fludd* evolves from the proportions of the parts of these pyramids the cosmic music, in which the following simple musical intervals play the chief part.

Disdiapason	= Double octave	*Proportio quadrupla*	4 : 1
Diapason	= Octave	*Proportio dupla*	2 : 1
Diapente	= Fifth	*Proportio sesquialtera*	3 : 2
Diatessaron	= Fourth	*Proportio sesquitertia*	4 : 3

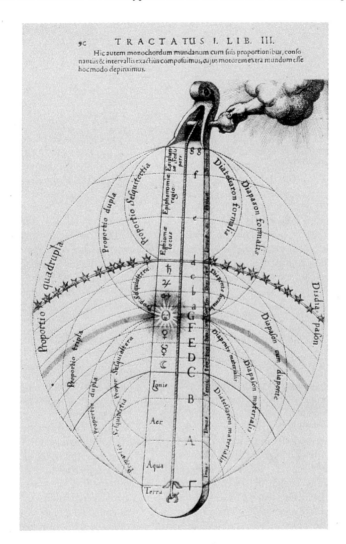

Monochordus mundanus.
Fludd, Utriusque Cosmi etc., p. 90

PLATE V

This is expressed in the characteristic figure in Plate V, representing the *monochordus mundanus*. It may be remarked that the idea of cosmic music also appears in the works of the alchemist *Michael Maier*.

Fludd's general standpoint is that true understanding of world harmony and thus also true astronomy are impossible without a knowledge of the alchemical or Rosicrucian mysteries. Whatever is produced without knowledge of these mysteries is an arbitrary, subjective fiction. According to *Kepler*, on the other hand, only that which is capable of quantitative, mathematical proof belongs to objective science, the rest is personal. It is already apparent from the concluding words of the appendix to Book V of the *Harmonices mundi*[35] that *Kepler* had to fight in order to justify the adoption of strict mathematical methods of proof:

From this brief discussion I think it is clear that, although a knowledge of the harmonious proportions is very necessary in order to understand the dense mysteries of the exceedingly profound philosophy that Robert [*Fludd*] teaches, nevertheless the latter, who has even studied my whole work, will, for the time being, remain no less far removed from those perplexing mysteries than these [the proportions] have receded [for him] from the accurate certainty of mathematical demonstrations.	Ex his paucis constare arbitror, etsi ad intelligenda mysteria conferta philosophiae profundissimae, quam tradit Robertus, cognitione proportionum harmonicarum omnino opus est, tamen illum, qui vel totum opus meum edidicit, adhuc a mysteriis illis perplexissimis abfuturum haud paulo longius ac ipsae ab accuratissima certitudine demonstrationum mathematicarum recesserunt.

Fludd's aversion to all quantitative mensuration is revealed in the following passages:

What he [*Kepler*] has expressed in many words and long discussion I have compressed into a few words and explained by means of hieroglyphic and exceedingly significant figures, not, to be sure, for the reason that I delight in pictures (as he says elsewhere) but because I (as one of whom he seems to hint further below that he associates with alchemists and Hermetic philosophers) had resolved to bring together much in little and, in the fashion of the alchemists, to collect the extracted essence, to reject the sedimentary substance, and to pour what is good into its proper vessel; so that, the mystery of science having been revealed, that which is hidden may become manifest; and that the inner nature of the thing, after the outer vestments have been stripped off, may be enclosed, as a precious gem set in a gold ring, in a figure best suited to its nature – a figure, that is, in which its essence can be	Quod igitur ille multis verbis et longa oratione expressit, hoc ego brevibus contraxi, figurisque hieroglyphis et valde significantibus explicavi; non sane ideo, quia picturis delector (ut ipse alibi dicit) sed quoniam multa paucis congregare et more Chymicorum (quippe quem cum Chymicis et Hermeticis versari infra innuere videtur) extractam essentiam colligere, faeculentam vero substantiam reiicere, et quod bonum est in suo proprio vasculo collocare decreveram, ut detecto sic scientiae arcano occultum manifestaretur, reique natura interna exutis vestibus, more gemmae pretiosae aureo annulo insertae, figurae naturae suae magis aptae includeretur, in qua eius virtus, tanquam in speculo, absque verborum plu-

---

[35] *Frisch*, V, p. 334.

beheld by eye and mind as in a mirror and without manyworded circumlocution.

For it is for the vulgar mathematicians to concern themselves with quantitative shadows; the alchemists and Hermetic philosophers, however, comprehend the true core of the natural bodies.

By the select mathematicians who have been schooled in formal mathematics nature is measured and revealed in the nude; for the spurious and blundering ones, however, she remains invisible and hidden. The latter, that is, measure the shadows instead of the substance and nourish themselves on unstable opinions; whereas the former, rejecting the shadow, grasp the substance and are gladdened by the sight of truth.

But here lies hidden the whole difficulty, because he [*Kepler*] excogitates the exterior movements of the created thing[39] whereas I contemplate[40] the internal and essential impulses[41] that issue from nature herself; he has hold of the tail, I grasp the head; I perceive the first cause, he its effects. And even though his outermost movements may be (as he says) real, nevertheless he is stuck too fast in the filth and clay of the impossibility of his doctrine and, perplexed, is too firmly bound by hidden fetters to be able to free himself easily from those snares without damage to his honour and ransom himself from captivity cheaply.[42] And he who digs a pit for others will unwittingly fall into it himself.

rimorum, circuitione oculo et animo conspiceretur.[36]

Nam mathematicorum vulgarium est circa umbras quantitativas versari; Chymici et Hermetici veram corporum naturalium medullam amplectuntur.[37]

A Mathematicis exquisitis et circa mathesin formalem versatis mensuratur atque revelatur Natura nuda; a spuriis autem et mendosis invisibilis et occulta manet. Hi ergo umbras pro substantia metiuntur, opinionibus variis nutriuntur; illi, umbra rejecta, substantiam amplectuntur, veritatisque visione gaudent.[38]

Sed hic tota latet difficultas, quod ipse motus rei naturatae exteriores excogitat, ego actus internos et essentiales ab ipsa natura profluentes considero; ipse caudam tenet, ego caput amplector; ego causam principalem, ipse illius effectus animadvertit. Et tamen ipse, quamvis motus eius extremi sint reales (ut dicit), magis coeno et luto impossibilitatis suae doctrinae inhaeret et perplexissimus obscuratis vinculis obligatur, quam, ut se facilis ex laqueis istis, salvo suo honore, liberare, captumque redimere queat minimo; atque qui foveam aliis fecit in eandem ipsemet ignoranter incidit.[43]

Such a rejection of everything quantitative in favour of the "forma" (we should say for "forma": symbol) is obviously completely incompatible with scientific thinking. *Kepler* replies to the above as follows:

---

[36] *Demonstratio quaedam analytica*, p. 5.

[37] L. c., p. 12.

[38] L. c., p. 13.

[39] *res naturata*: the actually existing natural object.

[40] *Kepler* "puzzles out" (ausklügeln), *Fludd* "beholds" (schauen).

[41] The *actus interiores* are the creative impulses occurring in "nature herself" (*ipsa natura*); the *motus exteriores*, resulting from these impulses, are the physical events occurring in "the created things" (*res naturata*).

[42] *minimo*: for a small price.

[43] Fludd, *Discursus analyticus*, p. 36.

... When I pronounce your enigmas – harmonies, I should say – obscure I speak according to my judgment and understanding, and I have you yourself as an aid in this since you deny that your purpose is subject to mathematical demonstration without which I am like a blind man.	... Quod igitur aenigmata tua, harmonica inquam, tenebrosa appello, loquor ex judicio et captu meo, et habeo te astipulatorem, qui negas, tuam intentionem subjici demonstrationibus mathematicis, sine quibus ego coecus sum.[44]

The disputants, then, can no longer even agree on what to call light and what dark. *Fludd*'s symbolical *picturae* and *Kepler*'s geometrical diagrams present an irreconcilable contradiction. It is, for example, easy for *Kepler* to point out that the dimensions of the planetary spheres assumed in *Fludd*'s figure of the *monochordus mundanus* illustrated above do not correspond to the true, empirical dimensions. When *Fludd* retorts that the *sapientes* are not agreed as to the ultimate dimensions of the spheres and that these are not essentially important, *Kepler* remarks very pertinently that the quantitative proportions are essential where music is concerned, especially in the case of the proportion 4 : 3, which is characteristic of the interval of the fourth. *Kepler* naturally objected, furthermore, to *Fludd*'s assumption that the earth and not the sun is the centre of the planetary spheres.

Fludd's depreciation of everything quantitative, which in his opinion belongs, like all division and all multiplicity, to the dark principle (matter, devil),[45] resulted in a further essential difference between *Fludd*'s and *Kepler*'s views concerning the position of the soul in nature. The sensitivity of the soul to proportions, so essential according to *Kepler*, is in *Fludd*'s opinion only the result of its entanglement in the (dark) corporeal world, whereas

---

[44] *Frisch*, V, p. 424.

[45] *Replicatio*, p. 27, on *Franciscus Georges Venetus*:

He concludes therefore that the soul is one and simple, but can be called divisible when descending to the lower things. And this is the reason for generation and corruption in the lower spheres. For this reason Pythagoras says, writing to Eusebius: 'God is in unity; but in duality is the Devil and evil, because in the latter is material multiplicity ... '	Concludit igitur, quod anima sit unica et simplex, ad res vero inferiores descendens divisa dicitur. Atque haec est generationis et corruptionis ratio in rebus inferioribus. Hic ergo dicit Pythagoras scribendo ad Eusebium: Deus est in unitate, in dualitate vero est Diabolus et malum quippe in quo est multitudo materialis ...

Replicatio, p. 37: Matter, expanding in multitude and not in form, which latter is always uninterruptedly connected with its shinning source ...	Materiam, quae sola in multitudine dilatatur et non in forma quae semper continua est ad suum fontem lucidum ...

its imaginative faculties, that recognize unity, spring from its true nature originating in the light principle (*forma*). While *Kepler* represents the modern point of view that the soul is a part of nature, *Fludd* even protests against the application of the concept "part" to the human soul, since the soul, being freed from the laws of the physical world, that is, in so far as it belongs to the light principle, is inseparable from the *whole* world-soul (see Appendix I).

Kepler is obliged to reject the "formal mathematics" that *Fludd* opposes to "vulgar" mathematics:

If you know of another mathematics (besides that vulgar one from which all those hitherto celebrated as mathematicians have received their name), that is, a mathematics that is both natural and formal, I must confess that I have never tasted of it, unless we take refuge in the most general origin of the word [teaching, doctrine] and give up the quantities. Of that, you must know, I do not speak here. You, Robert, may keep for yourself its glory and that of the proofs to be found in it – and how accurate and how certain those are, that, I think, you will judge for yourself without me. *I* reflect on the visible movements determinable by the senses themselves, *you may consider the inner impulses* and endeavour to distinguish them according to grades. I hold the tail but I hold it in my hand; *you may grasp the head* mentally, though only, I fear, in your dreams. I am content with the effects, that is, the movements of the planets. If you shall have found in the very causes harmonies as limpid as are mine in the movements, then it will be proper for me to congratulate you on your gift of invention and myself on my gift of observation – that is, as soon as I shall be able to observe anything.

Mathesin si tu aliam nosti (praeter vulgarem illam, a qua denominati fuerunt quotquot hactenus mathematici celebrantur), quae scilicet sit naturalis et formalis, eam ego fateor numquam delibasse, nisi ad generalissimam vocis originem confugimus, dimissis quantitatibus. De illa igitur scito me hic non esse locutum; habeas tibi, Roberte, laudem et illius et demonstrationem in illa, quae quam sint accuratae, quam certae, tute tecum judicabis sine me arbitro. Motus ego cogito visibiles sensuque ipso determinabiles, tu *actus internos considerato* deque iis in gradus distinguendis laborato; *caudam ego teneo* sed manu, tu caput amplectaris mente, modo ne somnians; ego contentus sum *effectis* seu planetarum motibus, tu si in ipsis causis invenisti harmonias adeo liquidas, quam sunt meae in motibus, aequum erit, ut ego et tibi de inventione et mihi de perceptione gratuler, ubi primum percipere potero.[46]

The situation is, however, not so simple as *Kepler* here represents it to be. His theoretical standpoint is, after all, not purely empirical but contains elements as essentially speculative as the notion that the physical world is the realization of pre-existent archetypal images. It is interesting that this speculative side of *Kepler* (here not avowed) is matched by a less obvious empirical tendency in *Fludd*. The latter tried in fact to support his speculative philosophy of the light and dark principle by means of scientific experiments

---

[46] *Apologia (Frisch, V, p. 460).*

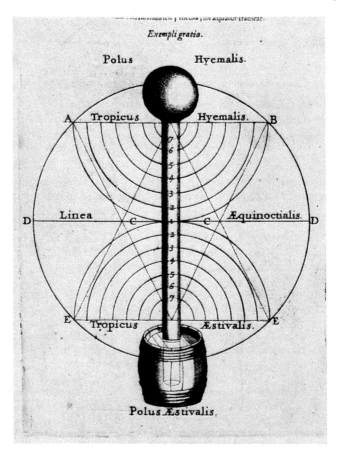

Fludd's weather-glass.
Fludd, Philosophia Moysaica, fol. 4

PLATE VI

with the so-called "weather-glass." Since this attempt casts light on what seems to us an extremely bizarre episode in the intellectual history of the seventeenth century, I should like to say something more about it at this point, although the relevant passages are only to be found in a late work of *Fludd*'s, the *Philosophia Moysaica* (Gouda, 1637), which did not appear until after *Kepler*'s death.

The weather-glass was constructed by immersing a glass vessel, opening downward, into a receptacle filled with water. The air contained in the vessel having been rarefied by heating, a column of water will rise within, its level determined by both temperature and air pressure. The latter concept, however, was not known before *Torricelli*, and the temporary variations in the water level, caused in part by variations in the air pressure, were usually interpreted as resulting from only the variations in temperature. On being warmed the column of water falls, on being cooled it rises, as a result of the expansion or contraction of the air remaining above the column of water. The instrument, a kind of combined thermometer and barometer, behaves, of course, in a way opposite of what we are used to.[47]

Plate VI and the following quotations from the *Philosophia Moysaica* make it apparent how *Fludd* regards the weather-glass as a symbol of the struggle between the light and dark principles in the macrocosm, a subject which has already been discussed here. The triangles on Plate VI are the same as those in the earlier figures (Plates I–IV).

That the instrument commonly called a weather-glass is falsely arrogated unto themselves by some contemporaries; that is, that they falsely boast of it as being their own invention.

So zealously avid of renown and greedy for fame and reputation is man that how and by what right he acquires them, still less whether by straight or crooked means, is of small concern to him. This alone was the reason why the heathen philosophers ascribed to themselves fraudulently those philosophical principles that by highest right belonged to the wise and divine philosopher Moses, and veiled and, as it were, gilded this theft of theirs by means of new names or titles, so that in this fashion they could show them off as having been due to their own invention (as will be enlarged upon below). In a quite similar way this experimental instrument or glass of ours has many spurious or illegitimate inventors who, by altering the form of the original somewhat, boast that they have first thought of this idea (*inventionem*) by themselves. As far as I am concerned, I judge it to be just and honest to attribute to anyone what is his: for it is no shame to me to ascribe the principles of my philosophy to my teacher Moses who received

Quod instrumentum vulgo speculum Calendarium dictum, falso a quibusdam nostri seculi hominibus sibimet ipsis arrogatur, utpote, qui illud propriam suam inventionem esse falso gloriantur.

Gloriae tam impense avidus atque famae et reputationis cupidus est homo, ut quomodo, quave ratione illam acquirat, nimirum an sit directe vel indirecte, parum refert. Ista sola erat causa, ob quam Ethnici philosophi sibi ipsis ea philosophiae principia more surreptitio ascripserunt, quae summo jure sapienti divinoque philosopho Moysi pertinebant, nominibusque sive titulis novis illam suam latrociniam velabant et quasi deaurabant, ut hac ratione ostentarent ea propriis suis inventionibus fuisse stabilita (ut infra dicetur latius); simili plane ratione instrumentum sive speculum hoc nostrum experimentale, plurimos habet inventores spurios seu adulterinos, qui, quoniam typi formam aliquantulum immutarunt, ipsius inventionem a seipsis prius excogitatam gloriantur. Quod ad me

---

[47] On the history of this instrument cf. G. Boffito: *Gli strumenti della scienza e la scienza degli strumenti* (Florence, 1929), where reference is made (Pl. 66) to an illustration and description of the "weather-glass" in *Giuseppe Biancani's Sphaera Mundi* (Bologna, 1620), p. 111, and also to Galileo's similar instrument called a "thermoscope" (Pl. 115). – I owe this bibliographical information to the kindness of Professor *Panofsky*.

them himself formed and written down by the finger of God. And therefore I cannot in justice arrogate to myself, or claim, the invention of this instrument, although I have made use of it (albeit in other form) in my history of the natural macrocosm and elsewhere in order to prove the truth of my philosophical argument. And I confess that I found it verbally specified and geometrically delineated in a manuscript at least fifty years old. First then, I shall explain to you the form in which I found it in that old record just mentioned; then I shall describe its shape and position as it is commonly known and used among us.

Before we proceed to our ocular demonstration, which will be performed by means of our experimental instrument, we ought first to consider that the general air, that is, the general element of the sublunary world, is the thinner and more spiritual portion of the "waters beneath the firmament" of which Moses makes mention. Therefore it is certain that any part of this air corresponds to its whole, and consequently the air enclosed in the glass of this Instrument is of the same nature and condition as the general world air. Wherefore it is clear that, because of the continuity between the two, the general air of the sublunary world behaves in its disposition exactly like the partial air enclosed in the glass which is a part of the general air; and this in turn behaves like the Spirit Ruach-Elohim that hovered above the waters, animated them by His presence, enlivened and informed them, and expanded them by giving them motion; so that in His absence, that is, upon

attinet, cuilibet quod suum erit tribuere aeqam atque honestum esse existimo: non enim erit mihi dedecus istius meae philosophiae principia praeceptori meo Moysi ascribere, utpote qui ipsa etiam divino digito formata atque designata accepit, neque jure mihi fabricam huius instrumenti primariam arrogare aut vendicare queam, quamvis illo in naturali Macrocosmi, mei historia et alibi ad veritatem argumenti mei philosophici demonstrandam (licet in alia forma) sum usus: et agnosco, me illud in veteri quingentorum saltem annorum antiquitatis manuscripto graphice specificatum, atque geometrice delineatum invenisse. Primo itaque formam, sub qua illud in monumento praedicto antiquo inveni, vobis exponam: deinde eius figuram atque positionem, quod vulgariter inter nos est cognitum atque usitatum hic describam.[48]

Priusquam ad ocularem nostram istam demonstrationem procedamus, quae erit in et per experimentale nostrum instrumentum facta, inprimis considerare debemus, quod Catholicus aer seu generale regionis sublunaris Elementum, sit subtilior et magis spiritualis Aquarum, infra Firmamentum portio, de quibus Moyses facit mentionem: Quare certum est quod quaelibet eiusdem aeris particula correspondeat eius toti, et per consequens aer inclusis in Instrumenti huius vitro est eiusdem naturae et conditionis cum aere Catholico mundano. Unde liquet, quod ratione continuitatis ipsorum, ut aer generalis mundi sublunaris in sua dispositione se habet, ita etiam eius aer particularis vitro inclusa, qui est Catholici pars, se habet iterum ut

---

[48] R. Fludd: *Philosophia Moysaica*, Gouda, 1637, I, 1, 2 fol. altera.

the cessation of His actuating force and active emanation or upon the contraction of the activity of His rays back into Himself, the waters then correspondingly contracted, condensed, darkened, and were rendered motionless and quiet.

Spiritus Ruah-Elohim, qui ferebatur super aquas, ipsas sua praesentia animavit, vivificavit, informavit, easque dando iis motionem dilatavit; ita quidem ipsius absentia seu actus et emanationis agilis cessatione, seu radiorum activitatis suae in seipsum contractione, aquae similiter sunt contractae, condensatae, obscuratae et immobiles atque quietae factae.[49]

In view of this description one would almost be inclined to call the weather-glass in *Fludd*'s sense a "noluntometer."

It is significant for the psychological contrast between *Kepler* and *Fludd* that for *Fludd* the number four has a special symbolical character, which, as we have seen, is not true of *Kepler*. A quotation from *Fludd*'s *Discursus analyticus*, given in Appendix II, will throw some light on this matter.

From what has been said above the reader has gained, we hope, some understanding of the prevailing atmosphere of the first half of the seventeenth century when the then new, quantitative, scientifically mathematical way of thinking collided with the alchemical tradition expressed in qualitative, symbolical pictures: the former represented by the productive, creative *Kepler* always struggling for new modes of expression, the latter by the epigone *Fludd* who could not help but feel clearly the threat to his world of mysteries, already become archaic, from the new alliance of empirical induction with mathematically logical thought. One has the impression that *Fludd* was always in the wrong when he let himself be drawn into a discussion concerning astronomy or physics. As a consequence of his rejection of the quantitative element he perforce remained unconscious of its laws and inevitably came into irreconcilable conflict with scientific thinking.

Fludd's attitude, however, seems to us somewhat easier to understand when it is viewed in the perspective of a more general differentiation between two types of mind, a differentiation that can be traced throughout history, the one type considering the quantitative relations of the *parts* to be essential, the other the qualitative indivisibility of the *whole*. We already find this contrast, for example, in antiquity in the two corresponding definitions of beauty: in the one it is the proper agreement of the parts with each other and with the whole, in the other (going back to *Plotinus*) there is no reference to parts but beauty is the eternal radiance of the "One" shining through the material phenomenon.[50] An analogous contrast can also be found later in

---

[49] R. Fludd: *Philosophia Moysaica*, fol. 27 v. (I, III).

[50] The controversy between these two definitions of beauty plays an important role particularly in the Renaissance, where *Ficino* took his stand entirely on the side of *Plotinus*.

the well-known quarrel between *Goethe* and *Newton* concerning the theory of colours: *Goethe* had a similar aversion to "parts" and always emphasized the disturbing influence of instruments on the "natural" phenomena. We should like to advocate the point of view that these controversial attitudes are really illustrations of the psychological contrast between feeling type or intuitive type and thinking type. *Goethe* and *Fludd* represent the feeling type and the intuitive approach, *Newton* and *Kepler* the thinking type; even *Plotinus* should probably not be called a systematic thinker, in contrast to *Aristotle* and *Plato*.[51]

Just because the modern scholar prefers in principle not to ascribe to either one of these two opposite types a higher degree of consciousness than to the other, the old historical dispute between *Kepler* and *Fludd* may still be considered interesting as a matter of principle even in an age for which both *Fludd*'s and *Kepler*'s scientific ideas about world music have lost all significance. An added indication of this can be seen in particular in the fact that the "quaternary" attitude of *Fludd* corresponds, in contrast to *Kepler*'s "trinitarian" attitude, from a psychological point of view, to a greater *completeness of experience* (*Erleben*).[52] Whereas *Kepler* conceives of the soul almost as a mathematically describable system of resonators, it has always been the symbolical image that has tried to express, in addition, the immeasurable side of experience which also includes the imponderables of the emotions and emotional evaluations. Even though at the cost of consciousness of the quantitative side of nature and its laws, *Fludd*'s "hieroglyphic" figures do try to preserve a *unity* of the inner experience of the "observer" (as we should say today) and the external processes of nature, and thus a *wholeness* in its contemplation – a wholeness formerly contained in the idea of the analogy between microcosm and macrocosm but apparently already lacking in *Kepler* and lost in the world view of classical natural science.[53]

Modern quantum physics again stresses the factor of the disturbance of phenomena through measurement (see the following section), and modern psychology again utilizes symbolical images as raw material (especially those that have originated spontaneously in dreams and fantasies) in order to

---

[51] In so far as scientific thought, based on the co-operation of experiment and theory, is a combination of thinking and sensation, its opposite pole can be more precisely expressed by the term "intuitive feeling." On *Plotinus* cf. also Schopenhauer, *Fragmente zur Geschichte der Philosophie*, 7: "Neuplatoniker" (in the *Parerga und Paralipomena*, ed. by *R. von Koeber*, Berlin, 1891).

[52] This is in harmony with the older alchemical texts according to which only the totality of all four elements makes it possible to produce the *quinta essentia* and the *lapis*, that is, the actual transmutation. Further remarks on the symbolism of the numbers three and four will be found in Appendix III.

[53] As modern parallels to this tendency toward unity and wholeness, cf. especially *Jung*'s study of synchronicity, and his essay, "The Spirit of Psychology," in *Spirit and Nature* (Papers from the Eranos Yearbooks, 1; New York, 1954; London, 1955).

recognize processes in the collective ("objective") psyche. Thus physics and psychology reflect again for modern man the old contrast between the quantitative and the qualitative. Since the time of *Kepler* and *Fludd*, however, the possibility of bridging these antithetical poles has become less remote. On the one hand, the idea of complementarity in modern physics has demonstrated to us, in a new kind of synthesis, that the contradiction in the applications of old contrasting conceptions (such as particle and wave) is only apparent; on the other hand, the employability of old alchemical ideas in the psychology of *Jung* points to a deeper unity of psychical and physical occurrences (Geschehen). To us, unlike *Kepler* and *Fludd*, the only acceptable point of view appears to be the one that recognizes *both* sides of reality – the quantitative and the qualitative, the physical and the psychical – as compatible with each other, and can embrace them simultaneously.

7

It is obviously out of the question for modern man to revert to the archaistic point of view that paid the price of its unity and completeness by a naive ignorance of nature. His strong desire for a greater unification of his world view, however, impels him to recognize the significance of the pre-scientific stage of knowledge for the development of scientific ideas – a significance of which mention has already been made at the beginning of this essay – by supplementing the investigation of this knowledge (Erkenntnis nach außen), directed inward (Erkenntnis nach innen). The former process is devoted to adjusting our knowledge to external objects; the latter should bring to light the archetypal images used in the creation of our scientific concepts. Only by combining both these directions of research may complete understanding be obtained.

Among scientist in particular, the universal desire for a greater unification of our world view is greatly intensified by the fact that, though we now have natural sciences, we no longer have a total scientific picture of the world (Weltbild). Since the discovery of the quantum of action, physics has gradually been forced to relinquish its proud claim to be able to understand, in principle, the *whole* world. This very circumstance, however, as a correction of earlier one-sidedness, could contain the germ of progress toward a unified conception of the entire cosmos (Gesamtweltbild) of which the natural sciences are only a part.

I shall try to demonstrate this by reference to the still unsolved problem of the relationship between occurrences in the physical world and those in the soul, a problem that had already engaged *Kepler*'s attention. After he had shown that the optical images on the retina are inverted in relation to the original objects he baffled the scientific world for a while by asking why then people did not see objects upside down instead of upright. It was of course easy to recognize this question as only an illusory problem, since man is in fact never able to compare images with real objects but only registers the sensory impressions that result from the stimulation of certain areas of the retina. The general problem of the relation between psyche and physis, between the inner and the outer, can, however, hardly be said to have been solved by the concept of "psychophysical parallelism" which was advanced in the last century. Yet modern science may have brought us closer to a more satisfying conception of this relationship by setting up, within the field of physics, the concept of *complementarity*. It would be most satisfactory of all if physis and psyche could be seen as complementary aspects of the same reality. We do not yet know, however, whether or not we are here confronted – as surmised by *Bohr* and other scientists – with a true complementary relation, involving mutual exclusion, in the sense that an exact observation of the physiological processes would result in such an interference with the psychical processes that the latter would become downright inaccessible to observation. It is, however, certain that modern physics has generalized the old confrontation of the apprehending subject with the apprehended object into the idea of a cleavage or *division* (*Schnitt*) that exists between the observer or the means of observation, on the one hand, and the system observed, on the other. While the *existence* of such a division is a necessary condition of human cognition, modern physics holds that its *placement* (*Lage*) is, to a certain extent, arbitrary and results from a choice co-determined by considerations of expediency and hence partially free. Furthermore, whereas older philosophical systems have located the psychical on the subjective side of the division, that is, on the side of the apprehending subject, and the material on the other side – the side of that which is objectively observed – the modern point of view is more liberal in this respect: microphysics shows that the means of observation can also consist of apparatuses that register automatically; modern psychology proves that there is on the side of that which is observed introspectively an unconscious psyche of considerable objective reality. Thereby the presumed objective order of nature is, on the one hand, relativized with respect to the no less indispensable means of observation outside the observed system; and, on the other, placed beyond the distinction of "physical" and "psychical."

Now, there is a basic difference between the observers, or instruments of observation, which must be taken into consideration by modern microphysics, and the detached observer of classical physics. By the latter I mean one who is not necessarily without effect on the system observed but whose influence can always be eliminated by determinable corrections. In microphysics, however, the natural laws are of such a kind that every bit of knowledge gained from a measurement must be paid for by the loss of other, complementary items of knowledge. Every observation, therefore, interferes on an indeterminable scale both with the instruments of observation and with the system observed and interrupts the causal connection of the phenomena preceding it with those following it. This uncontrollable interaction between observer and system observed, taking place in every process of measurement, invalidates the deterministic conception of the phenomena assumed in classical physics: the series of events taking place according to pre-determined rules is interrupted, after a free choice has been made by the beholder between mutually exclusive experimental arrangements, by the selective observation which, as an essentially non-automatic occurrence (Geschehen), may be compared to a creation in the microcosm or even to a transmutation (Wandlung) the results of which are, however, unpredictable and beyond human control.[54]

In this way the role of the observer in modern physics is satisfactorily accounted for. The reaction of the knowledge gained on the gainer of that knowledge (Erkennenden) gives rise, however, to a situation transcending natural science, since it is necessary for the sake of the completeness of the experience connected therewith that it should have an obligatory force for the researcher (für den Erkennenden verbindlich). We have seen how not only alchemy but the heliocentric idea furnishes an instructive example of the problem as to how the process of knowing is connected with the religious experience of transmutation undergone by him who acquires knowledge (Wandlungserlebnis des Erkennenden). This connection can only be comprehended through symbols which both imaginatively express the emotional aspect of the experience and stand in vital relationship to the sum total of contemporary knowledge and the actual process of cognition. Just because in our times the possibility of such symbolism has become an alien idea, it may be considered especially interesting to examine another age to which the concepts of what is now called classical scientific mechanics were foreign but which permits us to prove the existence of a symbol that had, simultaneously, a religious and a scientific function.

---

[54] Cf. on this matter the author's essay "Die philosophische Bedeutung der Idee der Komplementarität" in *Experientia* **6** (Heft 2), p. 72–75 [essay 2 in this collection]. The new type of statistical, quantum-physical natural law, which functions as an intermediary between discontinuum and continuum, cannot in principle be reduced to causal-deterministic laws in the sense of classical physics; and just in limiting that which happens according to law to that which is reproducible it must recognize the existence of the essentially unique in physical occurrences. I should like to propose, following *Bohr*, the designation "statistical correspondence" for this new form of natural law.

Appendix I

Fludd's Rejection of the Proposition that the Soul of Man is a Part of Nature

Replicatio in Apolog. ad Anal. XII (Frankfort on the Main, 1622), pp. 20 f.*

From these foundations of your *Harmonices* there arise, it seems to me, multifarious questions and doubts not easy to resolve, namely:

1. Whether the human soul is a part of nature?

2. Whether the circle with its divisions by the regular polygons is reflected in the soul because it [the soul] is an image of God?

3. Whether the determinants of the intellectual harmonies in the Mind Divine are established on the basis of the division of the circle which takes place in the essence of the soul itself, as *Johannes Kepler* would have it (p. 21), whose model here is the human mind, which has retained from its archetype the impress of the geometrical data since the very beginning of man?

4. Whether the sense of hearing is a part of nature and bears witness to the sounds and their qualities as represented [to the intellect] by the *sensus communis*?

5. Assuming that (on the basis of the aforesaid) the proportion is reflected in the mind from its origin, whether then the sounds should be considered harmonious and whether pleasure can be derived from them or not?

6. Whether the triangle is a part of the nature of the intelligible things, likewise the square and whatever else divides the circle into parts which by their quantity or length determine[55] any harmonious proportion, and whether all other natural factors that are present in artificial song, follow the numerical value, so established, of the consonances?

Ut mihi videtur, ex hisce Harmonicae tuae fundamentis quaestiones et dubia multifaria non facile dissolvenda oriuntur: videlicet

1. An anima humana sit pars naturae?

2. An in Anima reluceat Circulus cum suis divisionibus per regularia plana, propterea quia ipsa est imago Dei.

3. An ex divisione, quae sit in ipsius animae essentia, constituantur termini harmoniarum intellectualium in mente divina, ut vult *Johannes Keplerus* (p. 21) cuius exemplar est hic humana, characterem rerum Geometricarum inde ob ortu hominis ex Archetypo suo retinens?

4. An Auditus pars sit Naturae, testeturque de sonis eorumque qualitatibus, quas sensus communis repraesentat?

5. Si inveniretur proportio (ex praedictis) in intellectu ab origine relucens, an soni censeantur harmonici et utrum ab iis delectatio oriatur, necne?

6. An pars naturae rerum intelligibilium sit triangulum, pars quadrangulum et quodlibet distinguat circulum in partes, quae sunt quantitate seu longitudine sua termini proportionis alicuius harmonicae, et an ad numerum consonantiarum sic constitutum sequantur reliqua, quae insunt in cantu artificiali Naturalia?

---

* Cf. Kepler's *Appologia* (*Frisch*, V, p. 429).

[55] Literally: "are the *termini*", viz., determinants.

On the main points of these questions, my Johannes, I shall begin to speak in order, not intending to contradict you in any way or to do any damage to your *Harmonices* but only for the sake of discussion and as a philosopher stimulated by another philosopher to solve some questions, quite apart from his own opinion:

Whether the human soul is a part of nature?

This question I must answer in the negative, contrary to what you hope.

1. Because nature, in its capacity of universal soul, contains the formula of the whole and is not even divisible into essential parts, as *Plato* testifies.

2. *Hermes Trismegistus* says that the soul, or the human mind (which he did not hesitate to call the nature of God), can as little be separated or divided from God as a sunbeam from the sun.

3. *Plato* as well as *Aristotle* seem to affirm that the Creator of all things possessed as soul something whole [total] before any division. And *Plato* called this soul universal nature.

4. *Plato* says that the soul, when separated from the corporeal laws, is not a number having a definite quantity and cannot be divided into parts or multiplied but is of *one* form [a continuum].

5. And *Iamblichus* seems to maintain that the soul, though it seems to have within itself all orders and categories, is nevertheless always determined according to some unity.

6. Finally, *Pythagoras* and all the other philosophers who were endowed with some touch of the divine recognized that God is one and indivisible. Wherefore we can argue syllogistically as follows:

A. That which was a whole before any division is not a part of something.

B. Now, the soul was a whole before any division.

De harum, inquam quaestionum praecipuis, mi Johannes, ordine, non ut tibi in re aliqua contradicam, aut aliquid Harmonicae tuae damni afferam, sed disputandi solummodo gratia, atque ut Philosophus a Philosopho ad quaestionum quarundam resolutionem praeter opinionem suam irritatus, sic exordior:

An Anima humana sit pars Naturae?

Quaestio haec negative a contra me spem tuam tenetur:

1. Quia Natura quatenus anima universalis rationem habet totius, nec in partes quidem essentiales dividitur, ut testatur Plato.

2. Dixit Mercurius Trismegistus, Animam s. mentem humanam (quam Dei naturam appellare haud dubitavit), a Deo non minus separari aut dividi, quam radius Solis a Sole.

3. Plato cum Aristotele affirmare videtur, quod creator omnium possideret animam totale quiddam ante divisionem. Et Plato hanc animam Universalem naturam nuncupavit.

4. Plato dicit, quod Anima separata a legibus corporeis non sit numerus habens quantitatem, nec dividitur nec multiplicatur in partes, sed est uniformis.

5. Et Jamblichus adstipulari videtur, quod Anima, quamvis videatur omnes rationes et species in se habere, tamen determinata est semper secundum aliquid unum.

6. Pythagoras denique et omnes alii Philosophi divinitate aliqua praediti Deum agnoverunt esse unum et indivisibile. Sic ergo Syllogistice disputamus:

Quod erat totale quiddam ante ullam divisionem, non est pars alicuius rei,

At Anima erat totale quid ante divisionem,

C. Therefore it cannot be a part of nature.[56]

Ergo non potest esse pars naturae.

B is proved by the third axiom mentioned above. But if you say in objection to A that the Philosopher meant the world-soul or the universal soul, whereas you mean the human soul. I reply with the fourth axiom that the soul separated from the corporeal laws is not a number and not divisible. Now that world-soul, which in Plato's opinion according to axiom 3 is nature itself, is separated from the corporeal laws. Consequently the human soul can also not be considered a part of the former since it is indivisible (as is proved by axioms 2, 3 and 4). Or I can deal with you in another way, by taking my argument from your own mouth:

Minor probatur per tertium axioma supra allegatum. At si ad Maiorem dicis, Philosophum intellexisse de Anima mundi seu totali, te autem de illa humana, replicamus cum axiomate quarto, quod Anima separata a corporeis legibus non est numerus, neque dividitur: At Anima illa mundi, quae secundum Platonem iuxta axioma 3 est ipsa natura, separatur a corporeis legibus, ergo nec Anima humana potest recenseri pro parte illius, cum sit indivisibilis, ut per 2, 3 et 4. Vel aliter sic tecum agam, argumentum meum a tuo proprio ore desumendo:

A. *The image of God is not part of anything.*

B. *Now, on the basis of what has been granted, the human soul is the image of God.*
C. *Therefore, it is not a part of nature.*
A is clear because God is the One and Indivisible according to axiom 6. B is your own assertion as it is cited in the second question and as the speech of *Hermes Trismegistus* about the extent of the mind declares, according to axiom 2.
Now we shall go on to the second question: *whether the circle with its divisions by the regular polygons is reflected in the soul because the latter is the image of God?*

Imago Dei non est pars alicuius rei,
At vero, ex concessis, Anima humana est imago Dei.
Ergo non est pars Naturae.
Maior patet, quia Deus est unum et indivisibile, per 6. Minor est assertio tua, ut in quaestione secunda declaratur et Trismegisti sermo de Mentis amplitudine hoc declarat. Axioma 2.
Jam vero ad secundam Quaestionem properabimus, *An in Anima reluceat Circulus cum suis divisionibus per regularia plana, propterea quita ipsa est imago Dei?*

I shall not hesitate to answer this question also in the negative, supported by the strongest and most encouraging arguments of the Philosophers. Namely, because:

Hanc etiam Quaestionem validissimis Philosophorum suffragiis stipatus et ad hoc incitantibus negare non haesitabo. Videlicet quoniam

1. *Plato*, first of all, says that the soul, separated from the corporeal laws, is not a number having quantity and is neither divisible nor multiplicable. But it is uniform, revolving in itself, rational, and surpasses all corporeal and material things.

1. Imprimis Plato dicit, quod Anima separata a legibus corporeis non est numerus habens quantitatem, unde nec dividitur illa nec multiplicatur. Sed est uniformis, in se revertens, et rationabilis,

---

[56] I designate the parts of the syllogism by A, B, C. A is what *Fludd* later calls *maior*, the major premise, the more general statement; B is *minor*, the minor premise, the more specific statement; C is the conclusion.

quae superat omnes res corporeas
et materiales.

2. *Aristotle* and *Plato* say that the Creator maintained the soul as a totality before any division, and *Pythagoras* makes it a "one in itself" and says that it has its unity in the intellect.

2. Aristoteles ac Plato dicunt, quod Creator retinuerit animam totale quiddam ante divisionem: et Pythagoras ipsam in se ipsa unum facit, dicitque illam unitatem suam habere in intellectu.

3. *Pythagoras*, in his letter to *Eusebius*,[57] acknowledges that God is a unity and indivisible and says that duality is the Devil and evil, because in it lies multiplicity and materiality. And *Plato* holds that all good exists as One; but evil, he holds, comes from chaotic multiplicity.

3. Pythagoras ad Eusebium agnoscit, Deum esse unitatem et indivisibilem dicitque dualitatem esse Diabolum et malum, quippe in qua est multitudo et materialitas. Et Plato vult omne bonum esse per unum: at Malum vult esse propter multitudinem confusam.

4. *Cicero* says that it would not be possible for perfect order to exist in all the parts of the world unless they were united[58] by one single divine and continuous spirit.

4. Cicero dicit, quod non possit esse ordinis perfectio in omnibus mundi partibus, nisi de uno solo divino et continuo spiritu non essent continuatae.

5. God can neither be limited [defined] nor divided nor composed (according to *Franciscus Georgius*).

5. Deus nec potest definiri, nec dividi nec componi. Franciscus Georgius.

6. By the Platonic philosophers God is said to be present [lit.: poured into] in all things. [He is called] the world-soul (which, they say, contains the formula of the whole) inasmuch as He, universally diffused, fills and invigorates all things.

6. Deus infusus in omnibus rebus a Platonicis dicitur. Anima mundi [scil., dicitur], quam dicunt rationem habere totius, quatenus universaliter diffusus implet et vigorat omnia.

7. God can be determined neither according to essence nor according to quality nor according to quantity, inasmuch as no predication can comprehend Him. *Scotus.*

7. Deus est necque quid, necque quale, nec quantum, quatenus eum nullum comprehendit praedicamentum. Scotus.

8. The Pythagoreans and the Platonists regard the world-soul as being enclosed within the seven planetary spheres and say that within the first sphere it rests in the highest mind; and then, they say, it has become identical with it.

8. Pythagorici et Platonici includentes Animam inter 7. limites, dicunt ipsam in primo limite quiescere in summo intellectu et tum dicunt ipsam factam esse idem cum eo.

9. As all numbers are in the One, as all radii of the circle are in the centre, and as the powers of all the members are in the soul, so, it is said, is God in all things and all things in God. *Ars chymica.*

9. Sicut omnes numeri sunt in unitate, sicut in centro sunt omnes lineae circuli, sicut membrorum vires sunt in anima, sic Deus dicitur in omnibus et omnia in Deo. Ars Chym.

---

[57] See the letter quoted in footnote 45.

[58] *continuatae*: united, brought into continuous connection.

10. *Hermes Trismegistus* says that God is the centre of any one thing – a centre the periphery of which is nowhere.[59]

With the help of these axioms of the Philosophers I therefore argue thus against your assertions.

Argument I.

A. *That which in and of itself is neither a number nor has quantity*[60] *is not capable of receiving into itself any quantitative [measurable] figure (such as the circle).*

B. *Now the soul, which is freed from corporeal laws, is not a number and has no quantity.*

C. *Therefore the soul does not receive into itself from the very beginning a measurable figure (such as the circle); and consequently a circle is not in the least reflected in it.*

A is clear because a nonquantum[61] cannot receive into itself any quantities, as the One does not admit of multiplicity, and consequently is not a number.

B is confirmed by the first axiom and similarly by the second and third, according to which it is proved that the soul is one. But if you reply that the soul, as you conceive it, is not separated from physical laws since it is the human soul, then I say that you have meant the essence of the soul, as is apparent from your subsequent words; and in man, as he exists, this essence is not different from that soul of the macrocosm of which axiom 1 speaks in the second question, and according to axiom 2 of the first question where it is shown that the essence of the soul cannot be separated from God. Or also thus:

10. Mercurius Trismegistos dicit, quod Deus est cuiuslibet rei centrum, cuius circumferentia est nullibi.

Sic igitur super ista Philosophorum Axiomata contra vestram assertionem argumentamur.

Arg. I

Quod per se sumptum non est numerus nec quantitatem habet illud quidem figuram quantitativam (qualis est circulus) in se non recipit,

At Anima separata a legibus corporeis non est numerus, nec quantitatem habet,

Ergo anima figuram quantitativam (qualis est cirulus) in se ab origine non recipit, et per consequens, circulus in ea minime relucet.

Maior patet in eo, quod non quantum quantitates recipere non potest, quemadmodum unum non admittit multitudinem, et consequenter, non est numerus. Minor confirmatur per axioma 1 et similiter per 2 et 3, quibus Anima profatur esse unum. Quod si respondeas, Animam, quatenus a te accipitur, non esse a legibus separatam, quippe humanam; dico ego, te de animae essentia intellexisse, quemadmodum ex sequentibus apparet, quae in homine existente non differt ab illa magni mundi, de qua intendit Axioma 1. in secunda quaestione, et per 2. primae, ubi probatur animae essentiam non posse dividi a Deo. Vel aliter sic:

---

[59] A statement repeated many times by *Fludd*. This quotation comes from St. Bonaventura: *In Sententias*, I, d. 37, pars 1, a. 1, q. 1; but parallels abound in medieval literature. The source, it appears, is the pseudo-Hermetic *Liber XXIV Philosophorum* (12th century; see D. Mahnke: *Unendliche Sphäre und Allmittelpunkt*, Halle, 1937).

[60] Measurable size.

[61] A non-quantitative magnitude.

A. *If the soul is an image of God it is neither a quantity nor a number.*
B. *Now it is, as you yourself admit, the image of God.*
C. *Therefore it is not a number nor does it admit of quantity.*

A is established because God, according to axiom 7, cannot be determined according to essence nor according to quality or quantity, inasmuch as he stands outside of and above any predication.

As far as the confirmation of your statement (demonstrating that the soul is the image of God) is concerned, however, this is also proved by axiom 7, which testifies to the fact that the soul rests at all times in God and becomes one with Him in the highest terminating sphere of its being. And [it is also proved] by axiom 2 in the first question according to which the mind is not divided from God.

A. *If the circle with its divisions by the regular polygons is (as you say) reflected in the soul from the very beginning, then the soul is divisible and multiplicable.*
B. *Now the soul is neither divisible nor multiplicable.*
C. *Therefore . . .*

A is evident because, if the circle filled it [the soul] completely (whence it is also designated as circle by the Platonic philosophers, though only metaphorically speaking), and if this circle were divisible into parts by the regular polygons, it follows that the soul also would be divided by the divisions of that circle.

B is confirmed by axiom 1; furthermore it is shown clearly by axiom 2 that the Creator maintained the soul as a totality before any division, wherefore from the very beginning the circle was not reflected in it, nor did it admit of the divisions of the circle by the regular polygons. But this can be stated even more lucidly in the following argument:

Si anima sit imago Dei, non est quantitas nec numerus,
At, te confitente, est Imago Dei,

Ergo nec numerus est, nec quantitatem admittit.
Maior constat, quia Deus est nec quid, nec quale, nec quantum per axioma 7, quatenus extra et supra omne praedicamentum.

Quod autem ad confirmationem tuae sententiae (Animam Dei imaginem probanti) attinet, illud axiomate 7. comprobatur, quod testatur, Animam quandoque quiescere in Deo, et idem cum eo in summo essentiae suae limite factam esse. Et per Axioma 2. in Quaest. 1 mentem a Deo non esse divisam.

Si in Anima reluceat circulus cum suis divisionibus per regularia plana ab origine, ut dicis, tunc Anima dividitur aut multiplicatur.
At Anima nec dividitur, nec multiplicatur.
Ergo . . .

Maior constat, quia si eam impleat circulus, unde a Platonicis et circulus (quamvis metaphorica locutione) dicitur, et ille circulus dividatur in partes per regularia plana, sequitur, quod et anima per divisiones illius circuli etiam dividetur.

Minor confirmatur per Axioma 1. Praeterea per axioma 2. liquet, quod Creator obtinuerit Animam totale quiddam ante ullam divisionem, unde a primordio nec circulus in se relucebat, nec circuli divisiones per regularia plana admittebat. Sed et hoc luculentius Argumento isto sequenti declaratur:

[proportion], as 1 : 2, lies the octave; in the sesquialtera, i. e., 2 : 3, the fifth; and in the sesquitertia, i. e., 3 : 4, the fourth. Furthermore, from the number 4 and its root there result all the proportions of the composite consonances [chords]. The octave, for example, stands in relation to the fifth in the triple [proportion], i. e., as 2, 4, 6. For, between 2 and 6 a triple proportion is assembled from the double, namely 2 + 4, and the sesquialtera, i. e., 4 : 6. The double octave is found in the fourfold [proportion], as 2, 4, 8; the fourth, however, plus the fifth makes one octave, as 2, 3, 4. From this it can be seen that all musical proportions receive their properties from the quaternary and its root and either resolve themselves into its measures or arise from them. And, finally, if we consider mystic Astronomy we shall indeed perceive in it the whole power of the quaternary, and this most clearly; for its whole secret lies in the hieroglyphic monad which exhibits the symbols of sun, moon, the elements, and fire, that is to say, those four which are actively and passively at work in the universe in order to produce therein the perpetual changes whereby corruption and generation take place in it. The figure is as follows: [see Fig. 2]

producitur, quem ipse agnovit esse primigenium, et rationem totius habentem. Quod quidam cum ita sit, necesse erat, ut numerum quaternarium potius eligeremus in nostris divisonibus; quippe in quem Cubus resolvitur tanquam in prima sua elementa, videlicet quadrata, ex quibus triangulus et pentangulus secundum proprius illius confessionem eliciuntur. Proinde dividenda est potius res naturalis composita Cubo relata, in suas quartas, tanquam quadrata, quam in 3 tertias aut quinque quintas; quoniam in corruptione sit resolutio compositi seu Cubi in 4 elementa seu quadratum, sicut: a converso in generatione progressio naturalis a quadrato fit ad Cubum. Quam exactissime denique reperitur huius numeri vis in scientia Musica, quatenus ipse in se omnem Musica harmonicam comprehendit: Nam in dupla, ut 1 ad 2 consistit Diapason; in sesquialtera, ut 2 ad 3 consistit Diapente, et in sesquitertia, ut 3 et 4 Diatessaron se habet. Porro etiam ex numero quaternario et ejus radice omnes consonantiarum compositarum proportiones oriuntur; ut Diapason cum Diapente se habet in tripla, ut 2, 4, 6. Nam inter 2 et 6 proportio tripla est aggregata ex dupla, nempe 2 et 4 et sesquialtera, videlicet 4 et 6. Sed bis Diapason reperitur in quadrupla, ut 2, 4, 8. Diatessaron autem et Diapente unum constituunt Diapason, ut 2, 3, 4. Ex quibus videre licet, quod omnes proportiones in Musica ex numero quaternario, et ejus radice virtutes suas recipiant, et in ejus dimensiones vel cadant vel exurgant. Ad Astronomiam denique mysticam si respiciamus, totam equidem numeri quaternarii vim in ea perspiciamus, idque luculentissime; cum totum ejus arcanum in Monade hieroglyphica comprehendatur, Lunae, Solis, elementorum, et ignis symbola prae se ferente, tanquam quatuor illa, quae in mundo agunt et patiuntur ad inducendas assiduas in eo mutationes, quibus tam corruptiones, quam generationes in eo fiunt Figura est hujusmodi: [see Fig. 2]

Moon	Luna
Sun	Sol
Elements	Elementa
Fire	Ignis

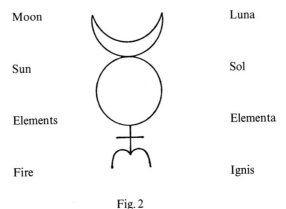

Fig. 2

In this symbolic image we see, first of all, an indication of the quaternary in the cross, four lines being arranged so as to meet in a common point. Joined with the number 3, which denotes the moon, the sun, and fire, this [quaternary] will produce the number 7, which can also be demonstrated by the four elements. And yet this number 7 is in itself none other than the quaternary considered formally.

In quo quidem symbolismo videmus primum in cruce numeri quaternarii indicium per dispositionem quatuor linearum in communi puncto, qui juncto numero ternario, Lunam, Solem et Ignem denotante numerum producet septenarium; id quod etiam ex 4 elementis praestari potest: Et tamen hic numerus septenarius in se est nihil aliud quam numerus quaternarius formaliter consideratus.

Furthermore, even the practitioners of ordinary astronomy have esteemed this matter as of great moment: in establishing the Zodiac, they divided it into four triads. We conclude, therefore, that the wise men called this number *Tetraktys* and gave it precedence above all other numbers because, as has been said, it is the foundation and root of all other numbers. Hence all fundamentals, both in artificial and natural things, and even in the realm divine as well, are squares, as has been explained above. It follows, therefore, that the division of a natural thing by the number 4, which is the order of nature itself, is preferable to a division by the numbers 3 or 5, which are by nature derived from the root of the quaternary and consequently subordinated to it. Finally, in dividing the earth into four parts, the water into three, the air into two, and the fire into one, one should not understand this distribution as the author [*Kepler*] does, as has been expounded above but with respect to the formal proportion in those elements. For I endeavour to show that the nature of the earth, since it is the basis and, as it were, the source and cube of matter, has little or nothing of form or vivifying light in itself; it is, so to speak, the vessel or matrix of nature and the receptacle of the celestial influences, so that the light that it has belongs to it more by accident than by nature, inasmuch as it [the earth] is very far removed from the source of light and is the coldest of all elements, and this in the fourth degree; water is also cold but to a lesser degree. For this reason it [the earth] admits of only *one* degree of light into itself and so also in the case of the others. The wise ought therefore to understand rightly before condemning rashly.

Porro etiam rem observaverunt Astronomiae vulgaris petitores magni momenti, creando Zodiacum in triplicitates 4 diviserunt. Concludimus ergo, quod Sapientes hunc numerum Tetractin appellaverint, ipsumque omnibus aliis numeris virtute praetulerint; quippe qui est fundamentum et radix omnium aliorum numerorum, ut dictum est. Unde omnia fundamenta, tam in artificialibus, quam in naturalibus, imo vero et in divinis quadrata sunt, quemadmodum in superioribus declaratum est. Sequitur ergo, quod praestantior sit rei naturalis per numerum quaternarium divisio, qui est ipsius Naturae ordo, quam per ternarium aut quinarium, qui natura sunt radici quaternariae et per consequens ipsi quaternario postponendi. In divisione denique terrae in 4 partes, aquae in tres, aeris in duas, et ignis in unum, distributio illa non est intelligenda authoris more, ut supra declaratum est, sed respectu proportionis formalis in illis elementis: namque demonstrare nitor quod natura terrae, quatenus est basis et quasi fons ac cubus materiae, parum aut nihil habeat formae seu lucis vivificae in se et quod fit quasi vas seu matrix Naturae, atque influentiarum coelestium receptaculum, ita est illa lux, quam habet, magis ei adsit per accidens, quam a natura, quatenus longius distat a fonte lucido, et est omnium elementorum frigidissimum, idque in gradu quarto; sicuti aqua etiam frigida est, sed in gradu remissiori; quare unicum lucis gradum in se admittit, et sic in caeteris. Sapientis igitur esset recte intelligere, priusquam inconsulte condemnare.

Appendix III

The Platonic and Hermetic Trends:
Johannes Scotus Eriugena (810?–877?)

The controversy between *Kepler* and *Fludd* is connected, from the point of view of the history of ideas, with the existence in the Middle Ages of two different philosophical trends which I may designate briefly as the *Platonic* and the *alchemistic* (or hermetic). Between these two trends there are, on the one hand, important points of agreement and even intermediary or transitional stages; but, on the other hand, there existed between them fundamental differences that seem to me to be more than mere shades of opinion. For the Platonist, the life of the Deity which he conceives in a more or less pantheistic spirit, that is to say as identical with the totality of the world, consists of a cosmic cycle which begins with the emanation from the Godhead first of the "ideas" and "souls," then of the corporeal world, and ends with the return of all things to God. The idea of the *opus* and its result, and thus the idea of transmutation (Wandlung), is foreign to the Platonist. The final stage of the cycle is identical with the initial stage,[63] and this process continues for ever and ever. What, then, is the meaning of this eternal cycle if it does not lead to any result? To this question the Platonist gives the answer: beauty. The prime cause of the cycle is unchangeable and unmovable, drawing things back into itself solely by virtue of its beauty.[64] The cycle pursues a self-sufficient beauty guaranteed by "rules of the game" which are determined once and for all, and it needs no result. The soul of the individual can do nothing but fit itself into this cosmic cycle in order to become a participant in the beauty of the universe.[65] This is the purpose of contemplation which always begins with melancholia, with the homesickness of the soul for its divine origin. (The parallel to the "melancholia" of the Platonists is the alchemists' "*nigredo*".)

   Despite all my respect for the philosophy of the Platonists, it seems to me that the attitude of the alchemists, with their *filius philosphorum* as a symbol

---

[63] Scotus Eriugena: "Finis enim totius motus est principium sui; non enim alio fine terminatur nisi suo principio a quo incipit moveri."

[64] Scotus Eriugena: "Ita rerum omnium causa omnia, quae ex se sunt, ad se ipsum reducit, sine ullo sui motu, sed sola suae pulchritudinis virtute."

[65] In the Renaissance Platonism of *Leone Ebreo* and *Marsilio Ficino* the circle appears specifically as the *circulus amorosus*. According to these authors the bliss of love lies in the fact that the lovers insert themselves into the cyclical current pervading the cosmos. The conception of love is broad enough to include both the desire for knowledge as *amor intellectualis dei* and the ecstatic states of the religious prophets as *amor coelestis*. For the alchemical parallels to this *circulus amorosus*, cf. the series of pictures in Jung's "Psychology of the Transference" (in *The Practice of Psychotherapy*, New York and London, 1954); and figure 131 in his *Psychology and Alchemy* (New York and London, 1953), which corresponds to the beginning of this circle.

of transformed totality, is closer to modern feeling. In particular, the Platonic idea of a primal cause that produces effects but cannot be affected in turn is not acceptable to the modern scientist, who is accustomed to the relativity of reciprocal effects (Wechselwirkungen). I believe also that this idea can hardly stand the test of psychological analysis; it seems to be determined by the particular and by no means generally valid psychology of its authors, a psychology that showed a tendency to deny the reciprocity between ego-consciousness and the unconscious.

The Platonists, as we have seen in *Kepler*'s case also, favoured in general a trinitarian attitude in which the soul occupies an intermediary position between mind and body. It may be of considerable interest to know, however, that in the earliest Platonic thinker of the Middle Ages, *Scotus Eriugena*, the idea of quaternity can also be found. In his work *De divisione naturae* (862–866), he introduces two pairs of opposites: a pair of active principles, viz., the *creans* (that which creates) as opposed to the *non creans* (that which does not create); and a pair of passive principles, viz., the *creatum* (that which is created) and the *non creatum* (that which is not created). By the aid of this terminology, which is very attractive to the mathematically minded, *Scotus* arrives at his four natures, a conception, that may be illustrated by the schematic drawing in Fig. 3, which also reveals the connection of *Eriugena*'s system with the Platonic cycle of emanation and re-absorption. In identifying Stages 1 to 3 of the cycle with the three Divine Persons, *Scotus Eriugena* attempted to compromise with the dogma of the Church. In the case of the fourth stage, however, that of the *natura nec creata nec creans*, he seems to have found himself in an embarrassing position. As a Platonist he could not do as the Hermetic philosophers did and allow a transformation (Wandlung) of the whole to appear simultaneously with this fourth stage. Since he wanted to return to the point of departure where no fourth Divine Person was at his disposal, he could think of nothing better than to act as though the *natura nec creata nec creans* were the same thing as the *natura creans nec creata* at the beginning, for which assumption no satisfactory reason is given.[66] To the question of what has happened to the fourth Person, therefore, the answer must be in the particular case of *Scotus Eriugena*: "He has disappeared in an identification with the first."

---

[66] It was Professor *Markus Fierz* who called my attention to this point.

1. *Natura creans nec creata.*
Origo: God the Father

2. *Natura creans creata.*
"Ideas": God the Son

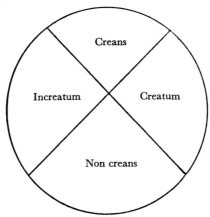

4. *Natura nec creata nec cre-*
ans. Goal: *theosis (deificatio)*

3. *Natura creata nec creans.*
"World": products of ema-
nation, the corporeal world,
matter; *theophaniai*, the Holy
Ghost. "God has created
Himself in the world"

Fig. 3. Quaternity as conceived by *Scotus Eriugena* in *De divisione naturae*

Printing: Mercedesdruck, Berlin
Binding: Buchbinderei Lüderitz & Bauer, Berlin